Praise for *Islam & Muslims* and Mark Sedgwick

"Sedgwick's long experience of living in the Muslim world and studying Islam gives authority to this book which successfully balances coverage of formal beliefs and actual practices. This realistic analysis is sympathetic but not apologetic. *Islam & Muslims* is a very helpful resource for anyone trying to understand the dynamics of Islamic history and contemporary Muslim life."

— John Voll, Professor of Islamic History at Georgetown University, and Associate Director, Prince Alwaleed bin Talal Center for Muslim-Christian Understanding, Georgetown University

"*Islam & Muslims* is really very, very good. I can attest that I truly enjoyed reading it, taking great satisfaction in the way that Mark Sedgwick managed time after time to 'get it right.'"

— L. Carl Brown, Garrett Professor in Foreign Affairs Emeritus, Princeton University

"Looking for a really good one-stop book on Islam and Muslims to recommend to friends and relations? *Islam & Muslims* is up-to-date, well-informed, insightful and sympathetic without being evasive."

— Michael Cook, author of *The Koran: A Very Short Introduction*

"Mark Sedgwick's *Islam & Muslims* is an accessible and informative survey of the way Islam is actually practiced today, written in a refreshingly direct style. It will appeal especially to the general reader seeking a knowledgeable but non-technical view of Muslim societies."

— Carl Ernst, Director, Carolina Center for the Study of the Middle East and Muslim Civilizations, William R. Kenan Professor of Religious Studies, University of North Carolina, Chapel Hill

continued . . .

D0003038

"*Islam & Muslims* is a most accessible, intimately informative, and thoroughly engaging read. Students and general readers alike will simply love this book. Whether one is wondering about how Muslims worship, what Muslims think about family and gender, why Islam has 'clashed' with the West, or all of these and more, this unique book is one that I would most highly recommend!"

— Bradley S. Clough, Abdulhadi H. Taher Chair in Comparative Religion,
The American University in Cairo

"*Islam & Muslims* draws on Mark Sedgwick's expertise and experiences as a scholar of Islam who has lived among Muslims for many years. The book stands out for its insightful focus on the everyday life of ordinary Muslims. Through comparisons between Islamic, Jewish and Christian traditions, *Islam & Muslims* succeeds in explaining to non-Muslims in the West not only the ideals of Islam, but also the diverse ways Islam is experienced by contemporary Muslims."

— Kambiz GhaneaBassiri, Assistant Professor of Religion and Humanities
Reed College

Islam
&
Muslims

Islam
&
Muslims

A Guide to Diverse Experience
in a Modern World

Mark Sedgwick

INTERCULTURAL PRESS
A Nicholas Brealey Publishing Company

BOSTON · LONDON

First published by Intercultural Press, a Nicholas Brealey Publishing Company, in 2006.

Intercultural Press, a division
of Nicholas Brealey Publishing   Nicholas Brealey Publishing
53 State Street, 9th Floor   3-5 Spafield Street, Clerkenwell
Boston, MA 02109 USA   London, EC1R 4QB, UK
Tel: (+) 617-523-3801   Tel: +44-(0)-207-239-0360
Fax: (+) 617-523-3708   Fax: +44-(0)-207-239-0370

www.nicholasbrealey.com

Cover photo courtesy of NATO images

Printed in the United States of America

20 19 18 17 16 15   4 5 6 7 8 9 10

Library of Congress Cataloging-in-Publication Data

Sedgwick, Mark J.
  Islam & Muslims : a guide to diverse experience in a modern world / Mark Sedgwick.
       p. cm.
  Includes bibliographical references and index.
  ISBN-13: 978-1-931930-16-1
  ISBN-10: 1-931930-16-3
  1. Islam—Theology. 2. Islam—Customs and practices. 3. Islam—Doctrines. 4. Islam—Essence, nature, genius. 5. Islam and politics. 6. Islamic countries—Relations—Europe. 7. Europe—Relations—Islamic countries. I. Title.
BP166.S43 2006

297—dc22

2006004414

For Laila

Contents

Preface

The first time I ever discussed Islam with a Muslim at any length was with a Turk named Mehmet, whom I met in a bar. I was surprised by the enthusiasm with which Mehmet explained and defended Islam, given the setting in which I had met him. After all, everybody knows that Muslims don't drink alcohol, and so I didn't expect anyone I met in a bar to be much of a Muslim. But Mehmet was, definitely. He may not have been a very observant Muslim, but he was still a Muslim.

There are many books introducing Islam to Western readers, but none I know of will help a reader to understand Muslims like Mehmet. Introductions to Islam generally explain the religion as it is meant to be, and perhaps as it is for the very devout. What I hope to do here is explain Islam not just as it is meant to be, but also as it actually is—I cover Islam in theory, and Muslims in practice.

This book is written for Westerners whose lives bring them into contact with Muslims, whether in the Muslim world or at home. It is also written for non-Muslims who want to better understand the world's most controversial major religion. I have assumed that the reader is a Christian or a Jew, as most probably will be. Followers of other religions and agnostics might try to put themselves in a religious position such as this.

Bridging the gap between the theory and practice of Islam is not an easy thing to do. In the first place, there is a lack of agreement about the theory. A Saudi Arabian religious scholar and an Iranian religious scholar would disagree on many things, if they ever spoke to each other. The variations in the theory of Islam, however, are insignificant in comparison to the variations in practice. There are so many Muslims in the world—Turks and Arabs, Iranians and Thais, and hundreds of other nationalities, including Americans. Some Muslims are research scientists, and some are illiterate peasants. Some are extremely devout, and some give their religion only an occasional thought. And yet all are, indisputably, Muslims. Their understandings of the world and their ways of living all have something in common. And that common ground brings us back to the theory of Islam, to the concept of how Islam is meant to be.

Like Mehmet, the Turk I met in the bar, this book sometimes defends Islam. Any attempt to explain Islam has to involve some element of defense. When I had my conversation with Mehmet, like most Westerners I knew more about Islam than I did about such religions as Zoroastrianism (which I knew I knew nothing about). But I now know that what I then thought I knew about Islam was not just hazy, but often plain wrong. Some Westerners question how an intelligent person could possibly be a Muslim. Part of the answer to that question is that no intelligent person could follow what the questioner understands by "Islam," because Islam as understood by the questioner does not actually exist.

"But you must admit that Islam isn't much of a religion for a woman," an intelligent and well-educated Western friend once protested to me, "since it says that women don't have souls." At the time I had no idea where my friend had found this information. I have since discovered that it was once a well-established medieval slander, a cousin to the story of Jews mixing Christian blood into their Passover wafers. How it had survived to reach my friend, I still have no idea. Most Western misconceptions about Islam are less dramatic, but there are many of them, as well as many areas where Westerners in fact know very little (right or wrong), but do not realize it.

It is not just lack of information that makes Islam and Muslims hard for Westerners to understand. It is also the types of Islam that Westerners tend to encounter. It would be hard for Martians to make much sense of Christianity if what they saw of it was the activities of Catholic bombers from the Irish Republican Army during its most violent period, and some sermons on hell-fire delivered by a certain sort of Protestant preacher. The Muslim equivalents of each of these are what get the most air-time on Western television. Beyond this, there are also certain areas where Islam and Western practice really do differ fundamentally—on gender relations, for example. It is not the purpose of this book to argue about whether Muslim or Western conceptions are right, but rather to show how Islamic conceptions make sense to Muslims, so even if a Western reader disagrees, that reader can at least try to understand. It is a sound principle of religious studies that one should try to understand beliefs and practices in the terms in which they make sense to those who believe in and practice them.

This purpose means that the book is written as much as possible from a Muslim perspective.[1] There are various theories among Western scholars, for example, about the origins of the Koran. Although interesting in their own right, few of them are of any help in understanding Islam or Muslims, since hardly any Muslims have even heard of them. What matters is not how the Koran actually came into being, but how Muslims *think* it came into being. What this book tries to convey is, in general, how Muslims see and understand things.

Different Muslims, of course, see and understand things differently. This book discusses groups of Muslims, but individuals are always individuals, even when they belong to groups. Italians, as a whole, eat a lot of spaghetti. That statement is true, but is of little use in predicting whether or not an individual Italian will eat a lot of spaghetti. An individual American I know likes reading about African wildlife. Again, that statement is true, but tells us nothing about Americans as a whole. This book tries to avoid this problem as much as possible by distinguishing between different types of Muslim, but even so it deals with groups, and therefore uses stereotypes. When it comes to understanding or dealing with individual Muslims, the reader is asked to remember that they are, above all, individuals.

The reader is also asked to remember that when I write of what is "Islamic" in this book I am referring to the theory of the religion of Islam, and when I write of what is "Muslim" I am referring to the practice of Muslim people. This distinction follows the usage in Arabic. In English, the two terms are not always used like this, so it is acceptable to say "Different Islamic peoples understand the Muslim religion differently," but I will not use the two terms in this way.

This book's treatment of Islam in theory is based on my own study of Islam and on a selection of the religious works which Muslims over the centuries have accepted as classics. My favorites have been Yahya bin Sharaf

---

[1] That does not mean that it is written from a pious or devout Muslim perspective — it is not. It deals with how things are, not with how things should be.

al-Nawawi's *Riyad al-Salihin,* Ahmad ibn Naqib al-Misri's *Umda al-salik,* and Muhammad al-Ghazali's *Ihya Ulum al-Din.* As much as possible, I have tried to let the contents of these works dictate the contents of this book. What Muslims such as these consider important about Islam is probably what interested non-Muslims should be looking at too. I have sometimes departed from this principle, however: for example, in spending more time on violence and on relations with the non-Muslim world than the classic authors did. These topics interest Westerners today more than they interested classic Muslim scholars in the past.

For Islam in practice, I have drawn partly on the published work of other scholars, but principally on the years I have spent in Egypt, probably the single most influential country in the Muslim world. I have also drawn on fieldwork I have performed in a dozen other parts of the Muslim world, from Morocco to Iran and Malaysia, as well as in America and Europe. Finally, I have drawn on the many discussions about different aspects of Islam which I have had over the years with students at the American University in Cairo, where I have been teaching for almost twenty years. The students I have taught there are far from being typical Muslims. They are generally from wealthy families, reasonably well educated, and often remarkably well traveled. In short, they are close in many ways to the typical readers of this book (all of whom are likely to be wealthy by the standards of the Muslim world, whether or not they are by their own standards!).

Islam was once the religion of the Arabs, and Arabs are still the single largest single group of Muslims (though Indonesia is the largest Muslim country). I generally start from an Arab perspective, but as much as possible include the theory and practice of non-Arab Muslims as well.

Spelling is always a problem when dealing with Islam. There are a number of systems for writing Arabic words in the Latin script, but none are entirely satisfactory. I have used an informal system that attempts to approximate words' actual pronunciations. Spellings according to the more formal system used by most scholars (and in many dictionaries and encyclopedias) are given in the glossary at the end of the book. I hope that the glossary itself will be useful.

I would like to thank all those who helped with this book, especially Brad Clough, Abdul Hayy Holdijk, Salima Ikram, Aleya Kerdany, Muhammad Legenhausen, Nur Ainah binte Mohammed Ali, and Yeşim Oruç.

Their comments helped me eliminate some of the errors that resulted from my attempt to generalize about the wide diversity of Muslim experience, and they were all most appreciated. Any remaining shortcomings in the final book are my responsibility alone.

Mark Sedgwick
Cairo, December 2005

1

A Cave in the Desert

What is Islam?

According to a book on the Iranian revolution published in the 1980s—a book that has now vanished into well deserved obscurity— the Ayatollah Khomeini was a paradoxical figure. He started a revolution, said this book, sitting on a prayer carpet but using a telephone. Since the 1980s, we have become used to the idea of Muslim revolutionaries using telephones. Osama bin Laden has often been pictured using his satellite phone, sitting outside a cave in Afghanistan or the wilder parts of North West Pakistan. The same contrast is there, though—between a hi-tech communications device and an ancient setting.

For most of his life, Osama bin Laden was more familiar with air-conditioned limousines and first-class departure lounges than with caves. He was, after all, a member of one of the richest families on earth, brought up in a luxury that most of us can only imagine. But his later cave setting matters. For Westerners who fear Bin Laden, the cave symbolizes the primitive and the barbaric, but for those Muslims who see Bin Laden as a hero, the cave means something quite different. Islam started in a cave, just as Christianity started in a stable. Going back to the cave is going back to the purity and simplicity and beauty of it all. The satellite phone he uses is an unimportant detail.

In the end, it is hard to say which matters more, the satellite phone or the cave. All religions are like this in some way, existing in the modern world but always referring back to the distant past, whether to a cave or to a stable. An American televangelist talks about life today, but also about the

Palestine of two thousand years ago, or even about the Sinai a thousand or more years before that. And so this book will have to start in the past.

Islam and Monotheism

Islam is one of the world's major religions, followed by just over one-fifth of humanity. It is either the major or the only religion in countries throughout the Arab world, in Iran (which is not part of the Arab world), in much of Asia, especially in Southeast Asia, and throughout Africa. There are Muslim minorities in America and Europe, and in almost every other country in the world as well.

As one might expect of such a widespread religion, Islam comes in many forms. There are big differences between the Christianity of a Texan executive, the Christianity of a subsistence farmer in Bolivia, and that of an Italian monk. There are similarly vast differences between various types of Muslim.

Islam is one of the world's three major "monotheistic" religions, in which believers acknowledge and worship a single Creator, the other two being Judaism and Christianity. Islam may sometimes seem very different from Christianity, but the differences between Islam and Christianity pale into insignificance when either religion is compared to a religion such as Hinduism. Scholars are not even sure whether "religion" (in the sense that Westerners understand the word) is the right term to apply to Hinduism, or whether there is even one single thing that can properly be called "Hinduism." These problems of definition do not occur with Islam.

Muslims, Christians, and Jews are all in full agreement on most of the basics, although they usually show little sign of this agreement. They agree that there is a single Creator who created the world and all that is in it, including human beings, starting with Adam. They agree that human beings have immortal souls, live only once, and should live their lives as their Creator wishes them to, as indicated in sacred scripture. After death, it is agreed, human beings will be judged by their Creator, but judged with mercy, and will ultimately be rewarded or punished for their intentions, acts, and omissions (though some Jews might differ here). To many readers of this book, this scheme will sound completely obvious. A Buddhist or a Hindu, however, would disagree with almost all of it.

Although in agreement on these basics, Muslims, Christians, and Jews disagree about details. Some of those details are of little significance: Jews and Christians maintain that it was Isaac whom Abraham did not in the end have to sacrifice, for example, while Muslims argue that it was another son, Ishmael. This particular difference does not have any important consequences, but other disagreements can matter more. Priests, for example, are essential for most Christians, once necessary but no longer significant for Jews, and out of the question for Muslims.

An important disagreement between these three religions is about the status of Jesus. For Christians, Jesus was the son of God; for Jews, Jesus was a human being who taught a religion of his own invention; for Muslims, Jesus was a human being who taught a religion revealed to him by God. Jesus changed nothing for the Jews, and everything for the Christians. For Muslims, Jesus changed some things, but the religion that had been established in his name was then in effect superseded by that revealed by God through another human being, Muhammad.[1] For Jews, Muhammad taught a religion of his own invention, just as Jesus had; for Christians, Muhammad taught a religion of his own invention; for Muslims, Muhammad changed everything. I will return to Muhammad later in this chapter, after we have considered more similarities and differences between Islam and the other monotheistic religions.

Muslims, Christians, and Jews all share the same basic concepts of virtue and vice. The good person is one who believes, worships, and lives properly; the bad person is one who does not believe or worship, and lives improperly. Life is a trial—in the sense that it is difficult, and in the sense that we are all tempted by evil, by Satan (called "Shaytan" in Arabic). When it comes to defining "living properly," though, there is an important difference between the monotheistic religions, since there is disagreement about the relationship between the letter of the law and the spirit of the law. For most Christians, what matters is the spirit, though the letter exists for certain

---

[1]Muslims do not quite believe that Islam *superseded* Christianity and Judaism. The actual position is more complex, and is discussed in more detail in chapter 12.

purposes and should not be ignored. Few Christians would agree to a baptism performed by email. For Muslims and Jews, the spirit of the law exists and matters, but the letter of the law matters far more on a daily basis than it does for Christians. Muslims, like Jews, have precise rules on matters where Christians have no rules—on food, on ritual purification before prayer, or even on how to sleep. These rules are not ends in themselves. Taken together, they underpin "living properly." They are not, however, *just* a means to an end. They are followed not only because they serve a purpose, but also—and most importantly—because they are God's commands, and no devout person disobeys God. This is one of the aspects of Islam that many Westerners find hardest to understand.

Disagreements on details such as these—the status of Jesus and Muhammad, and whether the letter of the law is important or not—matter. Which matters more, the points of disagreement or the points of agreement, depends on perspective. Once, Christians emphasized the differences between Christianity and Judaism, but now it is the agreements that tend to be emphasized. The phrase "Judaeo-Christian" is very much in vogue. It is usually the differences between Islam and Christianity that are stressed these days, however. I will examine some of the reasons for this trend in chapter 12. Even so, some Westerners prefer "Abrahamic" to "Judaeo-Christian," using a phrase that includes Islam by referring to the prophet whom all three monotheistic religions regard in much the same way.

The Early History of Islam

Just as the events of Jesus's life matter to a Christian, and just as the history of Israel matters to a Jew, so the events of early Islam matter to a Muslim. These events, then, are important for us as we try to understand Islam.

The Prophet Muhammad was born in 571 A.D. in a town called Mecca on the west side of the Arabian peninsula, a poor desert region largely ignored by the rest of the world. Mecca was an important town locally because it had one of the few sources of water in the area, making it a standard stop for traders and travelers going north toward the Byzantine and Persian empires. Its people were Arabic-speaking polytheists, worshiping various idols, many of which were housed in its central temple, the Kaba or "cube."

The Meccans prospered from the trade that passed through their town, and also from pilgrims visiting the Kaba. These traders and pilgrims were predominantly nomads who eked out a living in the desert. They were poor, and had to be tough to survive in such hostile conditions. Like most nomads, they were organized into tribes, networks of related families who depended on each other for help and defense. Skirmishes between tribes were frequent, and military virtues were highly regarded.

The Arabian nomads had little time for scholarship or writing, but loved poetry, which they learned by heart and recited in the evenings or to lessen the tedium of long journeys by camel (the only effective form of long-distance transport in the desert from antiquity until the Second World War). Some of the poems current at the time of the Prophet's birth still survive. They praise bravery and physical strength, hard drinking and amorous exploits, and—above all—the virtues of various beloved camels.

> So many singers before me . . . Are there any songs not yet sung?
> Do you, my sad soul, remember where she once lived?
> Speak of her, tents in the fair valley of Jiwa!
> Fair house of my true love Abla, blessing and joy to you!
> Doubting, I paused in the pastures, seeking the tracks of her camel,
> High on my swift-trotting mount, as tall as a citadel.

Like the other inhabitants of Mecca, the Prophet Muhammad was not himself a nomad. The lives of urban Meccans, however, were intimately linked to those of the nomads among whom they lived, and Muhammad spent part of his youth with nomads. The Meccans shared the tribal organization and the harsh values of their nomadic cousins.

Muhammad's early life was unremarkable, save that he took little part in the generally popular amusements of drinking, gambling, and chasing after girls. Something of a recluse, he would sometimes meditate in a cave outside Mecca. It was in this cave that he first heard spoken to him the words: "Recite! Recite in the name of your Lord." Muslims believe[2] that the Prophet Muhammad did not actually hear these words directly from God,

---

[2]For the sake of brevity, I will from now on drop the *Muslims believe that*, and merely say (for example) that the words of God were transmitted through an angel.

but rather that they were transmitted to him from God through the angel Gabriel. It is in this sense that he is a *prophet*—as a transmitter to humans of God's word—not as a foreteller of the future.

Although initially unsure and frightened after this encounter, the Prophet Muhammad did recite what he heard through the angel, then and over the following twenty years. What he heard, or more precisely what was "revealed" to him, later became the text of the Koran. The Prophet explained the significance of the words he had been given to recite, and gathered a small group of followers, who like him turned away from idolatry and debauchery toward the worship of the one true God. This God was identified by those first Muslims as the one God who is worshiped by the Jews and the Christians, though from the first it was made clear to Muhammad in the revelations he received that Jesus was neither divine nor the son of God. Only God himself, it was stressed, was in any way divine. Jews and Christians were both known in Arabia at the time, though there were more Jews than Christians. The Muslims at first turned toward Jerusalem when they prayed, just as the Jews did, but later this was changed, and the Muslims turned toward the Kaba instead. Thus, although some Christians and Jews deny that the God of the Muslims is the same as their God, this view cannot be justified from a historical point of view. As one Muslim put it forcefully, saying that the Arabs worship "Allah" is like saying that the Mexicans worship "Dios" or that the Germans worship "Gott."

At first, significantly more Meccans objected to Muhammad's preaching than accepted it. To most, he was a trouble-maker spreading a dangerous new religion and insulting their own gods. Muhammad's uncle was an important man and protected him from the general hostility (although he never himself became a follower of the new religion), but after this uncle's death Muhammad's small group of followers was subjected to various sorts of persecution. They eventually left Mecca and moved to a neighboring town, Yathrib. Yathrib was inhabited by different tribes from those found in Mecca, and was also a more religiously pluralistic society, partly because there was no Kaba and partly because many Jews had taken refuge there. Muhammad's preaching was better received in Yathrib than it had been in Mecca, and his following grew. Many of Yathrib's Jews initially inclined toward him, and practical agreements were reached between the Jews and the Muslims. Muhammad strengthened his position by means of such agreements and also by a number of marriages with women from important tribal factions.

As the Muslim community grew, the message of the Koran changed. In Mecca, the revelations that Muhammad received concentrated on generalities. It was explained that there is only one God, and that idols should not be worshiped. Muhammad's followers were told to pray to God, not to commit adultery, and to remember that they faced heaven or hell after death. In Yathrib, the revelations became more detailed, as did Muhammad's explanations of them. Regulations were introduced for such matters as the precise treatment of adulterers, the timing of prayer when traveling, and trusteeship arrangements for the inheritances of orphans.

The difference between the early and later revelations is often immediately obvious. Here is the beginning of a typical early, Meccan revelation:

> When the heaven is split open
> When the stars are scattered
> When the seas swarm over
> When the tombs are overthrown
> Then a soul shall know its works, the former and the latter.[3]

A typical later revelation from the Yathrib period is much more prosaic (and usually in something closer to regular prose):

> God will not take you to task for a slip in your oaths; but He will take you to task for such oaths as you swear in earnest. The expiation thereof is feeding ten poor persons with the average of that with which you feed your families, or clothing them, or setting free a slave.[4]

No translation of the Koran can convey anything of the power it has for Muslims who read it in Arabic. For these Muslims, even the most prosaic revelations are truly special and inspiring, just as the language of the classic versions of the Old Testament has extraordinary resonance for many Christians, but even more so. What reads a bit like a bureaucratic regulation in

---

[3]Koran chapter 82, verses 1 to 5, translated by Arthur J. Arberry.
[4]Koran chapter 5, opening of verse 59.

English is, for a Muslim who knows Arabic and is reading it in the original, beautiful.

Hostilities broke out between the Muslims and the Meccans, as they then often did between different groups in Arabia. The Muslims prevailed after six years and a number of skirmishes and battles. In 630, Mecca surrendered, and the victorious Muslims cleansed the Kaba of its idols, restoring it to its early purity—the Kaba was originally built as a temple for God by Abraham, not as a house for idols.

The victory of the Muslims over Mecca led to a substantial increase in Muhammad's following, and within a year Mecca and the surrounding section of western Arabia was entirely Muslim. Most of the Jews of Yathrib had broken their earlier alliance with the Prophet, and had been expelled; some were killed. Yathrib had been renamed *al-medina al-munawara*, "the luminous city," later abbreviated into plain "Medina," the name by which it known today.

Slightly more than one year after this victory, however, the Prophet died, at the age of about 61, in the year 632. The death of the Prophet marked the end of the revelation of Islam. The community of Muslims almost fell apart after his death, but then recovered and expanded. I will cover this history later.

Islam as it exists today is based largely on what happened between that first revelation in a cave outside Mecca in 610 and the death of the Prophet in 632. The community that the Prophet established in Yathrib (Medina) has been the ideal for all Muslims ever since. It was a community that must have offered its members extraordinary spiritual experiences. It also required total commitment, in peace and in war, and was often under attack. References to warfare abound in the story of early Islam, rather as they do in the Old Testament.

The Islamic Ideal

Like the community of Medina, the life and teachings of the Prophet have been part of the ideal for all Muslims ever since. There are occasional references to the Prophet in the Koran, but what the Prophet did and said is recorded mostly in the *hadith*. The *hadith* are collected in books quite separate from the Koran, and are of entirely human composition (though a small number are classified as divinely inspired). The *hadith* exist in several versions, rather as the New Testament gives four versions of the life of Jesus.

For devout Muslims, the example of the Prophet Muhammad and of the community he established is to be followed as much as possible. This concept is expressed in the word *sunna*, "exemplary tradition." *Sunna* has an opposite: *bida*, "innovation," defined as what the Prophet did *not* do. There are two sorts of *bida*. Some *bida* are unproblematic, like driving a car, which the Prophet obviously did not do but to which there is no objection. Some *bida*, however, are clearly problematic, like naming a tree after one's mother and making sacrifices to it on one's mother's birthday. The Prophet did not do this, and no Muslim should, either.

Attitudes toward *bida* vary. Many Muslims are relatively relaxed, and condemn *bida* only when they are as extreme as the tree example just given. Others, today mostly found in Saudi Arabia or in some way influenced by Saudi Arabia's Wahhabi movement (discussed in chapters 2 and 10), are extremely tough on *bida*, railing against things that most other Muslims regard as entirely acceptable (like building a tomb over a grave), or even against things that no other Muslim would consider at all problematic. The most extreme example in this category was in the late 1920s, when the Saudi government tried to set up a telegraph system, only to have the most extreme Wahhabis cut down the telegraph lines on the grounds that they were *bida*. Of course the Prophet never sent a telegram, but the idea that no one else should either struck all other Muslims as ridiculous.

The *hadith*, then, are as important as the Koran for Muslims—in fact, as a source of Islam as it exists today, the *hadith* are even more important. The Koran underlines the importance of prayer, for example, but nowhere does it specify exactly *when* or *how* to pray. For those essential details, the Muslim has recourse to the *hadith*. Because the early Muslims often asked the Prophet very specific questions, the *hadith* often record very specific answers. The Koran occasionally gives specific instructions too, but more frequently it just gives general exhortations. In general, the big ideas come from the Koran, and the detailed rules come from the *hadith*.

The *hadith* do not have a single fixed form. There are many different collections of *hadith* reports, usually arranged by subject. A single *hadith* report may be very short—along the lines of "A man asked the Prophet whether it was allowed to keep dogs for hunting, and the Prophet said, 'yes, it is.'" Others are longer and more complicated. New collections of these reports continue to be compiled from the older versions even today. Some can be found on the internet.

The Koran itself has a completely different form and status. The Koran was not written by the Prophet or by any other human; it was dictated by God (in Arabic), and is of exclusively divine authorship. As such, it is quite unlike anything else in the world, a sort of chink in creation through which God Himself is almost visible. The Koran does not contain the record of the life or teachings of the Prophet, though it does include scattered references to him.

The Koran is a relatively short text. It is not organized like a normal book, since its chapters are arranged by length: the longest come first and the shortest come last. The shortest chapters, which may be a page or less in length, usually deal with one single theme and often resemble prayers. The longest chapters mix passages that resemble the shorter chapters with divine admonition and exhortation, with stories such as that of the flood, and on occasion with detailed instructions like that about expiation of oaths in the section quoted above.

To a Westerner used to reading "properly" organized books, the Koran is not easy reading—but then no Muslim really reads it like a regular book. In daily life, the Koran is more important for what it is than for what it says. People keep copies of the Koran in their cars or houses, possibly never even opening them. Used in this way, the Koran works rather as a crucifix does for some Christians. Others recite passages aloud or listen to recorded recitations made by professional reciters, very often not understanding a word—most Muslims are not Arabs, and do not know Arabic. Arab Muslims of course understand much of what they recite or hear, though the language of the Koran is different enough from modern Arabic for sections to be very hard to understand even for them. For all Muslims, even those who know Arabic, it is the presence and beauty of the Koran (in spoken form) that really matters.

This is not to say that no one ever reads the Koran for its contents. Scholars study it, as do some individuals. Scholars learn classical Arabic to study it properly, but translations exist for those who do not have the time or ability to learn this difficult language. These translations, however, are not the Koran itself. All a translator can do is reproduce some of the meaning of the contents of the Koran. All translators have to choose between possible meanings inherent in an original text from time to time, but the nature of Koranic Arabic means that a translator of the Koran has to make these choices all the time.[5] Even more importantly, because God did not reveal the Koran in translation, the element of the divine that is present in the orig- inal text of the Koran—the little chink in creation through which God is almost visible—is not present in a translation. The original text is usually printed next to a translation; when it is not, as in most editions by Western publishers, the resulting book has no special value. To place a copy of such a translation in one's car would have as little significance as putting any other paperback there.

The Koran, then, is very special. Each copy of the original is more like the actual tablets on which the Ten Commandments were given than like a copy of the Bible. No Muslim will ever treat a copy of the Koran with anything other than respect, and any Muslim who publicly admits to doubts about its divine authorship is in effect denying that they are Muslim. Quotations from the Koran are frequently prefaced by "God said . . . ," though an alternative formulation (which I recommend for the use of non-Muslims) is "It is written in the Koran that. . . ." Anyone who says "Muhammad wrote in the Koran that. . . ." is uttering a gross blasphemy.

The Spread of Islam

Two things had to happen after the death of the Prophet for Islam to become a major world religion. First, the Prophet's followers had to use the raw materials of the Koran and *hadith* to build a formal religion through a process of interpretation which I will discuss in the next chapter. At the same time, Islam had to spread outwards from the small area of the western side of the Arabian peninsula where the whole of the early history of Islam had taken place.

---

[5]Yahya Alawi, a translator of the Koran into French working in Iran during the 1990s, decided to explain the choices he made and the alternatives he rejected, and found that the notes to his translation took up more than five times as much space as the actual text.

Religions spread in two main ways: an individual can encounter a religion, learn about it, and convert to it; alternatively, a state can promote a new religion, encouraging or even obliging individuals to convert to it. Christianity first spread outside Palestine through individual encounters, and then spread further and faster after the Roman emperor Constantine converted to Christianity in 312 and gave the support of the Roman state to the new religion. Islam spread in the opposite order, first as a state-sponsored religion, and then through individual encounters.

Shortly after the death of the Prophet, between 633 and 644, armies of Arab Muslims conquered most of the world around them. In 633, Arabia lay beyond the fringes of two great competing empires, the very ancient Persian empire (based in what is now called Iran) and the more recent Roman empire. Two centuries earlier, the original Roman empire had split into two parts, a Western Empire based on Rome and an Eastern Empire based on Constantinople. The Western Empire was Catholic, Latin-speaking, and the origin of the modern West. At the time of the Prophet, it was in a state of collapse after waves of barbarian invasions. The Eastern Empire, known as the Byzantine empire, was Orthodox, Greek-speaking, and the origin of the slightly different Christian cultures of Russia, modern Greece, and the Balkans. Both the Byzantine and Persian empires were sophisticated, civilized, and militarily advanced. By 644, both had fallen like houses of cards before the Arab Muslim armies. The Byzantine empire lost over two thirds of its territory, but struggled on for another eight centuries until its final extinction at Ottoman hands in 1453; the Persian empire collapsed altogether.

Slowly over several centuries, the peoples inhabiting the formerly Persian and Byzantine territories conquered by the Arab Muslims adopted the language and religion of their conquerors, inter-married with them, and so gave rise to the Arab world and Iran as they exist today. That process is not entirely complete: there are still groups within the Arab world that retain their earlier religions (usually Christianity, but sometimes Judaism), and keep earlier languages alive. On language, but not on religion, the inhabitants of the former Persian empire compromised, coming to speak what is today called "Persian"—a language so full of Arabic words and phrases that it would be as incomprehensible to a Persian from before the Arab Muslim conquest as German is to a speaker of English.

These conquests made a big difference to how Islam was seen, both by Muslims and by outsiders. For Muslims, the conquests were a clear sign of divine favor: God was with them. For outsiders, the conquests established Islam as a religion of war, spread by the sword. This view did not trouble Muslims until relatively recently, when it became necessary to defend Islam against modern Western views of it as a religion of violence. During the late nineteenth century, several explanations emerged in response to these views. One favorite explanation sees the conquests as defensive, which is hardly convincing given the immense territories conquered. Another explanation stresses that it was the political power of the Arab Muslims that was spread by the sword, not the religion of Islam. Non-Muslims were well treated by their conquerors and allowed to practice their own religions. In fact, they often had more freedom of worship and were generally better treated than they had been under their former rulers. From a historical point of view, this second explanation is a lot more plausible than the first. There is actually some evidence that the early Arab Muslim conquerors even discouraged conversions to Islam. They may have preferred to collect tribute from non-Muslim subjects than to accept conquered peoples as their equals. If this attitude did exist, it disappeared after a century or two. Like Christianity and unlike traditional Judaism, Islam today welcomes converts.

Some people have sought an explanation for these conquests other than divine favor. The standard alternative explanation given by Western historians is that the Persian and Byzantine empires had exhausted themselves in wars against each other, and had lost the loyalty of their subjects through bad administration and religious persecution. It is also worth noting that this is hardly the only case in history in which armies of nomads conquered apparently more sophisticated empires. That is what happened to the Western Roman empire at the hands of the barbarians, and what would happen to the remains of the Muslim empire in 1258 at the hands of the Mongols. What tends to happen after such conquests is that the conquering nomads fall apart within a few generations of their victory. From a historian's point of view, then, the really interesting question is not how the Arab Muslims conquered most of the world around them, but how they managed to keep united afterwards. This was probably because they shared an ideal beyond mere conquest—that of Islam. Perhaps it was also because the Arab Muslim leaders of the eighth century were also unusually talented.

For three centuries, the conquered territories were administered as a single, great, centralized Muslim empire.[6] This empire was a worthy successor to the Roman and Persian empires—rich, powerful, and sophisticated, with no possible rival closer than China (which was a long way away, separated by high mountains and cruel deserts). The Muslim empire has almost no significance from a strictly religious point of view, but has left memories of former greatness with Muslims today. The Muslim empire is today sometimes seen as the "golden age" of Islam. Few Muslims know much in detail about its history, however. That is perhaps fortunate, since the empire was actually more a golden age of Muslim civilization than of the religion of Islam (that was Medina under the Prophet). The civilization of the empire was Muslim in the sense that its rulers and elites were Muslim, but neither the rulers nor most of the elites were particularly devout. As well as producing great Islamic religious scholarship, the empire excelled in an unusual area of technology where it has never been surpassed: wine fountains.

Islamic scholarship and wine fountains were two extremes. The empire saw a flowering of the arts and sciences in many other areas related neither to piety nor to pleasure: architecture, satire, administration, hydraulic engineering, philosophy, medicine, poetry, astronomy, and mathematics. The English word "algebra" is a word of Arabic origin, as is "alcohol" a word which was probably first used in English in a scientific, medical context. Europeans looked to the Muslim world for expertise in all these areas until after the Renaissance. In fact, the modern West owes to the civilization of this great Muslim empire its original discovery of not only algebra and "Arabic" numerals, but a wide variety of devices. The astrolabe (the ancestor of the sextant), paper, carpets, variolation (the ancestor of immunization), and even Aristotle reached the West through the Muslims. So, unfortunately, did the plague. None of these, of course, have anything directly to do with the religion of Islam.

The Muslim empire finally broke apart, as even the greatest empires do sooner or later, bringing to an end the period of the Arab Muslims as a

---

[6] In fact, there were two empires, a short-lived Umayyad empire and then a longer-lived Abbasid empire, the names indicating two different ruling dynasties. Since the territories of the Umayyad and Abbasid empires were much the same, however, it is easier to think in terms of one empire.

superpower. The empire became a series of smaller states, many of which were then overrun by outsiders, notably the then barbaric Mongols. The Mongols destroyed the civilization of the Muslim empire, just as earlier barbarians had destroyed the civilization of the Roman empire. For centuries, Muslim history becomes—like European history during the Middle Ages—a mass of small battling states and rulers. None of these produced the wealth or the political stability that had once supported the cultural and scientific achievements of the old empire, and much that had once been known was forgotten. Although the imperial astronomers had known that the earth circled the sun, later astronomers believed that the sun circled the earth. Another great empire, the Ottoman empire, did emerge from the chaos to rule much the same areas as the Muslim empire had, but it never included Persia, and was more distinguished for its military than its cultural or scientific achievements. The Ottomans conquered their way up to Hungary, and came close to conquering the rest of Europe towards the end of the European Middle Ages, but when science and culture again revived, it was in Europe, not in the Ottoman empire. The symbolic contribution of the Ottomans to world civilization is not algebra, but military music.

Though Islam first spread out of the Arabian peninsula in the wake of conquering armies as the religion of a powerful and sophisticated state, it later spread through encounters between Muslim preachers and followers of other religions, usually not monotheistic ones. This is how Islam spread among the Turks, the Africans, the Malays and the Indonesians. In all these cases, its fortunes were secured once it became the religion of the local state, as it usually did. Even before this occurred, it probably helped that the Muslim preachers and traders who spread Islam were seen as the representatives of a more powerful and sophisticated civilization, rather as Christian missionaries were often seen in nineteenth-century Africa.

It is wrong to think of Islam as a religion spread by the sword, then. On the whole, Islam spread peacefully, like most other religions, even though Muslim rulers often acquired territory by conquest, just as non-Muslim rulers did. The early conquests of the Arab Muslims and the achievements of the Muslim empire ended with the invasions of barbarian Mongols, but still matter today as reminders to Muslims of the divine favor they once enjoyed, and as a troubling contrast to the position of Muslim states in the modern world.

Where Muslims Live Now

At the time of writing, there are about 6.3 billion people on earth. About 22 percent of these (1.4 billion) are Muslim. 1.3 billion of the 1.4 billion Muslims live in a belt of land stretching half way round the earth, from West Africa through North Africa and the Middle East, on through Central Asia and Iran, south across the Indian subcontinent to Indonesia. Outside this belt, significant numbers of Muslims are found in Russia and China—about 20 million in each country. Then there are about 25 million Muslims living in the West: some 5 million in North America, and some 20 million in Western Europe. One or two percent of the population of most prosperous European countries is Muslim, and about 7.5 percent of the French population is Muslim—one French person in fifteen. Islam started off in the Arab world, but today only one of the eight countries with the largest Muslim populations, Egypt, is Arabic-speaking (see table 1, overleaf).

Map of the Muslim population of the world

■	Mostly Muslim (75% to 100% of population)	▦	Muslim Minorities (7 to 19% of population)
▦	Many Muslims (20% to 70% of population)	□	Few or No Muslims (0% to 6% of population)

Table 1: Countries with Muslim populations over 50 million.

Country	Muslims (millions)	Total Population (millions)
Indonesia	204	231
Pakistan	143	148
India	124	1,034
Bangladesh	119	136
Egypt	69	73
Turkey	67	67
Iran	66	68
Nigeria	65	130

The world's largest Muslim country is now Indonesia. The next three largest Muslim country are the three main parts of the Indian subcontinent (Pakistan, India, and Bangladesh). More than a quarter of the world's Muslims live in these three countries and neighboring Afghanistan, even though most Indians are Hindu rather than Muslim.

As table 2 shows, the territories of the old Muslim empire (the Middle East and North Africa, i.e., the Arab world plus Turkey and Iran) now come second after the Indian subcontinent. Despite this, the Middle East and North Africa is still the Muslim heartland, with a population that is 95 percent Muslim.

Table 2: Muslim populations by region.

Region	Muslims (millions)	Total Population (millions)
Indian sub-continent	415	1,375
Middle East & North Africa	380	400
Sub-Saharan Africa	240	685
Southeast Asia	230	600
Central Asia	50	80
Europe	40	730
China	20	1,310
North America	5	320
Elsewhere	0	770

Muslim minorities exist in many countries. These minorities have three possible origins. In Africa, they are often the result of the same processes of conversion that produced Muslim majorities elsewhere—but the process was interrupted before it could produce a majority. A second possible origin, mostly in China and Russia, is foreign conquest. One or two centuries ago, Muslim majority areas were conquered and their territory and populations then incorporated into larger, non-Muslim empires, in which a former independent majority became a subject minority. This is what happened to areas such as Chechnya. The third possible origin, which generally applies to Muslim minorities in the West, is immigration over the last fifty years or so. This process is continuing at the time of writing.

More demographic data, for those who are interested, are given in an appendix.

Summary

Islam is a monotheistic religion that has much in common with the other monotheistic religions, notably Judaism and Christianity. It has the same basic understanding of birth, life, death and judgment, and its scriptures tell much the same stories: Adam and Eve, Noah and the flood, Moses and Mount Sinai. The biggest difference between Islam and Christianity is that Islam sees itself as the accurate and final expression of God's will and plan for humanity, more perfect than Christianity or Judaism. Where Islam differs from those two religions, Islam is right and the others are wrong.

Islam started in seventh-century Arabia, and is based on the Koran—revealed by God to Muhammad through an angel—and on the teachings and example of the Prophet Muhammad, as recorded in the *hadith*. The circumstances of Islam's birth have left their mark on Islam as it exists today, in ways ranging from the reverence paid the pre-Islamic temple in Mecca (the Kaba) to many references in the Koran to warfare and loyalty in battle. The references to battle are a reflection of the fighting endemic in seventh-century Arabia, fighting in which the first Muslims were engaged.

At his death, the Prophet Muhammad left a small community of Muslims, the Koran and the *hadith*. The Koran was never read in isolation, but was always part of a growing and changing religion that was incorporated in the later Muslim community. After the Prophet's death, the concepts of *sunna* (exemplary tradition) and *bida* (innovation) encouraged Muslims to imitate that first community, and the Prophet himself. Muslims try to follow the example of that earliest community as closely as possible, but most make a distinction between innovations (*bida*) that are acceptable (motorcars) and ones that are not (ancestor worship). Only a very few Muslims put everyday aspects of modern life into the "not acceptable" category.

The Prophet is enormously important in Islam, and to all Muslims. Although in the end God matters more, and although in the end Islam is God's religion (not the Prophet's), in daily life reference is made more often to the Prophet than to God. In most sermons, the name of the Prophet comes into at least every other sentence. The significance of the Prophet is such that his name is never mentioned by devout or even semi-devout Muslims (and never appears in print in a Muslim language) without the addition of the phrase *sal'Allahu aleyhi wa salim*, which is generally translated into English as "peace be upon him," or—more accurately—as "may God bless him and give him peace." Sometimes this phrase is added a little perfunctorily, but often the speaker dwells almost lovingly over these syllables.

For anyone (Muslim or not) to insult the Prophet, may God bless him and give him peace, is generally considered unendurable. Almost universal outrage resulted in 1988–1989 when the British author Salman Rushdie was widely reported to have insulted the Prophet, may God bless him and give him peace, in his book *The Satanic Verses*, and again in 2005-2006, when an obscure Danish newspaper was even more widely reported to have done the same.

On both occasions, many Westerners had difficulty understanding what all the fuss was about. This was partly because, for most Westerners, there is now no figure who has the same significance as the Prophet still has for nearly all Muslims. Although Jesus has similar significance for devout Christians, devout Christians are now a minority in most parts of the West, and have gradually grown used to living in a society where the concept of the sacred—and so also the concept of blasphemy—has almost vanished. In the West, the days are now long gone when blasphemy was a crime that might be punished by death. In the Muslim world, the concepts of the sacred and of blasphemy still matter.

On both occasions, there was more to it than just blasphemy and outrage. There was also mutual incomprehension. Just as many Westerners could not understand what all the fuss was about, most Muslims could not understand that Westerners might think that novels or cartoons didn't really matter that much. Also, certain individuals on both sides, and even certain states in the Muslim world, thought that political advantage might result from fanning the flames, and did fan them, successfully. Finally, the "Clash of Civilizations," which I will discuss in chapter 12, also played an important part. For reasons I will examine in more detail later, Muslims today often feel attacked and misunderstood by the West. For many Muslims, the Danish cartoons were the last straw: when would Westerners learn to show a little respect for Islam and for Muslims? Death threats and television pictures of chanting crowds and burning embassies were never, of course, likely to increase Western understanding of Islam or Western respect for Muslims. But then people do not always act in their own best interests.

2

Who's in Charge Here?

The Construction of Islam

Most European states like to have some kind of official relationship with each major religious group. Usually, there is an archbishop or two who is in regular contact with the highest levels of government—perhaps a Catholic one and a Protestant one. Then there is a Chief Rabbi who enjoys similar levels of access, though perhaps less frequently. But when it comes to the Muslims . . . in European states, there is probably an Islamic Council, a National Islamic Council, a Federation of Councils, a National Federation, and perhaps even a Federation of Federations. My favorite was a Council of Italian Muslims in the late 1990s that represented all of thirty people.

It is not just in Europe where it is unclear who is in charge of Islam. Islam is a religion with no priests, and has acknowledged no single leader since the death of the Prophet. And yet there are plenty of Muslims who are happy to speak in the name of Islam: muftis, mullahs, ayatollahs, shaykhs, "community leaders," and even the President of the Council of Italian Muslims who had only thirty followers. Many Westerners find it difficult to decide which of these, if any, are worth taking seriously. Understanding who speaks for Muslims requires an understanding of the somewhat unusual, and often somewhat complicated, authority structures within Islam—of how what started in a desert cave turned into the worldwide religion we know today as Islam.

Islam rests on the Koran, the *hadith*, and the example of the Prophet, as we saw in chapter 1. After the death of the Prophet, all of these elements had to be put together somehow to form a comprehensive system. All new religions have to go through such a stage.

There are passages in the Koran that have only one possible meaning, but there are also passages that have several possible meanings. In the early years of Islam, one problem was how such passages should be understood. Likewise, there are *hadith* that are completely clear, but there are also subjects on which there are several *hadith* that seem to say different things, as well as slightly different versions of the same *hadith*. All this mass of material had to be interpreted and reconciled, just as Christian doctrine had to be worked out by the early Church. There was never exactly a Church in Islam, but something not vastly different evolved—a body of men (very occasionally including a few women) who were the guardians of the proper interpretation of Islam, called the Ulema (discussed later in this chapter).

Denominations

As in Christianity and Judaism, there are different denominations within Islam. A denomination is a major subdivision of a religion, such as Greek Orthodox or Episcopalian. Confusingly, the word "Church" is used to mean both denomination (e.g., most Italians are in the Catholic Church) and the hierarchy, or authority, within a denomination (e.g., the Catholic Church forbids contraception). Although Islam does not have a Church in the sense of a hierarchy, it does have Churches in the sense of denominations, though the word "Church" is not usually used. I will examine differences in the views of Islam's denominations from time to time throughout this book.

The basic division in Islam is between the Sunni denomination, which is the largest one (and has subdivisions of its own), and the Shi'i denomination, which is the second largest. Most Muslims worldwide are Sunni. For centuries the Shi'a were a minority in all parts of the Muslim world, never a majority. Only in the sixteenth century did they become the majority in certain areas: Iran and then, even later, in much of Iraq. The Shi'a are also found as substantial minorities in other Muslim countries, notably Lebanon and Pakistan, and in the West.

Like Catholics and Orthodox Christians, Sunnis and Shi'as generally recognize and accept each other as different. This mutual recognition and acceptance is often easier when the two denominations do not actually live together. In recent years, Sunnis and Shi'as have come into violent conflict in Pakistan and Lebanon, and then in Iraq. Similarly, Catholics and Orthodox Christians have come into violent conflict in recent years in what was once Yugoslavia, as have Catholics and Protestants in Northern Ireland. In all these cases, there was a religious element to the conflict, but the conflict was not really about religion.

The split between Sunnis and Shi'a started shortly after the death of the Prophet (as discussed further in chapter 10). Since then, there have been further splits, producing a number of smaller denominations and sects. Most of these, like the Druze, are of Shi'i origin. Some, like the Ahmadis, are of Sunni origin.

At the start of the nineteenth century, a new movement emerged among Sunnis in what is today Saudi Arabia, called Wahhabism by outsiders. The Wahhabis (who call themselves by other names, such as "Unitarian" or even plain "Muslim") are not exactly a denomination, but are something similar to one. Originally, Wahhabism started as a radical sect of Sunni Islam, in the sense that what they believed differed significantly from what other Muslims around them believed, and that these differences of belief gave rise to tension and conflict. This period involved much loss of life and property, and ended with the virtual destruction of Wahhabism. Wahhabism survived, however, though in less radical form. Today, it is a denomination in the sense that it is the official religion of Saudi Arabia, and is increasingly influential elsewhere in the Sunni world. Wahhabi Islam differs from mainstream Sunni Islam in being unusually strict and puritanical. Just as differences between the views of Sunni and Shi'i Muslims will be indicated from time to time throughout the book, so will differences between the views of Wahhabi and non-Wahhabi Muslims.

Interpretation

Regardless of denomination, Muslims today will often claim to be reading the Koran directly, without intermediation. Muslims may say "it says in the Koran that . . . ," just as Christians sometimes say "it says in the Bible that . . ." However, in both cases, whether he or she realizes it or not, the person who claims to be reading the Koran or Bible directly is in fact reading it through a lens influenced by principles and teachings they have previously absorbed. The Koran, for example, says "intoxicants and games of chance and stones set up and arrows are only an uncleanness, Satan's work."[1] These words clearly condemn alcohol and gambling, but do they actually forbid them? The reference to stones presumably indicates the worship of idols—but what is this about "arrows"? Might that require pacifism? Any Muslim today will have no difficulty at all in understanding the passage, however. They will tell you that it "obviously" forbids alcohol, gambling, idol-worship, and attempting to divine the future, whether by casting arrows or by any other means, such as crystal balls. For that "obvious" reading to be possible, however, someone at some point had to put the passage together with other passages from the Koran and the *hadith* and with what they knew of the early Muslims' way of living, had to then *decide* on its meaning. Once the decision about the passage's meaning had been made and accepted, however, it became possible for later generations to read the passage and *think* that they were understanding it directly.

In the case of Christianity, decisions such as these were made by bishops at early Church Councils. Islam had rejected priests and bishops, and there were never any councils. Islam's system was by necessity less formal (which may be one reason why unorthodoxy was better tolerated). At first, it seems, people just asked someone older—what did the Prophet do? What did the first Muslims do? Soon, however, some people began to specialize in answering these questions, in collecting and studying the *hadith*, and in teaching and preaching. By the start of the Muslim empire, these religious scholars became Islam's religious specialists. They are known as the Ulema (a word which is plural, indicating the group, not individuals within it).

The Ulema

"Ulema" literally means "scholars," but the Arabic term is probably already familiar to many readers, and will be used to avoid confusion between religious scholars and other, later types of scholars (like geologists). In some

---

[1]Koran chapter 5, verse 90.

parts of the Muslim world, but not in others, the word "mullah" is used to indicate an individual member of the Ulema. An alternative title is "shaykh." These and other terms, like "mufti" and "ayatollah," will be discussed later in the book.

The Ulema are like Judaism's rabbis, and they are in a sense Islam's priests, but are very different from priests in important ways. Firstly, the Ulema have no sacramental functions. There are no ritual acts that they can do that any other Muslim cannot also do. When a group of Muslims prays together, for example, someone has to lead the prayer. In a big, modern mosque in a major city today, there will usually be a professional prayer-leader (*imam* in Arabic), appointed and paid by the government, and he will usually be from the Ulema. But in a small neighborhood mosque or in a village, prayer will be led by the oldest and most respected man present, who might well be a local shopkeeper. In a private house, prayer will usually be led by the householder. In all cases, the prayer-leader is an Imam, though perhaps only for five minutes. Similarly, if a non-Muslim wishes to become Muslim, he or she has to repeat the "testimony of faith" (the recognition that there is no god other than God, and that Muhammad is the Prophet of God) in front of two witnesses. Any two sane adult male witnesses will do, so long as they are themselves Muslim (gender relations in Islam are discussed in chapter 6). For practical reasons, someone wishing to become Muslim nowadays will probably choose witnesses who can issue a formal certificate with a rubber stamp, and if in the Muslim world will probably therefore choose government employees who will be from the Ulema; but this is merely a question of administrative convenience. Members of the Ulema are more likely than ordinary Muslims to be leading prayer in a major mosque, or certifying conversions or marriages, but this is because modern states like to have matters of importance done in an official way and within their control, not because of anything to do with Islam or holy men.

The second big difference between the Ulema and priests is that they are not organized into any sort of a formal hierarchy (except, to some extent, in Shi'i Islam, as is discussed in chapter 10). Their internal organization is more like that of physicians than of priests. Some of the Ulema are more highly respected than others, of course, and some will report to others within particular institutions (a school, for example), which will all have some sort of a director. There may even be national or regional councils of Ulema, just as there are medical councils. But no one member of the Ulema has anything like the authority over other members that a bishop has over priests, or a pope over bishops.

The Sharia

The conclusions that the Ulema come to on particular questions have from time to time been collected, and these collections come close to being formally considered as codes of law. Two words are used to describe these codes. The closest to a Western conception of "law" is what is called the *fiqh*, which consists of rules on such topics as contracts, land ownership, theft, and inheritance, as well as rules on topics such as prayer and fasting. There is also the *sharia,* a term often confused with *fiqh*, but that in fact has a much wider meaning. The Sharia is everything a human needs to live properly—not just the *fiqh*, but also moral and ethical rules. This book, in a sense, is a book about the Sharia.

The Sharia also covers criminal law, and the word "Sharia" is nowadays often understood in the West to mean simply Islam's criminal law, or even just certain penalties in criminal law, notably stoning and amputation. There are reasons for this misunderstanding (discussed in chapter 11), but that is not what the word really means. In this book, the word "Sharia" will be used in its real, original sense, as the rules and perspectives that guide (or should guide) Muslims through life.

The Sharia establishes five categories for any act. Two will be immediately familiar to Western readers: the forbidden (*haram*) and the required (*fard*). It is forbidden to kill, to marry one's sibling, or to enter into a contract to sell something one does not have. It is required that one pray, look after one's spouse, and pay one's debts. The opposite of *haram* is *halal*, "allowed," a word which means much the same as Judaism's *kosher*. A *halal* butcher is one who sells meat that a Muslim is allowed to eat (i.e., that has not been slaughtered contrary to the Sharia).

A third category is that of "recommended," *mustahabb*, often called *sunna*. The *sunna*, as we saw in chapter 1, is the exemplary practice of the

Prophet. The word is also used in a slightly different sense: a *mustahabb* or *sunna* act is an act that one is not required to do, but that it is a good idea to do. In this sense, someone might say, "It is *sunna* not to drink until you have finished eating." This means that the Prophet and the early Muslims are known not to have drunk until they had finished eating, and that Muslims today should follow that example, but are not obliged to do so. To pray in a mosque at noon on a Friday is required, not *sunna*—there is no choice in the matter, and anyone who fails to pray in a mosque on a Friday without a legitimate excuse will have this held against him when he comes to be judged after death. To pray before setting out on a journey, on the other hand, is *sunna*, as it is to give money to beggars one meets in the street. Failing to do so will not be held against one, but doing it will be held in one's favor.

A fourth category is the reverse of *sunna*: *makruh*, discouraged. It is discouraged to drink before one has finished eating, to cut one's hair on a Friday, or to speak harshly to a beggar. Just as one is rewarded for doing something that is *sunna* but not punished for not doing it, so one is rewarded for not doing something that is discouraged, but not punished for doing it. It will not be held against a person if he or she has his or her hair cut on a Friday, but it is better to wait until Saturday (unless the person in question is in some parts of Southeast Asia, where the Ulema argue that Friday is actually preferable to Saturday).

The final, fifth category is a neutral one, called *mubah*, allowed. Talking on the telephone is allowed—unless one happens to be comforting someone who is ill, which is *sunna*, or making a Friday appointment with the hairdresser, which is *makruh*.

These multiple categories give Islam a certain flexibility. Everyone is expected to pay attention to the two extreme categories, forbidden and required, and people generally do. This does not mean that every Muslim prays when he or she is required to, and that no Muslim ever enters into a dodgy contract, but every Muslim at least knows the status of these actions. The extent to which two intermediate categories, *sunna* and *makruh*, are observed, is a matter of personal choice. A very religious person will try hard to practice the *sunna* and avoid the *makruh*, but most Muslims do not bother. Hairdressers have plenty of customers on Fridays, most of whom probably have no idea that having their hair cut on that particular day is discouraged; many know, but do not much care. In many Muslim households, water and soda are not presented until the meal has ended, but more because that is the way things have always been done than for any religious reason. Few people probably realize that the custom they are following has a religious basis.

Even for the extreme categories, there are exceptions. It is forbidden to kill, but not if someone is trying to kill you and the only way to stop them is to fight back. It is required to fast, but not if a medical condition means that fasting will damage your health.

The Sharia was once the main basis for the legal system in Muslim states, but for reasons I will discuss in chapter 11, it has today been replaced in most places by legal systems that are more similar to Western ones: a case for breach of contract will no longer be judged according to the Sharia in most Muslim countries. The Sharia, however, remains the standard which all Muslims live by in their daily lives—or which they ignore, depending on the type of Muslim. For observant Muslims, what the Sharia says on a particular issue matters more than what national law says. For example, national law in most Muslim countries says nothing about the consumption of pork, but the Sharia forbids it. No Muslim will eat pork simply because national law allows it. A popular black-market money changer in one Arab city is a devout Muslim, on whose premises tapes of the Koran are always playing. This mixture of religiosity and criminality seems odd to many of his Western customers, but it makes somewhat more sense in Islamic terms: the money-changer follows the Sharia, and the Sharia has nothing to say on the subject of exchange control. Some would argue, however, that the Sharia requires Muslims to follow all state laws and regulations, as long as they do not require something that is forbidden by the Sharia. Even though the Sharia is no longer the basis for the legal system of the state, it is still very important to Muslims today.

Sunni and Shi'i Muslims have somewhat different versions of the Sharia, partly because the Ulema of each denomination developed their version without much reference to the conclusions of the Ulema of the other denomination (for reasons discussed in chapter 10), and partly because they used different sources and methods in developing their versions of the Sharia. The Shi'i Ulema doubted the accuracy of many *hadith* that the

Sunni Ulema accepted, and more importantly, the Shi'a regarded their own early leaders, whom they called "Imams," as infallible interpreters of the Sharia and of Islam. The Shi'i Ulema considered their interpretations as important as, and gave them as much weight as, the *hadith* of the Prophet. For Sunni Muslims, what the Prophet said about Islam was, by definition, right—even when he was not passing on the Koran that had been revealed to him, he was still speaking on behalf of God (though not in the actual words of God). Since his death, no one (according to Sunnis) has spoken on behalf of God, though of course some people have been closer to the truth than others. For Shi'i Muslims, the Imams also spoke on behalf of God just as the Prophet did, in the sense that their words were divinely protected from error. For Sunni Muslims, the Imams did not have any such protection.

In practice, most of the disagreements between the Sunni and Shi'i Ulema are not considerable. They disagree about how to time fasting, for example, not about the need to fast. In the remainder of this book, "Muslims" covers both Sunni and Shi'a, and where the Shi'a take a different view, this will be indicated.

Another group that understands the Sharia somewhat differently is the Sufis. It is important to understand that the Sufis are *not* a separate denomination, although many people get confused about this. Sufism is an option *within* Sunni and Shi'i Islam, not an alternative to either.

For Sufis, Sufism is a collection of understandings and practices that allow them to come closer to God in this world, to achieve a sort of foretaste of heaven before getting there. For Wahhabis and some other Muslims, in contrast, Sufism is also one vast *bida*, an irregular innovation of the most problematic kind, and has no place in Islam. They believe Sufism should be excised from Islam completely.

Along with doing everything that all other devout Muslims do, a Sufi normally also belongs to a Sufi order, called a *tariqa*, that is run by a "Shaykh" (elder), often called a "guide." In some orders, the Shaykh is a full-time professional who gives his followers (or only very occasionally, *her* followers) detailed guidance as they advance step by step along a difficult spiritual path that leads to the spiritual experience of God himself. More frequently, however, the Shaykh is a part-timer who does little more than hold a weekly ceremony called a *hadra* (or *majlis*), at which Sufis gather for a special form of liturgy known as *zikr*. Each order has its own peculiarities of liturgy and practice. The *hadra* and *zikr* are discussed in chapter 5, in the context of Islamic worship.

Sufism encourages people to look at inner meanings rather than outer appearances, and Sufis emphasize the Sharia as a means to an end, rather than as an end in itself. As a result, they have often been accused of ignoring the Sharia, or at least of paying less attention to it than they should. While this sometimes happens, it is unusual, and in general Sufis follow the Sharia in the same way that other Muslims do.

The Ulema Today

For most of Muslim history, the Ulema were respected, influential, and wealthy. They controlled not just the interpretation and preaching of Islam, but also education and the legal system. There was no education other than that provided by the Ulema, save for apprenticeship. A baker learned how to bake by working for a baker, and a builder learned by working for a builder, and a physician or a clerk by working for a physician or a clerk. But anyone who wanted to be a physician or a clerk needed to be literate first, and primary education was provided by the Ulema. The Ulema also had a virtual monopoly over intellectual life.

The Ulema remained wealthy because their schools and the major mosques were supported by endowments that paid decent salaries to the Ulema who worked there. The Ulema themselves controlled these endowments and could draw extra income from them as fees and expenses. One of the Ulema who ended up in a village school might be financially little better off than the peasants whose children he taught, but the preachers and prayer-leaders of major mosques and the teachers at major schools lived comfortably.

The Ulema still keep some of that prestige today, and are usually still spoken of with respect, but—except in Saudi Arabia and Iran, discussed later—the modern Ulema have lost most of their former position. For a start, they are no longer wealthy, since the endowments from which they once benefitted have almost everywhere been taken over by the state. The

Ulema are often now paid by the state like bureaucrats, and in most Muslim countries, bureaucrats are paid very poorly indeed. Economically, then, the Ulema have descended from the elite to the lower middle class, which naturally has had implications for recruitment. Once upon a time the cleverest and most ambitious Muslims aspired to join the Ulema; now the cleverest and most ambitious Muslims aspire to work for multinational corporations.

Secondly, the Ulema have lost their monopoly over intellectual life. Throughout the Muslim world, there are newspapers, journalists, television and radio stations, universities and professors, novelists, and directors of art galleries. These play leading parts in intellectual life, just as they do in the West. Even in the area of religion, the Ulema now have rivals. Newspapers occasionally print articles by members of the Ulema, but regular journalists see no reason why they should avoid the topic of religion. Smaller mosques traditionally had preachers who were not of the Ulema, but those preachers lacked the education to do much more than fill a gap. Now they may well have university degrees and be just as strong at general intellectual training as the Ulema. In fact, people often prefer their preaching to that of the Ulema. Across the Muslim world, recordings of preachers are popular listening for many. There are no exact figures, but at a rough estimate more than three quarters of such recordings are by preachers who are not Ulema. Equally, there are no exact figures for the sales of books on religious subjects, but probably only one in ten of the best-selling authors on religious topics are from the Ulema. Instead, they are journalists, or lawyers, or physicians, and occasionally university professors. Increasingly, even engineers and computer scientists are coming to the fore.

The situation is not the same everywhere. In Saudi Arabia, always a special case because of Wahhabism, the Ulema maintain their former position in society. In Iran, too, the Ulema recovered their former position after the Iranian Revolution of 1979. Iran is unique as a long-established Shi'i state, and the special nature and organization of Shi'i Islam is one of the reasons why the state never quite managed to take away the economic and social status of the Ulema there. Admittedly, though, even in Iran, the Ulema could not keep its former monopoly over education and intellectual life. They kept enough of their former position to be able to take part in, and benefit from, the Iranian revolution. The revolution, however, proved a mixed blessing for the Iranian Ulema, since it meant that after it they became closely associated with the new regime. As the regime became less and less popular, so did the Ulema. At the time of writing, popular feeling in Iran is such that younger members of the Ulema sometimes take off their distinctive clothing and don ordinary clothes before traveling on public transport.

In much of the Sunni world, the place of the Ulema has to some extent been filled by a mixed group of journalists and self-appointed intellectuals. On the whole, religious authority in most Muslim countries is no longer in the hands of any one identifiable group of people. To some extent, this is also true in the West, where journalists and other "lay" people are happy to write on religious subjects. Churches in the West, though, still have more authority for most Western Christians than any single body or organization now has for Sunni Muslims everywhere.

Summary

Most Muslims today are Sunni, but some—especially in Iran and Iraq—are Shi'i, a separate and different group. There are also a number of other, much smaller, denominations. The Wahhabi movement is in some ways a separate denomination, with its strongest base in Saudi Arabia. It favors the most literal possible interpretation of the Koran and *hadith*, and since the end of the Second World War has been becoming increasingly influential among Sunni Muslims.

Although many Muslims today claim just to be simply following what it says in the Koran, their understanding of what they find in the Koran is conditioned by a process of interpretation carried out in the first centuries after the Prophet. This process was conducted by religious scholars called the Ulema, on the basis of the Koran, the *hadith*, and their own logical methods.

The Ulema are not priests, because they have no sacramental functions. They are scholars, and once were powerful and important. Today they are much less important, and no longer attract the finest talent available. They are in general poorly paid bureaucrats, except in Saudi Arabia and Iran, where they still have power.

The totality of all the conclusions of the Ulema make up the Sharia, which has rulings on almost every aspect of life. It covers what in the West would be criminal and civil law, but also the details of ritual and worship, and optional *sunna* recommendations about almost every aspect of human behavior. The Sharia is no longer the national law in most Muslim countries, but even so it is still the standard to which Muslims refer in their daily lives.

Some Muslims, whether Sunni or Shi'i, are also Sufis, who are organized into orders and emphasize the inner aspects of Islamic spirituality, but do not ignore the Sharia.

The Sharia matters as much as it ever did, but the Ulema matter less. Except in a few countries, they no longer have the authority they once had, or the financial standing that went with it. With rare exceptions, ambitious and clever young men no longer embark on careers as Ulema. Instead, when they do not go into business, they become journalists and intellectuals — and may then interpret Islam for the public just as the Ulema used to, but without the Ulema's formal religious training.

3

Smiles and Frowns
Types of Muslim

As I started writing this book, I noticed some of the reader reviews of introductions to Islam on Amazon.com. I was struck by the complaint of one American reader. His last two girlfriends had been Muslim, and he wanted to understand a bit more about their religion. He'd bought a book from Amazon, and it had been no use at all. I wasn't totally surprised by his disappointment. Muslims are not supposed to have girlfriends and boyfriends. Whoever that disappointed reader's girlfriends had been, they must have been pretty non-standard Muslims.

Of course, many Muslims are non-standard. In fact, "standard" Muslims may even be in a minority, especially in the West. Muslims, like everyone else, have doubts; Muslims, like everyone else, make their own compromises with reality—comfortably or uncomfortably. Some of my Muslim friends live exemplary lives, and some do not. And even those who lead exemplary lives provide very different sorts of examples. Some have beards and stern expressions; some have beards and soft expressions. Some cover their hair and laugh, and some cover their hair and frown. And they laugh and frown at different things.

There are many types of Muslim. Most of these types have much in common, but the differences between them are also important, and so before we can look at other aspects of Islam, it is necessary to consider the different varieties of Muslim. This was probably always complicated, but the picture today is more complicated than it used to be, because of the impact of modernity on the Muslim world and on Muslims everywhere.

When I first visited the Muslim world, I shared the common view of most outsiders, that Islam is medieval. On my fourth evening in Egypt, I was sitting with some other foreigners in a hotel bar, and I explained to one of them how I thought Islam really needed a reformation. One man there was a European scholar of Islam, and his expression, as he said to me, "It's a bit more complicated than that," was enough to discourage me from making any more instant judgments for the rest of the evening. He was right: it is more complicated. Later, as a historian, I spent years trying to unravel the complications. The conclusion I finally reached is that in some ways Islam has already had a reformation, but no one really noticed. And, certainly from a Western point of view, this invisible reformation was the problem, not the solution.

One of the telltale signs of this reformation is the changes in the status of the Ulema as the Muslim world modernized. These were dramatic, as we saw in chapter 2. But modernity has not just changed the status of the Ulema: it has also changed other Muslims, and it has changed Islam. Islam has entered the modern age.

What people usually mean by "the modern age" is a tolerant, liberal and rational society, like America. Of course, there are ways in which even American society can be intolerant, illiberal and irrational, and there are ways in which Sweden (for example) is different from America without being any less modern. "Being modern" does not have to mean "being like us." But the main point is that if America is generally tolerant and liberal and rational, this is not because of the Reformation. It is because of what happened *after* the Reformation. While early Protestant society much preferred God to reason, and was in many ways extremely illiberal and intolerant, the Enlightenment preached reason and liberal tolerance. Western modernity needed the Enlightenment more than the Reformation, and it needed other events during the nineteenth century as well. Industrialization and mass literacy were certainly important, for a start.

Tradition

Three important things happened in the European Reformation. One was that the Catholic Church lost its former authority, and members of a new and newly literate middle class started reading the Bible on their own. The second was that Christianity itself changed—more for the new Protestants than for Catholics, but for Catholics too, as a result of the Counter-Reformation. The last thing that happened was that Europe divided into Protestant and Catholic countries, which then often fought each other.

Much the same three things happened to Islam during the second half of the nineteenth century, though in less obvious ways. Firstly, as we have seen, the Ulema lost their former authority, and the old interpretations of Islam were to a large extent replaced with independent understandings by the new and newly literate middle class. Secondly, Islam itself changed, with the introduction of new understandings that I will discuss at various points throughout this book. Thirdly, like Europe centuries before, the Muslim world split. The split was not by region as with Protestant and Catholic Europe, but by class, into "modern" and "traditional" Muslims. The educated inhabitants of the towns and cities today generally follow a quasi-Protestant reformed Islam, which I will call "modern," while the less educated inhabitants of the countryside generally follow the old, traditional Islam.

In their religious lives, traditional Muslims typically concern themselves with matters such as prayer, divine grace and the saints. Sufis are nearly always traditional Muslims. Modern Muslims regard many traditional beliefs as superstitious, and concern themselves especially with the application of the Sharia, to themselves and to society as a whole. I will discuss Islam and politics in chapter 11, but I should emphasize one important difference between traditional and modern Islam immediately: traditional Islam was never particularly political, while modern Islam has an emphasis on society that often makes it very political.

Traditional Muslims and modern Muslims generally live fairly happily side by side. In many countries, for example, an office manager will typically be a modern Muslim, and the man who makes the tea will typically be a traditional Muslim. Each thinks of the other as Muslim, but the modern manager sees the man who brings the tea as superstitious and ignorant, while the traditional man who brings the tea thinks that the manager fails to understand some very important things about life, God, and religion. The manager may be a lot richer than the traditional Muslim with the tea tray, but if the manager can't even understand the operation of divine grace in the world, the traditional Muslim would not swap places with him for anything. Each man will normally avoid offending the other, though. If any lecturing happens, it will normally be the modern Muslim taking advantage of his university education and higher status to lecture the traditional Muslim, with the traditional Muslim seeming to listen politely, but probably not paying much attention. The post-reformation conflicts in the Muslim world are not between traditional and modern Muslims, but between sections of modern Islam and the state. I will go into this more in chapter 11.

The difference between traditional Muslims and modern Muslims is of great importance, and will be referred to again and again in the remainder of this book. Both are Muslims, but in very different ways. Formally, they are not separate denominations, but in practice they might almost be. The differences between them are often more important than differences between Sunni Muslims and Shi'i Muslims.

Modernity

An event which changed Christianity even more than the Reformation was the coming of modernity during the nineteenth century. The challenges modernity presented to religion were felt mostly in the West, but they had some impact in the Muslim world as well.

The first and most obvious challenge to religion came from nineteenth-century natural science, which offered all sorts of problematic discoveries—most notably about the origins of the earth and of humanity. Evolution was and is the test case: Did God make man in a way that His "intelligent design" can be discerned, or did man evolve in random fashion from some sort of ape? A second challenge was the growth of other sources of knowledge, from sociological research to novels, that began to suggest views of human nature that were at variance with those of religion. The third challenge to religion was little noticed by the general public, but had a profound impact all the same: scholars in history and linguistics began more and more to understand religion as something that developed and changed over time. Not only could human authors be discerned in the Bible, but so could human editors, trying to reconcile divergent points of view, and not always succeeding.

Western Christians have responded to these challenges with varying positions. At one extreme, it is possible to hold that God made man, and that anything which suggests evolution is either a misunderstanding or a trick of Satan. Typically, Christians taking this line will also hold that sociology and novels have nothing to teach us, and that their Christianity today is precisely what was taught by Jesus. At the other extreme, one can accept evolution, and conclude that everything else in the Bible is wrong too. Agnostics taking this line generally see sociology and novels as more useful sources of understanding than the Bible. For them, the study of history can perhaps tell us how the mass illusion of Christianity developed in the first place.

In between these extremes, some argue that the Bible describes the most important aspects of the relationship between God and humans in symbolic terms. The Bible does not actually make any precise scientific claims about the technical mechanism of the appearance of human life on earth, but it is still a divine text of unique importance. For those taking this line, sociology and novels may be seen as useful sources of knowledge, but they should not be treated as sources of absolute truth. For such Christians, certain aspects of Christian doctrine reflect the conclusions of past Church councils, and those conclusions are subject to revision. There is no reason why a question that was decided one way a thousand years ago should not be decided another way today.

A fourth position, which is perhaps the most nuanced one, may be called "postmodern" (though actually it was first developed in the nineteenth century). This position holds that the Bible is a document composed by our more distant ancestors. It contains much that reflects their outdated views, not just on a scientific level but also on sociological and theological levels, but it also contains truth. Independent sources of knowledge, from novels to the study of other religions, can help us unlock that truth. The Bible may be of human origin, but that does not stop it being one of the best available means of access to the divine.

At the extremes, Muslims are faced with the same alternatives as Christians. They can decide that either the Koran is right (and evolution is an error or a trick), or at the other extreme they can decide that the Koran is all wrong. For those who maintain that the Koran is right, one ingenious idea helps in the evolution debate: the remains which appear to be "missing links" are in fact the remains of long-dead humans who were changed into simian form by God as punishment for their great sins.

However, it is difficult for Muslims to occupy either of the two intermediate positions. For Muslims, the text of the Koran is entirely the work and word of God. It is possible for a Muslim to hold that the Koran uses symbolic language and is describing the essence of things, not their technical form, but it is difficult to hold that the Koran reflects the views of our more distant ancestors. This would imply that the Koran is not God's word, and to imply that is almost universally understood as abandoning Islam. The closest to this position comes from a number of Muslim intellectuals who maintain that the views of our ancestors are present in the Koran to the extent that God paid attention to the general level of understanding of the time and place in the same way that He paid attention to the language of the time and place: God revealed the Koran to seventh-century Arabs in seventh-century Arabic, using seventh-century concepts. Such intellectuals are at present found mostly in Iran, both among the Ulema and in the universities, and occasionally in the West.

The status of the Koran, then, means that the positions that Muslims can occupy differ from those that Christians can occupy. Muslims also differ from Christians because of the belief that Islam is God's final revelation, good for all times and all places. Hence, while times may change, Islam itself cannot change—and cannot have changed in the past. At most, the details of the application of certain rules may have been, and still may be, modified, but the rules themselves are eternal. This makes it very difficult for Muslims to see Islam as developing and changing over time.

A further reason why only a tiny minority of Muslims understand Islam as developing over time is that although some scholarly research has been done on the historical development of Islamic doctrine, it is very basic, at least in comparison to the research that has been done on Christianity. Most active scholars of religious history are Westerners, and Westerners are more interested in Christianity than Islam. When historical research into Islamic doctrines has been done, it has almost always been done either by Westerners or by Muslims who were very obviously not practicing or believing Muslims. This means that when the conclusions of such research are known to Muslims, they are generally rejected out-of-hand as entirely lacking in legitimacy, or even as an attack on Islam by outsiders aiming to destroy Islam and the Muslims. To some extent, this reaction results from the conflictual relationship between Islam and the West, which I will consider in chapter 12. As a result, the historical understandings of religion that are widespread in the West are simply not available in the Muslim world. Only a few Muslims encounter them and are in a position to even consider them.

The result is that while it may seem obvious to many Westerners that Islam was originally the religion of tribes that dwelt in the desert in ancient times, and then of a sophisticated but essentially pre-modern society, and that it bears the traces of its history, only a tiny minority of Muslims are in a position to take this view. Although it will be interesting to see what consequences the positions currently being developed in Iran and the West will have over the years to come, at present "postmodern" Muslims are so few as to be of no real significance. They are really a category all on their own.

Another reason why Islam does not strike Muslims as the religion of desert tribes is because the mental world of any Muslim encompasses seventh-century Arabia, just as the mental world of any Christian encompasses first-century Palestine. Babies in mangers and kings following stars are very distant from the world in which modern Westerners live, but even so do not feel alien. In exactly the same way, tribal battles in the desert do not feel alien to Muslims living in high-rise apartment blocks and watching satellite televison.

Religiosity

As one would expect, the degree of commitment to Islam of both traditional and modern Muslims varies from the extremely devout to the merely nominal, with an infinite number of gradations in between. There are extremely devout Muslims whose every action is guided by an awareness of the Sharia, and merely nominal Muslims who pay little if any attention to Islam on a daily basis. There are also, of course, former Muslims—people who were brought up as Muslims, and later became atheists or converts to other religions.

The Sharia offers two principal categories for measuring religiosity: "righteous" (*salih*) and "corrupt" (*fasih*), roughly equating to observant and non-observant. In practice, most Muslims measure religiosity in slightly more subtle terms, recognizing degrees of observance between these two alternatives. In everyday life, the concern is not so much with whether or not people are "righteous" as with how often they pray.

As I will explain in chapter 5, adult Muslims are required to pray a ritual prayer five times a day in a particular way at particular times. For most of the five ritual prayers, there is a period of three or four hours between the earliest time the prayer can be performed and the time after which the prayer has been "missed." The most devout Muslim is one who prays all five prayers immediately when they become due—which, for the first prayer of the day, involves getting up before sunrise. Such a person only misses a prayer in the most unusual and extreme circumstances, and is fairly scrupulous in following the Sharia (including many of the parts of it that are merely *sunna*). The next gradation of piety corresponds to one who prays all five prayers, but sometimes misses one if he or she is busy with something, and "makes it up" by praying it later. Such a person may routinely miss the first prayer of the day, making it up when he or she wakes up rather than getting up for it before dawn. Such a person will observe most aspects of the Sharia, and some *sunna* practices. Both these gradations of observant Muslim would be considered "righteous" by the Sharia, and represent piety which is generally admired, but not unusual.

The next gradation is of partly observant Muslims, those who do not pray on a daily basis, but may sometimes pray the Friday prayer in a mosque if male, or may sometimes pray at home on Thursday nights if female. Perhaps they pray the five prayers for a few days or weeks when they are going through a difficult period in their lives, or during the fasting month of Ramadan (see chapter 5), but then stop again. They will be aware of many aspects of the Sharia, and observe some of them. After this gradation comes someone who only prays twice a year on the major festivals, and then comes someone who has not prayed at all for years. Such a person may or may not still observe some other aspects of the Sharia, especially fasting during Ramadan. Both these gradations of partly observant Muslim would be condemned as "corrupt" by the Sharia, but are regarded more tolerantly by almost all Muslims, and almost all Muslim societies.

One problem with this way of measuring commitment to Islam is that the effort required to pray the five prayers varies depending on circumstances. In Wahhabi Saudi Arabia, an exception among Muslim countries, the state enforces religiosity by such means as obliging shops to close at the time of prayer. Customers then have little alternative but to go to a mosque and pray. The operatives of the Virtue Promotion and Vice Prevention Committee (often known to Westerners as "the religious police") actually chase pedestrians into a nearby mosque, sometimes with sticks, if they find them in the streets at prayer time. Regular prayer in Saudi Arabia, then, does not explain much about an individual. Even an Arab Christian I know once found himself praying in a mosque in Saudi Arabia, since it was simpler to do what he was told than to tangle with the Virtue Promotion and Vice Prevention Committee. This was not any sort of attempt to make a Muslim out of the Arab Christian, but simply a failure to ask questions. In Turkey, on the other hand, visible religiosity is frowned upon by the elite, and under certain circumstances praying can even be a breach of military discipline. Failing to pray regularly in Turkey, then, has a very different meaning from failing to pray regularly in Saudi Arabia.

Saudi Arabia and Turkey are extreme cases, but even in other countries, circumstances vary. It is easy to pray the dawn prayer on time if one lives in a village where everyone gets up at dawn anyhow, but not if one is working a late shift in a town where electric light has displaced the patterns of nature. Similarly, if one's workmates all stop work to pray together, it is easy to join them; if one is living in a Western country, there is unlikely to be a praying area at one's place of work, and considerable determination may be required to brave the astonished stares of other people as one prays in a corner of the office. All these factors need to be taken into account when attempting to deduce religiosity from praying practices.

It is hard to estimate what percentages of the world's Muslims fall into each of the above categories, though it is probable that more Muslims do not pray the five prayers on a regular basis now than was the case in past centuries. The medieval Ulema generally held that someone who did not pray at all had left Islam, and so could be punished for apostasy. This punishment was rarely if ever applied, but the fact that the argument was made in the first place suggests that at that time only a small minority of Muslims did not pray. There is, however, really no way of telling. Today, it is probably the case that most traditional Muslims living in circumstances where prayer is easy do pray regularly, and that many modern Muslims living in circumstances where prayer is more difficult do not. Is even possible that most Muslims today do not actually pray regularly, and therefore are "corrupt" in the Sharia's terms. As devout Muslims say, "But God knows best." The vast majority of Muslims do, however, fast Ramadan, another index of religiosity.

That someone does not pray regularly does not mean that he or she is not a believing Muslim. Many Muslims who pray only occasionally, or even not at all, still observe many of the prohibitions and requirements of the Sharia in their daily lives and their family lives, especially during Ramadan, and their world view and ethical systems are still formed by Islam. Equally, that a Muslim is found in a bar drinking beer certainly means that he or she is not very devout, but it does not necessarily mean that he or she is not religious at all, especially if the bar in question is in a Western country.

There are, however, also a small number of non-observant Muslims who pay no attention at all to the Sharia, and whose world views and ethics have little to do with Islam. In the West, there are many non-observant Christians, and in some European countries almost the entire population could be described as only nominally Christian. The situation is very different in the Muslim world, however. Entirely non-observant Muslims are comparatively rare, except in some sections of Turkish society. In many European countries, and even in some parts of the United States, to be anything more than a nominal Christian is unusual, and takes some effort. In the Muslim world, in contrast, it takes some effort *not* to be somewhat religious. Openly non-observant Muslims are found most frequently in the West, where social pressures operate in the opposite direction.

Non-observant Muslims still tend to be more Muslim than nominal Christians tend to be Christian, precisely because there are so few of them. The friends and family of a non-observant Muslim may include other non-observant Muslims, but will also invariably include more observant Muslims. Even purely nominal Muslims will not want to distress their grandparents or offend strangers if this can be avoided. Non-observant Muslims, then, will not normally admit explicitly that their Islam is only nominal. Turks will on occasion stress that religion is a purely private matter, which sometimes amounts to such an admission, but other Muslims will not usually even go that far. This extreme reluctance to be openly non-religious is more a question of discretion than of hypocrisy.

It is possible for a non-Muslim to offend even a non-observant Muslim by saying something outrageous about Islam, like suggesting that the Koran was written by Muhammad or that the Sharia is primitive and barbaric. The non-observant Muslim might think such things himself or herself, but that is different. I may think my mother is irritating, but that does not mean that I want to hear you say it.

The lowest stage of religiosity is that of the former Muslim, whether an open atheist or a convert to another religion. Converts from Islam are extremely rare, and normally found only in the West and in other parts of the world where Muslims are a small minority and sometimes know little or nothing of their religion. During the nineteenth century, Christian missionaries put serious effort into the Muslim world, but generally ended up converting only Arab Christians (for example from Coptic Orthodoxy to Catholicism).

It is not entirely clear why so few Muslims convert to other religions. In part, it may be because Christianity already existed at the time of the first Muslims, and so the Koran has many references to Christianity and to the relative superiority of Islam. All Muslims are therefore somewhat familiar with many basic Christian doctrines (or one version of them) from an early age, and are also familiar with the reasons for rejecting them. A Christian friend of mine was struck by a Muslim acquaintance's conviction that Christians worshiped three gods: one in heaven, one on earth, and one flying around in between. The Muslim in question was not well educated, and was not following even the Koranic version of the doctrine of the Trinity, but clearly considered at least one aspect of Christianity self-evidently ridiculous. More educated Muslims generally have a similar attitude toward Christianity, though backed with more sophisticated logic.

Another reason for the lack of conversions from Islam is the way Muslims define communities in religious terms. Anyone who joins another religious community thereby leaves their own original community, of family as well as of friends. There is also the problem that the Sharia prescribes the death penalty for a Muslim who leaves Islam. This penalty is not often written into modern national law codes, and is only carried out very rarely, but it does exist. In the early 1990s, a Kuwaiti Muslim converted to Christianity, which was so remarkable that he was invited to appear on a Kuwaiti television talk show. When he did appear, proudly using his new Christian name, the national outrage was such that the Kuwaiti state felt it had to do something. Executing him might have caused all sorts of problems, so the Kuwaiti government simply persuaded him to slip out of the country, turning a blind eye while he did so. Converts from Islam and open atheists of Muslim origin exist, then, but are so rare that this book will make no further reference to them.

Some Muslims spend their whole lives in the same stage of religiosity, especially if they are brought up as devout, traditional Muslims. Others become devout only in old age. Some oscillate: somewhat devout as children, non-observant until early middle age, and then increasingly devout again. "I really used to like Pink Floyd then, before all this . . ." one Muslim man told me, gesturing with a wry smile at his large beard, a mark of modern religiosity. It can also go the other way, from a religious adolescence to a non-observant middle age, and on again to something else. The Egyptian husband of an American friend of mine started at 20 as the Imam of the (illegal) Muslim Students' Association at Cairo University, passed from there to Marx to Freud, and then by the age of 50 had moved from Freud to the classics of medieval Islamic mystical philosophy.

Tolerance

Degree of religiosity is largely independent of how tolerant or intolerant a Muslim is, though a non-observant Muslim will generally be tolerant of non-observance and of non-Muslims, at least except when it comes to matters such as politics—but more on politics later (see chapter 12). Traditional Muslims are generally more tolerant than modern ones, as traditional Islam discourages the making of hostile judgments against others. Traditional Muslims are also generally more confident in their faith, and so have less need to be tough on themselves, or on others. Because Sufism encourages people to look at inner meanings rather than outer appearances, Sufis are often more tolerant than other Muslims. In general, Sufism discourages hostile judgments against other people. Hostility to others, Sufis often say, should be used as a mirror: what you hate in someone else is probably the reflection of a fault in you. Traditional Islam, however, also encourages righteous Muslims not to associate with the corrupt—which includes non-Muslims, by definition—any more than is strictly necessary. In countries where Muslims are a minority, this can lead to something of a ghetto mentality, or even to areas which are real ghettos. Sometimes, of course, even devout Muslims prefer making friends with non-Muslims to a self-imposed ghetto.

Although there has not yet been anything like an Enlightenment in the Muslim world, plenty of Muslims have spent enough time in the post-Enlightenment West to absorb many of the views and values that Westerners generally have, and to know the West well enough to understand what is going on there. These Muslims have not come together to form a distinct and visible group, but they exist all the same. They tend to be the most tolerant and liberal of all.

This is not to say that Muslims living in the West are all liberal, or that all liberal Muslims live in the West. Liberal and tolerant Muslims may equally live in the Muslim world, where they are most likely to be found among the rich, largely because it is the rich who have most contact with the West. Some Muslims in the West, in contrast, are anything but tolerant—they may be "real crazies," as one American put it. This is partly because the experiences they have had in the West may actually have made them *less* tolerant than they were originally. Muslims arriving in the West experience culture shock just as Westerners in the Muslim world often do, and in some cases this culture shock leads to anti-Western reactions and more radical views. First-hand experience of the problems that exist in the West, which a Muslim arriving there from the Muslim world may know little about in advance, sometimes leads people to question their former liberal views. This phenomenon is not restricted to Muslims: it used to happen to some Soviet defectors as well.

Alternatively, Muslims of more traditional backgrounds may simply find the West incomprehensible, and retain their original traditional views for this or for some other reason. Many elderly traditional Pakistani Muslims haunt British mosques, never having learned more than a few words of English, disoriented by their experiences and grasping at the few things in their new environment that are familiar. Someone who has only just worked out how to buy a bus pass will hardly absorb anything very subtle from their surrounding culture. In America, however, Muslims are generally better educated than in Europe, as a result of differences in immigration policies and histories, but even a well educated U.S. Muslim may stick close to traditional views.

The Western visitor to the Muslim world is usually struck more by intolerance than by tolerance. This intolerance derives partly from ignorance. Muslims without experience of the West may easily be shocked to see a young Western man and a young Western woman holding hands in public, because they read the scene very differently from the way a Westerner would. Such a thing would not happen in most parts of the Muslim world unless the young woman were a prostitute and the young man were intent on flaunting his debauchery (though in some parts of the Muslim world, courting couples do sometimes hold hands). Western visitors, in turn, are sometimes shocked—or at least surprised—to see Muslim men holding hands, assuming that this indicates a sexual relationship. It does not: it simply indicates friendship.

Intolerance, then, can be a reaction more to what somebody *thinks* is going on than to what is *actually* going on. It is also because a Muslim in the Muslim world is less likely to say, "well, that's their business." This is partly a question of cultural difference, but also because Islam—especially modern Islam—is concerned with virtue promotion and vice prevention, as I will discuss in chapter 8.

Westerners living in the Muslim world generally learn fairly quickly to behave in public in ways that do not provoke intolerance. If it is the local norm, even husband and wife do not hold hands in public, and unmarried couples either present themselves as married or as brother and sister. Neighbors may suspect that the young man who has arrived to stay with his "sister" is not actually her brother, but they will usually keep such suspicions to themselves, and disapprove less than they would had the young woman been—in their terms—flaunting her debauchery.

Likewise, Muslims who are used to Western customs sometimes learn to apply different standards to Westerners. This is not always successful. I once introduced an elderly and respectable friend in the Sudan to two visiting American academics, one male and the other female, who were not romantically attached. After they had left us, my friend enquired politely, searching for the right word, "Is she his . . . mate?" Less respectable Muslims who think they know Western customs sometimes make the mistake of assuming that Western women are sexually available to anyone who asks nicely. Many Muslims, however, understand Western customs perfectly well—though they might not want their own children to behave like their Western friends.

It is usually what is seen as immorality that most attracts Muslim intolerance. Muslims also tend to be less tolerant than Westerners in questions of religion and politics. As we have seen, criticism of Islam by a non-Muslim is almost never acceptable, and atheism is as objectionable in a Westerner as anyone else.

Summary

Muslims come in many varieties, but the most important distinctions are between traditional and modern Muslims, and between the devout and the less devout. The distinction between the devout and the less devout is one commonly made by Muslims themselves. The distinction between traditional and modern Muslims is one made mostly by scholars studying Islam, and not even by all of them. But most Muslims would understand what was being referred to if it were explained to them. They might, however, reject the distinction, because Muslims prefer to think of there being one true Islam, not several different varieties.

Views of sacred texts as containing primarily symbolic truth, and of the tenets of religion as historical developments, are widespread in the West, and allow many Christians to understand Christianity as an important source of truth about life, but as one source among many, and thus subject to considerations that come from outside the Bible. Such views are barely known in the Muslim world, and thus the choice for almost all Muslims is between agnosticism and accepting the Koran as an absolute, just as some American Christians take the Bible as an absolute.

Muslims, then, can be plotted on a chart with two axes, like a compass rose. One axis (say, between North and South) measures religiosity, from the devout to the non-observant. The other axis (say, between East and West) measures the impact of modernity, from the traditional to the modern, or even to the postmodern—the sort of nuanced view of religion as developing in history. Sufis are almost always traditional and pious Muslims, and postmodern Muslims are rare in the extreme. What are generally called "fundamentalists" are modern and devout. Beyond that, major groups (as opposed to individuals) cannot be plotted, with any accuracy, on only one part of the chart.

4

God and Angels

The Muslim Worldview

One afternoon, a young man who introduced himself as Dr. Abdullah came to see me. He wasn't really a doctor, it turned out, but rather a student of veterinary medicine, studying in Denmark thanks to the Danish foreign aid budget. I later learned that he was famous at his Danish university for his constant denunciations of Danish immorality, which he usually ended with a proposal of marriage to the female student whom he had been lecturing.

Dr. Abdullah had been asked by a Danish student I knew to deliver a cassette to me (I never discovered why she chose that particular messenger). After giving me the cassette, he lectured me for almost an hour—on Danish immorality, and on the existence of heaven and hell and the nature thereof, and on the sad fact that I was probably destined to hell. And then he left, and went back to Denmark.

A year later, Dr. Abdullah visited me again. Mysteriously, he seemed to have been transformed into a relatively normal Westerner. We chatted pleasantly about mutual acquaintances in Denmark. This time, no lecture.

When Dr. Abdullah appeared outside my door again a month or two later, I was almost pleased to see him . . . until the lecture started. After the lecture came the explanation—proof of the truth of everything he had been saying, at least for him. Had I noticed the dreadful state he had been in on his last visit to me, he asked. Well, shortly after that visit he had gone home to his family. They too had noticed his state, and had called a Shaykh. The Shaykh had spotted immediately that Dr. Abdullah was possessed by a jinn, an evil spirit. Praise God, the Shaykh had carried out a ceremony, and driven the jinn out. It turned out to be a female jinn, and a Jewish one at that. Probably picked up in Denmark.

Dr. Abdullah was far from a typical Muslim, but all varieties of Muslim — devout and less devout, traditional and modern, and Wahhabi — share more or less the same worldview, which includes jinn as well as heaven and hell. In this chapter, readers will notice many similarities in the worldviews of other monotheistic religions, but also some differences.

God and Creation

The start and end point of Islam is God. God is called "Allah," which is the same word that Arab and even Maltese Christians use to refer to Him. The Koran makes clear that Allah — whom I will from now on simply call "God" — is the same as He who is worshiped by Jews and Christians, who created Adam, saved Noah from the flood, guided Moses out of Egypt, and so forth. Some Christians and Jews may not accept that they worship the same God as Muslims do, but all Muslims accept that they worship the same God as the Jews and Christians — though Muslims disapprove of Christians also worshiping Jesus, which they see as a form of polytheism.

There is also another word in Arabic, *ilah*, which means "god" with a small g — as Westerners would use the word when referring to "the gods of the Romans." One of the most important and most often repeated statements in Islam uses both forms: "There is no *ilah* other than Allah," *la ilah il'Allah*. This statement echoes the first of the Ten Commandments, and is the first of two things that any Muslim is required to believe — the first part of the testimony of faith. It is something that all Muslims do believe. If they did not, they would be atheists or converts to polytheism.

The most important point about God is that He is One. That is how one of the best known chapters of the Koran starts: "Say [O Muhammad]: He, God, is one."[1] Almost immediately, this point is expanded: "[He] has not begotten, and was not begotten," in part a contradiction of the Christian understanding of Jesus (though in terms that few Christians would them-

---

[1]Koran, chapter 112.

selves use) and in part a statement of another important characteristic of God—that He is eternal, not created, but the Creator.

In English, God is sometimes referred to by a characteristic such as "the Creator," or perhaps "the Judge." In Islam, many more such characteristics are used to describe God. He is the Creator and the Judge, but also the Merciful, the Life-Giving, the King, the Delightful[2] . . . ninety-nine of the most important such adjectives applied to God in the Koran have been collected to make a list of the ninety-nine "names" of God. Some of these are more commonly used than others. Any sentence in Arabic that refers to "the Merciful" could only refer to God, whereas a reference to "the Delightful" would cause confusion.

God's mercy is emphasized in another important and oft-repeated phrase, "in the name of God the Merciful, the Compassionate." This phrase starts every chapter of the Koran, and is repeated by devout Muslims as they start any statement and almost any action.[3] The more devout the Muslim, the more frequent the use of the phrase. It is not thought in any way strange to announce: "In the name of God the Merciful, the Compassionate: the bus will now stop for twenty minutes." According to many Ulema, there is a single exception: when the action about to be started involves killing, as when slaughtering an animal, in which case the mention of mercy would seem inappropriate. Another phrase is then used. Some Muslims may privately question God's mercy at difficult moments in their lives, but—if devout—they will do their best to drop such ideas.

God, then, is One, and He is also Merciful. The third most important characteristic of God, to judge at least from the phrases most often repeated by Muslims, is that He is Great (or, literally, "incomparably and most uniquely Great"). This phrase, "Allahu akbar," is used on numerous occasions. God's greatness is in some ways the complement to His mercy.

---

[2] Actually, a grammatical modification which does not exist in English is used to change "Merciful" into "incomparably and most uniquely Merciful," "Delightful" into "incomparably and most uniquely Delightful," and so on, but this is cumbersome in English. I will simply say "Merciful" and "Delightful."

[3] In fact, the Arabic really means "by the name of God," but the erroneous translation "in the name of" has become so well established among Muslims as well as observers that there is no point in resisting it.

One aspect of that greatness is stressed immediately after God's mercy in the most frequently used Islamic prayer, the "Fatiha," the equivalent of the Lord's Prayer in Christianity (and the first chapter of the Koran): God is also "Master of the Day of Judgment."

Another important consequence of God's greatness is that everything that happens does so only by God's will, or at least by His permission. This immediately brings Muslims, like other monotheists, up against the problem of good and evil. If God is all-powerful and all-merciful, how can such evil and suffering exist in the world? The standard Muslim response to this question is little different from the standard response of other monotheists: suffering is a test.

No devout Muslim can ever imagine anything happening independently of God. Many Muslims, especially devout traditional ones, see the hand of God in everything. An earthquake is a sign of God's displeasure, and a delicious fruit is an expression of God's bounty. A Muslim geologist, however, will inevitably see the hand of God acting somewhat more remotely, but an understanding of plate tectonics may simply mean that God is seen as the ultimate cause rather than the immediate one. In some cases, of course, God can become such a remotely ultimate cause as almost to vanish for all practical purposes, but this is unusual.

God's presence in everything that happens is emphasized by devout Muslims in ways that can strike Westerners as strange. On the morning on which I wrote this chapter, I took a taxi in Cairo. Upon arriving at my destination, I found that neither I nor the taxi driver had change for the smallest denomination bill I had in my wallet. The taxi driver asked a passer-by to change the bill, which he did. As I got out of the taxi, the driver remarked "Praise and thanks be to God because He sent us someone to ease our difficulty." The driver did not really mean that God had interested Himself in our minor problem and wrought a miracle specially for us. He was simply making the routine point that God is all-powerful and that His mercies extend to all of His creation, and that He should be praised and thanked.

All but the least devout Muslims constantly remind themselves and everyone else of the importance of God's permission by use of the phrase *in sha Allah*, "if God so wills." It is *sunna* never to make a statement of any sort about the future without adding this phrase as a rider; to omit it while speaking a Muslim language implies a denial of the need for God's permission.

The full version of the announcement about the bus, then, would be "In the name of God the Merciful, the Compassionate: the bus will now stop for twenty minutes, *in sha Allah*" (because announcing a twenty-minute stop implies that in twenty minutes the bus will start again).

The phrase *in sha Allah* is in some ways just part of the future tense in Muslim languages, but it is not just that. In Arabic, a devout Muslim will often reply to a statement including *in sha Allah* by saying *Bi izni'Llah*, "with God's permission." There is nothing remarkable about an exchange such as

"Oh no! I'm late. I'll catch a taxi, if God so wills."
"With God's permission. Don't forget your coat."

Devout Muslims speaking English will sometimes add the Arabic phrase *in sha Allah* to an English sentence. Alternatively, they may avoid the need for it by reformulating a sentence: "I intend to catch a taxi" is a statement about the present, and so needs no rider.

The phrase *in sha Allah* gives rise to endless misunderstandings between Muslims and Westerners resident in the Muslim world, since Westerners have great difficulty in not understanding it as indicating uncertainty.[4] When a Muslim telephones a Westerner and says "Sorry, it isn't ready today, but it will be ready tomorrow, *in sha Allah*" the Westerner tends to think that he or she is being told that it probably won't be ready tomorrow either. That is not what the phrase means at all. It is simply an acknowledgment of God's all-powerfulness.

Because everything happens by God's permission, everything that does happen is God's will and should be welcomed as such — even misfortune. To rail against misfortune is to rebel against God. The proper approach to misfortune is to try to see the wisdom in it. By definition, there must be good

---

[4]Westerners in Egypt who know the country insufficiently well often say that Egypt is run by IBM — "*in sha Allah, bukra, malesh.*" *Bukra* means "tomorrow," and is often used to mean "tomorrow or at some time in the future." *Malesh* is a phrase that has no English equivalent. Depending on context, it can mean either "it doesn't matter," "don't get upset" or "sorry." When an Egyptian secretary says "*malesh*, I forgot your report, but I'll do it now, *in sha Allah*," she will often be understood by a Westerner to have said "I couldn't care less about your report. I might do it now, or I might not." What she has actually said is "Sorry about your report. I'll do it right now."

in everything that happens, even the death of someone one loves deeply. Eventually, one should be able to thank God for everything that happens, however hard that may be.

Misfortune happens by God's permission, but the stress is on fortune rather than misfortune, on God as Creator and Provider. Muslims thank God far more often for good things than for bad: for food, for its taste and variety, for beauty both human and natural, and for the general perfection of His creation. Everything in creation has its reason and purpose, and it is often argued that only the most stubborn or the most blind can contemplate the many miracles of creation without seeing in them the hand of the Creator.

No Muslim can ever conceive of anything as being on a level with God. One might expect this to be uncontroversial, since the worshipers of idols vanished from Mecca after the city's surrender to the Prophet, and idol-worship has not been known in the Muslim world since then. There are other ways to stray from the proper conception of God, however. One is to imagine that humans can achieve anything independently, without His permission—though all Muslims agree that humans have to try, too. It is often said that the fisherman has to put the line into the water at a suitable place with suitable bait; whether or not a fish is caught is then up to God.

Another way to stray is to ascribe divine powers to humans. This risk is emphasized especially by modern Muslims and Wahhabis, who consider the regard that Sufis pay their Shaykhs or spiritual masters as wicked, since it raises humans above the human level. Traditional Muslims are less concerned, arguing that everyone knows that what is special about a Shaykh is the favor shown him by God, and knows that a Shaykh is a human being like any other.

The second thing that all Muslims are required to believe is that Muhammad is the Prophet of God. This is the second part of the testimony of faith, after "There is no god other than God." All Muslims agree that Muhammad was the last prophet of God, and also agree that Muhammad was purely human; not all Muslims, however, agree on quite *how* Muhammad was (or is) human. For many Sufis, the Prophet was created by God of pure light, and this Prophetic light was the first thing that God created; for them, this light still exists today. For modern Muslims and Wahhabis, such views are little less than idolatry. A constant struggle goes on at the tomb of the Prophet in Medina between the Wahhabi custodians of the tomb, appointed by the Saudi Arabian state, and more traditional Muslim visitors. The visitors want to stand at the tomb and pray, and if possible to touch the tomb of one who was and is closer to God than any other human being. The Wahhabi custodians wield batons to prevent this happening. For them, this tomb is just the tomb of a human like any other, and their plain duty is to save the misguided from actions that suggest otherwise.

Shi'i Muslims and traditional Sunni Muslims have much the same regard for the Prophet, but Shi'i Muslims also have almost as much regard for the Imams—Ali, Hussein, and so on. Again, this seems to the Wahhabis to be a form of idolatry, and the Shi'i minority in Saudi Arabia suffers various forms of persecution as a result.

All Muslims see God as One, Merciful, and Great. Even if they ignore God in their daily lives, to the extent that they do conceive of God, this is how they will conceive of Him.

Angels and Jinn and Unseen Forces

God created the world and all that is in it. He also created two classes of being that are not quite in the world: angels and jinn. Angels are purer beings than humans, but unlike humans do not have free will—they cannot choose between good and evil. They are superior to humans in that they are always good, but inferior to humans in that they cannot choose good, which is what really matters. Jinn, like humans, can choose. As a result, there are good jinn and bad jinn, Muslim jinn and Christian jinn, and so on. Jinn are also, in the end, a lesser type than humans. If any proof of this were needed, it is that God's Prophet, Muhammad, was human, not a jinn.

For most devout Muslims, angels and jinn are as real as humans, even though they are not quite of this world. Only the most devout give much time or thought to angels. The jinn, in contrast, are very present in most Muslims' worldviews, and are generally feared. They usually keep to themselves, but sometimes intervene in human affairs, for example in forms that Westerners would recognize as poltergeists. There are even stories of sexual relations between humans and jinn. Although in theory there are good, Muslim jinn, in practice it is bad jinn that people tend to encounter. Everyone has heard of cases of persecution and even possession by bad jinn, who are usually thrown out of the person they were afflicting later, during ceremonies involving the Koran. Every town has its experts in expelling jinn — usually talented amateurs, but sometimes members of the Ulema. Some Muslims educated in the modern Western tradition maintain that mentions of angels and jinn in the Koran should be taken allegorically rather than literally, but they are in a small minority, and even they never quite lose their fear of the jinn. As a notable exception to the general rule, educated Iranians pay less attention to the jinn than most other Muslims.

The most important non-human being is Satan. As other monotheists also believe, Satan disobeyed God and was cursed and cast out into darkness. On the face of it, Satan appears as a fallen angel, but since angels cannot chose good or evil and so cannot disobey God, and since Satan is made of fire while angels are made of light, most argue that Satan is in fact a jinn, not an angel. Regardless, Satan is very present in devout Muslims' thoughts, as the enemy of good and the tempter of humanity. Temptation may often be understood in very personal terms: "'In that case,' whispered Satan in my ear, 'why should I not drink just one glass of beer?'" Satan, it is often said, is most likely to be found waiting outside a mosque — there is little reason for him to waste his time on visiting a bar or a brothel. As if to confirm this, more devout Muslims are more aware of Satan than are less devout Muslims, and non-observant Muslims hardly concern themselves with him at all.

Just as there are unseen beings, so there are unseen forces. The most important of these is divine grace, *baraka*. *Baraka* gives both spiritual and practical assistance — it encourages health and prosperity, for example. It is an immaterial force for good that may be received directly from God, or may be received indirectly. Food cooked with love is said to transmit *baraka* to the person who eats it; a burger from a fast-food restaurant, in contrast, has less *baraka*; a burger bought with the proceeds of crime has no *baraka* at all. A good deed confers *baraka* on the person who does it, and *baraka* may be gained from simply visiting the righteous. More devout Muslims are more concerned with *baraka* than less devout ones, but even partly observant Muslims are aware of it.

A second unseen force, in a sense the opposite of *baraka*, is envy, *hasad*, sometimes called in English "the evil eye." Just as *baraka* encourages health and prosperity, *hasad* encourages illness and misfortune. The source of *hasad* is purely human: a person looks with envy on something or someone—perhaps even a baby—and thereby blights it. If someone has cooked food for another person with love, but as that other person is about to eat it a stranger passes by and looks on the meal with envy, then that food loses its *baraka*. Especially among Arabs, one practical way of stopping this happening is to offer food to a stranger immediately upon seeing him or her look at it, in which case the stranger will either take some or, more likely, refuse politely. In either case, the stranger can hardly be envying the food any longer.

Traditional Muslims, whether devout or not, take *hasad* very seriously. All sorts of phrases and objects are deployed to ward off envy. Certain varieties of incense are widely considered to be very effective—so much so that, in many Muslim cities, poor men in search of tips are more likely to be equipped with rough-and-ready incense burners than with materials for washing windshields. Throughout the Arab world, objects used to ward off envy often involve the color blue. The "hand of Fatima," a hand showing five fingers, is very popular as well (though in Pakistan it has a totally different significance, indicating Shi'ism). Modern, Wahhabi, and many Shi'i Muslims, while not denying the existence of *hasad* and its powers of blighting, commonly regard many of these precautions as *bida*. More educated Muslims sometimes see such precautions as superstitious, but even so sometimes make use of them. Other measures to ward off *hasad* might include hiding an object that might attract envy, offering it for sale, or offering it as a gift, as with food that a stranger looks at. In some parts of the Muslim world, admiring any object will result in it being offered to one as a gift. Although the offer is genuine, there is usually an expectation that it will not be accepted. When an old car has a "for sale" sign on it, the owner may actually want to sell the car, or may simply want to ward off envy by means of an offer for sale (having decided that *hasad* is why the car keeps breaking down).

Some individuals are thought to be especially capable of blighting with their envy. Some Muslims tell the story of a farmer who, in the course of a quarrel with his neighbor, asks such a man with him up a hill to blight his neighbor's crops. "Where are his fields?" asks the man. "Just over there," replies the farmer, pointing into the distance. "Ah, what good eyes you have!" replies the man enviously, to the farmer's horror.

An alternative way of hurting an enemy is through the use of magic. Traditional Muslims, as well as many modern Muslims, take magic very seriously. Like jinn, magic is mentioned in the Koran, and so must exist. Like deliberate blighting, the use of magic is strictly forbidden. Regardless, less devout traditional Muslims often cast spells. Spells are used especially by women, and especially in connection with romantic difficulties—whether to hurt a rival or to make a man fall in love. Certain countries, especially in Africa but also including Indonesia, are infamous for the magic practiced there.

Saints and Miracles

Just as there are persons especially known for their *hasad*, there are also persons especially known for their *baraka*. These persons are associated with miracles, and in this book will be called "saints." The Arabic term is *wali*, a word which signifies someone especially close to someone—in this case, close to God. All types of Muslim accept that saints exist, since they are mentioned in the Koran; modern and Wahhabi Muslims, however, are generally very cautious about saints, worrying about regard for them turning into the cult of saints, which they see as a dangerous form of idolatry. Less devout modern Muslims pay little attention to saints, rather like most Westerners today. All varieties of traditional Muslim are very conscious of the existence and role of saints, though. For many such Muslims, saints are an important part of their worldview.

There is no formal canonization process for recognizing saints in Islam. "Saint" is not a title, but a description. Many saints are never recognized as such by anybody, or perhaps they are just recognized by a few other saints (saints are best equipped to recognize one of their own). Others recognize saints either by their miracles or simply by sensing their *baraka*.

It is God who makes saints, not humans, and God might in theory transform anyone into a saint. In general, it is the most devout and the most holy who become saints, but persons who would strike a Westerner (or even many Muslim physicians) as simple-minded or deranged are often classified by traditional Muslims as saints. In one village in Upper Egypt, there is a man who never speaks and never wears clothes—a serious infraction of the Sharia, which is strict on human nakedness. But he is thought by the villagers to be a saint, and so he is allowed to roam the village as he wishes, and is treated with great respect. His photograph (or at least the photograph of his head and the uppermost part of his torso) even adorns the village bus.

Besides the most devout, a second type of saint that might strike Westerners as strange is the hereditary saint. Although there is little basis for this in the Koran or *hadith,* many less educated traditional Muslims believe that *baraka* passes from father to son. The remote descendants of saints, then, are often treated with great respect, for no reason other than their ancestry. Similarly, the descendants of the Prophet, known as *sayyids* or *sharifs,* are treated with special respect. There are probably by now at least a million people in the Muslim world who are, or believe they are, descended from the Prophet. I have known *sayyids* who were very devout, and *sayyids* who were anything but devout. By the nineteenth century, in some parts of the Muslim world, *sayyids* had become a sort of hereditary aristocracy, powerful and wealthy as well as respected.

Great Sufi Shaykhs are commonly regarded as saints. In fact, it is unlikely that any Sufi Shaykh who was not also a saint would be a seen as a particularly great Shaykh. The miracles of such saints are often fairly modest— for example, appearing in their followers' dreams or knowing the truth when someone is trying to lie to them. If a course of action recommended by a saint meets with success, that is a sort of miracle; if a course of action forbidden by a saint ends in disaster, that is also a sort of miracle. Other miracles are more dramatic: examples include being in two places at the same time, curing illnesses in humans and animals, and even (though this is unusual) raising the dead.

Sufis and other traditional Muslims stress that these miracles are not the work of the saint, but of God. They distinguish three varieties of miracle. The greatest miracles are those which people often do not think of as miracles—the rising of the sun each morning, for example, or the beauty of the moon. The devout see such miracles as "signs" of God, as evidence of His power, beauty, and majesty. Then there are miracles performed by God for prophets as proof of those prophets' missions: the classic example is an occasion when Moses turned a staff into a snake in front of Pharaoh. Finally, there are miracles performed by God for saints, the ones I have been discussing. Such miracles are seen as an overflowing of God into the world.

In theory, then, saints do not work their own miracles, and have no supernatural powers of their own. In practice, however, supernatural powers are frequently ascribed to saints either in effect or even explicitly. Such powers can also be ascribed to places associated with saints, normally their tombs, since *baraka* remains with a saint after death. This is one important reason why modern and Wahhabi Muslims object so strongly to the traditional conception of sainthood—because it so easily turns into what they see as a form of idolatry. Modern Muslims and Wahhabis accept that *baraka* exists, and can, for example, be acquired through good deeds. They condemn the visiting of tombs and of living persons for their *baraka*, and see the saints' alleged miracles as deceptions. Shi'i Muslims in search of *baraka* visit not the tombs of saints, but their infallible Imams.

Birth, Death, Destiny, and Judgment

Baraka is the otherworldly sustenance of the human soul while it is in exile in the created world. The human soul is immortal, and enters the created world by passing into a fetus some four months after conception. Since the soul is immortal and comes from outside creation, at the moment of its arrival in creation it still remembers God. Only later does creation intervene between it and God, veiling God, and making possible ignorance, error, and evil. More poetically, it is said that a little after birth, an angel places its finger over the baby's lips, warning it to keep the secrets it knows. The baby then gradually forgets them. The very same story is used by some Jews to make much the same point.

 The single purpose of life on earth is to worship God by living properly. Living properly involves doing what God requires of us, which is synonymous with what Islam tells us He requires of us—following the Sharia. Other religions are not reliable guides. The most important thing that God requires of us is to worship Him, in ways I will discuss in chapter 5. It is not that God needs our worship—clearly, God needs nothing—but rather that we need to worship God, because He has told us to, and because worship does us good. In addition to worship, we are also required to act in certain specific ways in our daily lives, again as indicated in the Sharia. Living properly requires a fairly disciplined daily life: doing certain things and not doing certain things. Thus, we must not forget God, or turn away from Him. We must not commit murder, fornication, theft, consumption of alcohol, and so on. The list of forbidden actions is much the same in all monotheistic religions, but the list of required actions is longer in Islam than in Christianity, and shorter in Islam than in orthodox Judaism.

As I said earlier, the Sharia does not just express God's instructions in terms of forbidden and required. There are also intermediate categories: *makruh* and *sunna*. The more devout the Muslim, the more attention is paid to these intermediate categories. It is not always certain which acts fall into which categories, but devout Muslims generally follow what is called "the way of precaution." If an act might be forbidden or might be *makruh*, it is safer to assume that it is forbidden. Less devout Muslims sometimes follow the reverse of this approach. This has no acknowledged name, but consists of hoping that an act that many see as forbidden is actually no more than *makruh*.

Traditional Muslims, and especially Sufis, understand the need to follow the Sharia somewhat differently, in terms of the ego, or *nafs*. A human consists of body, heart (which is the center of the emotions, as well as a physical organ), mind (the center of reason, as well as an organ), soul, and ego. Of these, only the soul is immortal; the ego passes away at death, as do the body, mind, and heart. Though it has a consciousness of its own, which may be transformed, the ego is really the lower self. It is where the passions reside, where desires develop. A wild animal is pure ego; desire or passion translate instantly into action. A baby similarly has no control over its ego, but an adult human must struggle to control the ego. The importance of this struggle is emphasized by describing it as the greater of the two Jihads. The lesser Jihad is that fought on the battlefield; the greater one is that which we all fight against our own egos.

God will assist us in the struggle to master our ego, both directly and indirectly—directly with *baraka* or sometimes with more direct intervention of a miraculous variety, and indirectly through the Sharia. Much of the Sharia, including the requirement for worship, can be seen as training in controlling the ego. The ego demands that we eat; the baby grabs whatever food is nearby without a second's reflection; the Muslim in training fasts, and even when not fasting, always pauses and pronounces the words "in the name of God, the Merciful, the Compassionate" before eating. Eating then takes place under the control of the mind, not of the ego.

An uncontrolled ego is an obstacle to finding God (or, technically, to being found by God). Someone who is a slave to their passions is reduced to the level of an animal, and is closed to the appreciation of the divine and to receiving God's help.

Sufis often think in these terms, but for them, as for all devout Muslims, the central reason for following the Sharia is not that it serves a purpose, but that it is God's command that we follow it. Sunni Muslims are not required to understand, but rather to obey. Shi'i Muslims are required to understand as well, but in the end they too are required to obey, whether or not they understand. God has forbidden us to eat pork, and that is that. Christians learn that the spirit of the law is more important than the letter of the law. Muslims learn that the spirit of the law matters, but that the letter of the law must be observed in its own right, anyhow.

Some Westerners have argued that it made sense to avoid pork in hot climates before the invention of refrigeration, but that it is no longer necessary to avoid it today. This argument strikes nearly all Muslims as irrelevant. If God had meant us to eat pork in cold climates or with the benefit of refrigeration, He would have said so. He did not, and that is that. A secondary and interesting point is that pigs are unclean (a concept I will discuss in chapter 7). They were created to serve as scavengers, not as food. Muslims who heard about pigs being involved in the transmission to humans of influenza and SARS were not surprised, but such considerations are not the main point.

We can, however, choose not to live properly, because we have free will. God, however, is Great in the sense that nothing happens except by His permission—including our wrong choices. In fact, everything that we will do or fail to do in our lives has always been known to God; it is said to be "written" on a "hidden tablet." The combination of these two observations raises the familiar problem of predestination: if God knows in advance how we will act, and if we can only act by His permission, how can we have free will? If we are destined to evil, how can God punish us for what is not really our fault? There have been various attempts to unravel this apparent paradox, which was not clearly addressed either in the Koran or by the Prophet in the *hadith*. The most accepted solution is the idea that we voluntarily adopt or assume acts which were predestined for us. Not all Muslims find this compromise entirely satisfying. In practice, the emphasis is on free will more than predestination.

Finally, at the hour appointed and known to God from before the day of our birth and written on the hidden tablet, we die. It is absolutely forbidden to hasten this hour, so neither suicide nor euthanasia may be contemplated. The prohibition on euthanasia runs so deep that it is even extended to animals—to put a suffering and dying animal "to sleep" is not an act of mercy, but an interference with God's will. To kill a human being in the name of mercy is even more unthinkable.

Having died, we await the Day of Judgment. There is disagreement about what happens while we are waiting for the Day of Judgment, but most Muslims believe that in our graves we will feel a foretaste of what our lot will be on that terrible Day. Suffering in the grave will be remitted from suffering in hell after judgment. If we are destined to heaven, according to some, while in the grave we will feel a breath of fresh air as through an open window.

On a day that no human can predict, the world will end and Judgment will come. It may be tomorrow, or it may be in a thousand years or more. The outline of preceding events will be familiar to other monotheists—a titanic struggle between good and evil, between an evil one and a Messiah (the same word is even used). One of the most chilling images is that, at the end, the combatants will fight each other with sticks and stones, as there will be nothing else left with which to fight. Some of the details of these events are disputed between Muslims and other monotheists, and even between Muslims. It is not entirely clear, for example, whether or not the Jews will all be on the opposite side to the Muslims. One difference between Muslims' vision of these days and the one familiar to most readers is the role to be played by the Mahdi, a title which means "the guided one." It is the Mahdi who will lead the fight against the Evil One, with the assistance of the Messiah, who is identified as Jesus. The main role is that of the Mahdi, not Jesus.

After the struggle between good and evil, the world will end and we will receive our final judgment, which will be just but tempered with mercy. None of us, in fact, can be saved without mercy, since none of us can achieve salvation by our own unaided efforts. Those judged as among the good will go to heaven, and those judged as among the bad will go to hell. There is disagreement about whether there is some intermediate category, and about whether some or even all of those condemned to hell may at some later point be allowed to pass into heaven.

The Islamic conception of hell as a place of fire and torment needs no explanation. The Islamic conception of heaven is less familiar. Heaven is described in the Koran as a place of gardens and cool streams, peopled with the good and with *houris*, mysterious and voluptuous female lovers, where there is wine that does not intoxicate. The first part of this image was probably more evocative to the dwellers in hot and arid deserts to whom the Koran was first revealed than it is to dwellers in the northern parts of America or Europe. For those who are used to rain, snow and dark, heaven might more easily be imagined in terms of golden beaches and an unclouded sky. The idea of *houris* scandalizes many Westerners, who may also wonder what women do, since there is no mention of a male equivalent of the *houri* (some argue that such an equivalent must exist, though perhaps it is not sexual, and others argue that *houris* are not gender specific). Westerners are usually less worried by the idea of wine in heaven, however. To a Muslim, wine is of course forbidden, as are voluptuous lovers. The central point is that heaven contains all the possible pleasures of earth, only better—without any of the drawbacks of earthly indulgence.

The images that have been discussed above are, for some Muslims, precisely that—images. For others, they are not images but literal descriptions, just as fire and torment is a literal description of hell for many Christians. The Wahhabis insist that everything in the Koran, from the description of heaven to the occasional mention of God's "throne," be understood literally, or at least as it would have been understood by the first Muslims to whom the Koran was revealed. Further enquiry is forbidden.

A more subtle picture of hell is suggested in the following story, well-known among traditional Muslims. A saint one day met the Caliph, who asked him where he was coming from. "From hell," replied the saint. "What were you doing there?" asked the Caliph. "Fire was needed," explained the saint, "so I thought of going to hell to ask if they could spare a little. But the guy in charge there said, 'We have no fire here.' I asked him 'How's that?'

Isn't hell the place of fire?' He answered, 'I tell you, there really is no fire down here. Everybody brings his own fire with him when he comes.'"

Judgment, heaven, and hell are much dwelt on by Muslim preachers of all varieties, and are therefore very present realities for all devout Muslims. For the less devout, they are less present, just as they are less present for other less devout monotheists. Some Muslims, just like some Westerners, are occasionally aware that hell might exist, but rather hope that it does not.

The awareness that the Day of Judgment may come tomorrow is more present for many traditional Muslims than it is for other varieties of monotheist. This is partly because preachers tend to dwell on it, but also because the Koran constantly refers to it. At any one time, there are substantial numbers of Muslims who are convinced that the Final Days are upon us, and even that the Mahdi has been born and is living somewhere in hiding, awaiting the right moment to emerge.

In troubled periods of Islamic history, figures claiming to be the Mahdi have often attracted large followings. In the nineteenth century, such a person led armies that conquered the whole of the northern Sudan. This alleged Mahdi died shortly after this conquest was completed, giving his followers some serious explaining to do. Somewhere in the Muslim world, at this moment, there is surely at least one figure recognized as the Mahdi, but with only a handful of followers. No alleged Mahdis have gathered large followings for over a century, but this could certainly happen again. Many Muslims are inclined to understand current tensions between the Islamic world and the West in terms of the approach of the Day of Judgment.

Summary

The Islamic worldview is, in its outlines, quite similar to that of other monotheistic faiths. This common ground matters, since it implies that ultimately Muslims are not so different from Christians and Jews. But the differences matter, too.

As any Muslim can tell you, God is One, Great, and Merciful. His creation is a miracle in which He Himself may be seen. Nothing happens save by God's permission, including your reading to the end of this sentence.

Everything that does happen is also by God's permission, which means that if you drop this book before getting to the end of the paragraph, you should welcome it as God's will. This view of God's will once supported a standard Western view of Muslims as "passive" and "fatalistic," a view to which there is some truth—certainly in comparison with the average modern American. To most Muslims, though, determination to overcome all odds and un-limited confidence in one's ability to do so is not a virtue, but a sign of im-maturity.

The Prophet was a regular human being, though some Muslims as-cribe very unusual characteristics to him. God communicated with him through an angel, and angels are as real as humans, though of a lesser order because they cannot choose between good and evil. Jinn are also real, and often feared, even though they can and sometimes do choose good, just as humans can. Satan may be a fallen angel, but is probably a jinn. He is to be found more often outside a mosque than in a bar.

There are also unseen forces: *baraka* or divine grace which brings spir-itual benefits, health and prosperity, and *hasad* or envy which blights. *Baraka* is valued by much the same people as those who value the angels, and *hasad* is feared by much the same people as those who fear the bad jinn. Saints are endowed with *baraka* and may be the agents of miracles, whether they are alive or dead, and whether they are devout persons such as Sufi shaykhs or other persons who some might regard merely as simple-minded.

Humans are born to live properly, which in practice means living ac-cording to Islam, as indicated by the Sharia. They are born sinless, knowing God, but the world washes this original knowledge away. There is no con-cept of "original sin," but humans inevitably do sin, not being angels. They may rely on God's mercy, to a certain extent, when it comes to the Day of Judgment. Heaven and hell are more prominent in the sermons of Muslim preachers than they are in those of most modern varieties of Christian preacher, but are ignored by the less devout, just as they are everywhere.

5

How to Do Islam

Worship

Any visitor to the Muslim world is immediately struck by the amount of praying that goes on. It is almost impossible to spend a day in a large Muslim city without seeing someone praying somewhere, and even those who stay at home hear the Call to Prayer several times a day. This is quite a contrast to much of the West, where religion tends to be more or less invisible, except perhaps on Sundays.

Christians can be Christian even if they do not go to church, applying—or attempting to apply—Christian principles in their daily lives. For most Christians, what matters is how they live and what they believe. Actually going to church (or not) is less important, though still important. Muslims, in contrast, stress worship more than belief. The daily worship of devout Muslims is as complicated as the daily worship of a medieval Catholic monk. It is central to Islam.

In Islam, worship is the main purpose of human life, as we saw in chapter 4. For a small number of very devout Muslims, this may actually be the case. Other devout Muslims try to make it the case. Even those Muslims who are not especially devout and do not actually worship on a regular basis are familiar with the main components of Muslim worship discussed in this chapter, and if ever they become more religious, it is to these forms of worship that they will turn. One act of worship—fasting—affects the less devout almost as much as the devout, though in different ways.

In this chapter, I will review the most important components of Muslim worship, following at first the order known to all Sunni Muslims, that of the "five pillars" of Islam. The Shi'a count either three or ten pillars, depending on what they wish to emphasize, but in practice agree with Sunni Muslims on the importance of these five components.

The first of the five pillars is not really what most Westerners would consider an act of worship: the recognition that there is no god other than God, and that Muhammad is the Prophet of God. This recognition, expressed in the "testimony of faith," is the starting point of Islam. Its many implications make up the essence of the Muslim worldview, as we discussed in chapter 4. This recognition should be, and sometimes is, continuous. There is no special time set aside for it, though its verbal formulation is repeated on several occasions, notably during prayer.

Prayer

The second pillar of Islam, and so the most important of the acts which in Western terms constitute Muslim worship, is prayer—but in a special sense. There are two words in Arabic (and in other Muslim languages) that are translated into English as "prayer." One, *dua*, is closer than the other to what is generally meant by "prayer" in English. A *dua* is an appeal to God, and most Muslim *duas* differ little from the prayers of other followers of monotheistic religions. "O God, save us from the fire [of hell]," pray Muslims, as might many others. A Muslim may pray a *dua* silently on his or her own, or listen to it as a member of a congregation, repeating "Amen" at its end (though pronouncing "Amen" slightly differently, as "ah-meen"). The only real difference between a Muslim's *dua* and a Christian's prayer is that many Christians prefer free-form prayer using their own words, while most Muslims prefer to use well known phrases in their *duas*. The Shia prefer *duas* composed by the Imams.

The prayer that Muslims are required to pray five times a day, however, is not a *dua* but the *sala*. This is also translated into English as "prayer," but is actually closer to "rite." Just like a Catholic priest performing the mass, a Muslim performing the *sala* must follow a set form, not only of words but also of movements. Just as a mass would not "work" if the priest forgot to consecrate the bread, so a *sala* does not work and needs to be done again if certain crucial elements are left out.

To perform the *sala*, Muslims must first ensure that they are in a state of ritual purity, a concept I will examine further in chapter 7. This state is obtained by washing certain parts of the body in a specified manner and order; it is lost in various ways, most frequently by using the lavatory or even by passing wind. Clothes too must be ritually clean—mud is not a problem, but blood is. The ritual washing needed to restore a state of purity takes about two minutes.[1]

Once in a state of purity, Muslims must find a suitable place for performing the *sala*. Having a mosque nearby is convenient, but almost anywhere else will do equally well. There is no need for the space used for *sala* to be secluded. If at home, a Muslim is as likely to use the dining room as the bedroom. If at work, a corner of the office will do fine—a corner rather than a corridor simply because performing *sala* in the corridor is likely to create an obstacle for passers-by. The owner of a vegetable stand in the street will usually pray on the sidewalk next to the stand. The only places that are not acceptable for *sala* are those that can hardly be clean—animal stalls and bathrooms are specifically excluded. To make absolutely sure of cleanliness, most Muslims will unfold a special prayer mat, which they will fold up again and keep somewhere out of harm's way after the *sala*. The vegetable seller on the sidewalk may use a piece of cardboard instead. In addition to a prayer mat, Shi'i Muslims will also place a small clay tablet in front of them.

The Muslim then turns toward Mecca, or rather toward the Kaba in Mecca, and starts the *sala* by raising his or her hands and saying "Allahu akbar," God is great. The Muslim then repeats some verses of the Koran, bows, rises, and prostrates twice, with his or her forehead touching the ground—or, in the case of Shi'i Muslims, touching the clay tablet. This procedure is repeated a number of times for each *sala*—usually four times, but only twice for the *sala* at dawn, and three times at sunset. Each movement within the *sala* is accompanied by specified phrases. Sunni Muslims then end the *sala* by turning the head to the right and then to the left, and Shi'i Muslims end the *sala* by raising and lowering the hands three times. The whole procedure

---

[1]There is also a state of "major" impurity, resulting mostly from sexual intercourse, that requires longer and more elaborate ablutions.

takes about five minutes. More devout Muslims add some non-obligatory (*sunna*) *sala* before and after, adding five or ten minutes more.

This *sala* is at the heart of Muslim worship. It is usually performed individually, but is also often performed in congregation, either in a mosque or elsewhere (for example on the sidewalk or in a house). In a large mosque, a designated prayer-leader or "Imam" will lead the prayer. The title is the same as that used by the Shi'a for their infallible leaders, but the sense of the title is here very different. The Imam for *sala* stands in front, with other worshipers arranged in lines behind, following the Imam's lead in bowing, prostrating, and so on. In a small, local mosque or in an office or private house, an Imam is selected for each *sala* — a male if any males are present, since women are not allowed to lead men in prayer. The Imam should be the most respected person present — usually the oldest but sometimes the most learned. On Fridays at midday, the *sala* must if possible be performed in congregation, and is preceded by a sermon and some *duas* — on this occasion the procedure takes about an hour, most of the time being taken up by the sermon.

The subject matter of the sermon varies. It may legitimately discuss anything of interest to the community, including politics. At certain times of year, most sermons will be on a certain subject. Sermons at the start of Ramadan, for example, generally deal with fasting. Most sermons deal with ritual, moral, or ethical issues, referring frequently to the Koran and *hadith* to support the point being made. Even in small mosques, the style of delivery used by most preachers is one that was developed in the age before microphones to make an address audible across a large open space. Few Muslim preachers take advantage of their microphones to use the more conversational style Westerners are now used to; microphones are generally used only to broadcast sermons into the street outside. As a result of this style of delivery, Muslim preachers — whatever their topic — often remind Westerners of political orators from the Europe of the 1930s, who used a similar old-fashioned style of open-air delivery. Very few Muslims have heard recordings of European orators of the 1930s, and so for them this style has no unfortunate associations. It is simply the style generally considered appropriate for sermons.

The Friday midday *sala* is in many ways like a church service, but the other *salas* have no obvious equivalent in Christianity. They are best understood as a repeated turning to God, with elements of meditation. Performing the *sala* involves interrupting daily life, making a space for God. This is not always easy, and can sometimes be very inconvenient. A report needs to be finished, customers are waiting to be served, children are waiting to be fed . . . but time still must be found for the *sala* despite this. Performing the *sala* also means turning one's concentration away from the task at hand to other, greater things, and recognizing that what seems to be important and urgent is, in fact, far less important and urgent than God.

In the Muslim world, the time of prayer is announced by the Call to Prayer, nowadays usually broadcast from loudspeakers mounted on mosques, relayed from an often crackly microphone below. In some places, a Caller to Prayer still climbs a minaret and gives the Call from there without electronic amplification—which, many would agree, generally sounds nicer. Muslims once divided the day by these Calls for Prayer. Although Chinese-made watches are now generally the norm, an inhabitant of the Muslim world is still subconsciously aware of time in terms of prayer. The absence of the Call to Prayer in the West is at first quite disconcerting to people from predominantly Muslim countries. In Saudi Arabia and a few other places, the Call to Prayer is reinforced by laws requiring all business to cease for about twenty minutes, but elsewhere normal time continues, with what academics call "ritual time" briefly superimposed. It is better to perform the prayer as soon as the Call to Prayer is heard, but it is acceptable to perform it at any point until the following Call to Prayer begins.

Although the *sala* is generally obligatory, there are exceptions. No one is obliged to pray before adulthood (defined as puberty), or if insane. Women may pray at home instead of going to the mosque for the Friday midday *sala,* which is sometimes a mercy (what would the younger children get up to if both parents were absent for an hour?) but may also reflect a rather dismissive view of women. Whether or not women pray in mosques voluntarily depends more on local custom than on Islam. Travelers are allowed to perform shorter *sala,* and have extra latitude about when to perform them. The ill may pray in bed.

Sala is *sala,* however, and almost without exception the *sala* have to be performed sooner or later. Many Muslims do not bother to perform the *sala* at all, but many do perform them scrupulously, every day for the whole of their adult lives. Some perform the *sala* for a few years, stop, and start again in later life. Except in the West, those Muslims who do not perform the *sala* cannot avoid being aware on a daily basis that many others do perform them. For those who do perform the *sala* regularly, it is a constant revalidation and confirmation of their faith.

Alms

The giving of charity is generally regarded in the West not so much as an act of worship but as something that one should do, and the focus is often more on the object—the homeless, cancer research, or the rainforests—than on the act of giving. In Islam, the giving of alms is seen more as worship, and is the third pillar of Islam. The emphasis is not so much on the objective or the recipient as it is on the act of giving—that is to say, on the donor. In fact, the recipient is technically God Himself, and whoever receives the alms is in theory benefiting not from the generosity of the immediate donor but from the mercy of God. The greater benefit is to the donor. It is good to give away part of one's money, since it lessens one's attachment to the rest. Such a donation is said to "purify" what remains. It is also, like the *sala*, a periodic acknowledgment of one's duty to God.

The rules for calculating the amount a Muslim should give in alms (*zakat* and, for the Shi'a only, *khums*) are as precise as those for calculating one's income tax. They are also even more obscure, since most of them relate to economic situations more common in earlier centuries—not to salaries and pension plans, but to flocks of goats and date harvests. In essence, *zakat* is payable on different categories of income at between 2½ percent and 10 percent, on top of which the Shi'a also pay *khums* at 20 percent after deduction of living expenses. Alms only become payable once a certain threshold has been passed, and so are not payable by the poor. For those required to pay alms, they must be calculated and paid once a year. It is also good to give money or one's time in excess of this requirement, but that is not obligatory, and is called by a different name—*sadaqa*, not *zakat*. The devout often give *sadaqa*, even if they are not especially rich. If a vegetable seller gives away his partly spoiled stock at the end of the day, as many do, that is *sadaqa*.

In theory, *zakat* and *khums* (like *sadaqa*) are paid to God. In practice, some Muslims pay their *zakat* to public or private funds or charities which then distribute it, and some pay it directly to the poor themselves, often employing some intermediary to disguise their identities. Shi'i Muslims pay their *khums* to any one of their leading Ulema, the "models for emulation" (see chapter 10). These Shi'i figures thus have considerable economic power as well as prestige; the fund established by one Ayatollah, administered from London, has the financial weight of a small international bank.

It is hard to say how many Muslims today pay alms as they should. Muslim commentators sometimes remark that if rich Muslims really paid the *zakat* that they were obliged to pay, there would be no problem of poverty and no need for any state programs of social relief. In general, the more devout the Muslim, the greater the likelihood of *zakat* being paid in full.

Fasting

The fourth pillar of Islam (and so the third most important element of Muslim worship) is the fast. The *sala* means giving up five blocks of time each day to God; *zakat* means giving up money once a year; fasting requires giving up even more than either of those sacrifices. During the month of Ramadan, from dawn to dusk, all adult Muslims who do not have a legitimate excuse are required to fast. Fasting in Islam means abstaining from anything that is taken by mouth—not just food, but also from drink and medicine and, for Muslims who smoke (as many do), also from tobacco.

This sacrifice is not, for most people, as difficult as it might sound—what has to be done is done, and one gets used to it—but it changes the nature of the day. During Ramadan, in towns and cities in the Muslim world, people become more and more taciturn as the day goes on, and shops and businesses close early. The streets become emptier and emptier, save for the sometimes erratically driven cars of those hurrying to get home by dusk. And then, as the last rays of the sun vanish, fasting becomes feasting. Food has never tasted more delicious, water has never been sweeter. Conversation becomes animated, crowds gather in the streets. Everyone goes to bed late and happy—and everyone is bleary-eyed the next morning, more taciturn than ever.

For the non-Muslim, Ramadan in the Muslim world is rarely an enjoyable month, as it is hard to get anything done. Everyone else's attention wanders, and everything seems to be shut when the non-Muslim wants it to be open. Worst of all, perhaps, is the subtle but pervasive feeling of being out of joint with everything, as if day had become night, and night day. For the Muslim, in contrast, Ramadan is almost a holiday—work goes on, but from the perspective of the evening, the events of the day seem almost like a dream. Normal life recedes, and something almost magical replaces it. Ramadan is a bit like a Christmas that goes on for a whole month, with the indulgence balanced by abstinence. This is especially true in countries like Egypt; Ramadan in Pakistan, in contrast, is a more sober affair.

For Muslims in the West, the experience of Ramadan is necessarily very different. Life in the surrounding world goes on as normal, and most people Muslims meet are not even aware that it is Ramadan, and still less aware of what Ramadan involves. Muslims are expected to work normal hours, and to work with normal dedication. The feast at the end of the fast may not be the family celebration that it is in the Muslim world, but rather a sandwich and a can of Coke consumed silently at work at what seems to others an odd hour of the day. The evening brings no general feeling of elation in which to join, but merely an evening like any other. Fasting Ramadan in the West is for many a lonely and often alienating experience.

In some parts of the West that are farther north, it is not even possible to fast the full period. The timing of Ramadan is fixed by the lunar calendar, based on months starting with the new moon. This is shorter than the solar calendar used for the familiar, Western year, which is based on years starting just as the days start to grow longer. Because the lunar calendar is shorter than the solar calendar, Ramadan falls about ten days earlier each solar year. In 1998, Ramadan started in December and ended in January. In 2015, Ramadan will start in July. Anyone who tries to fast from dawn to sunset during July in northern Canada or northern Sweden is unlikely to be alive at the end of the month. Muslims in such northern latitudes thus generally fast only until the sun sets on some more southerly land. A young woman, an Arab Muslim friend of mine, was studying at a Swedish university in 1980, when Ramadan ended in August. She used to retire to her dormitory room as the sun was about to set in her own country. Getting a picnic ready on her bed, checking her watch, she would finally draw the curtains to pretend that it was dark, and sometimes cry in her loneliness as she broke her fast.

Sometimes, Muslims in the West arrange to break the fast together in a mosque or community center, especially at times of year when sunset is after working hours. When this happens, Ramadan is a less lonely affair. The local Muslim community then becomes the focus of the evening, rather than (as in the Muslim world) the family.

Ramadan as described so far may not strike the reader as especially religious. In fact, it is and it isn't—like Christmas in the West. The celebration is there for everybody, and everybody is aware that there is some religious significance to it. Nearly everyone fasts; it is almost harder not to fast than to fast when everyone else is fasting. Many Muslims who do not normally pray regularly begin to pray, and some Muslims who normally drink alcohol stop doing so. Devout Muslims who normally pray regularly add extra prayers, and may spend part of their evenings in their local mosque, praying the special Ramadan "tarawih" *sala.* Others stay up late reading the Koran rather than walking among the festive crowds or watching the special Ramadan quiz shows on Egyptian television (usually very secular shows, by the way, and now available everywhere by satellite). Some devote part of their time to works of charity, especially the "Table of the Merciful." During Ramadan, wealthier Muslims give money and time to the preparation of the sunset meal for the poor, and as sunset nears, tables (called "of the Merciful," i.e., of God) appear in public places. Anyone who so wishes can seat themselves and be fed their sunset meal for nothing.

Attitudes to the non-religious aspects of Ramadan vary. Traditional Muslims are usually happy that feasting succeeds fasting, but modern Muslims sometimes rail against the festivities. If Ramadan is meant to be a month of fasting, they ask, why is it that total food consumption actually goes up rather than down? What have Egyptian television quizzes about the activities of movie stars got to do with God? Rather the opposite!

Even in the Muslim world, of course, not everyone fasts. Children need not fast, though as they grow older they generally try to show their maturity by fasting at least part of the day. The old and the sick do not have to fast if it will damage their health, and pregnant women never have to fast. Travelers and women who are breast-feeding may delay the fast until a more convenient time, and women do not fast during their periods. Some people do not fast because they choose not to, or because they are not Muslim in the first place. Even those who are not fasting, however, do not usually eat, drink, or smoke in public. In some countries it is actually illegal to do so, while in others it is simply a question of good manners—eating, drinking, or smoking in front of someone who cannot eat, drink, or smoke makes their task harder, and so should not be done.

Pilgrimage

The fifth and last pillar of Islam is pilgrimage. The *sala* prayer is performed (or not) five times a day; alms are given and Ramadan is fasted once a year; but pilgrimage happens once a lifetime, and then only if possible.

The main pilgrimage, called the Hajj, differs from the Christian concept of pilgrimage. For most Christian pilgrims, the journey is as or more important than the actual arrival at the pilgrimage site; for the Muslim, it matters little how a pilgrim gets to the vicinity of Mecca (usually, these days, by airplane). What matters for a Muslim on Hajj is what the pilgrim does in Mecca—especially at the Kaba, the "house of God"—and then in the region of Mecca, over a period of several days. A precise and detailed series of rituals is prescribed. Most of these rituals seem to have existed before Islam—as did the Kaba itself—and were adopted into Islam; equally, most of them have no parallel elsewhere in Islam.

At a certain point as the pilgrim approaches Mecca, for example, not only is ritual purity required (as it is for the *sala*), but a whole set of very special rules have to be followed. Although a woman can wear more or less what she likes, a man is allowed to wear only two pieces of cloth, the edges of which must not be hemmed with stitches. Shoes, too, may not contain stitches. Besides stitches, all sorts of other normal things become forbidden, such as letting fall any part of one's body, whether a fragment of a fingernail or a single hair. Not only may the pilgrim not cut his or her fingernails or hair, but he or she may not even scratch—a scratch might dislodge a hair. A pilgrim is also not allowed to carry a weapon or kill any animal—not normally an issue nowadays, but relevant once, when weapons were routinely carried for personal protection, and travelers would if possible add any passing edible animal to their evening meal for a bit of variety.

The Hajj can only be performed during the lunar month named after it, Dhu'l-Hijja, which is three months after Ramadan (and, like Ramadan, falls a little earlier each solar year). Each year, at the start of Dhu'l-Hijja, millions of Muslims converge on Mecca from every part of the world: some from neighboring cities in Arabia, some from nearby Egypt and Syria, some from as far away as Indonesia and China, and—in recent decades— some from America, Argentina and Belgium. Before cheap air travel, less than a quarter of a million Muslims assembled each year; before steamships, only 50,000. Today, the Hajj causes the single largest annual movement of people on earth (though many Americans would guess Thanksgiving may come a close second).

Once in Mecca, the pilgrim goes to the Kaba, which is located in the vast open courtyard of an even vaster mosque. After entering the mosque, the pilgrim walks—along with thousands or even millions of others—seven times around the Kaba in an anticlockwise direction, attempting on each circuit to kiss a large black stone set into one of the corners of the Kaba. The pilgrim then runs seven times up and down a corridor in the mosque; at either end of this corridor are exposed the rocky surfaces of two ancient hillocks. The first part of the Hajj is then complete.

The second part of the Hajj, which is performed on the ninth day of the month of Dhu'l-Hijja, takes place some 13 miles from Mecca, on the plain of Arafat, at the foot of a small mountain. Here the pilgrims spend the afternoon in one vast crowd, in prayer and meditation, just as the Israelites once waited below Mount Sinai for Moses. The following day, at Mina (between the plain of Arafat and Mecca itself), the pilgrims first throw small pebbles at some ancient stone pillars, and then slaughter (or have slaughtered on their behalf) a small animal, usually a sheep. Much of the meat is later distributed to the poor.

After returning to Mecca from Mina for a final circuit of the Kaba, the Hajj is complete. Although not part of the Hajj ritual, the pilgrim will normally then take the opportunity of going north to Medina, spending about a week in the city of the Prophet, praying the *sala* in the mosque built around the Prophet's tomb. Some pilgrims instead choose to go to Medina before going to Mecca.

Many attempts have been made to explain the sense and significance of these various rituals, which are believed to have been established by Abraham, who struggled against idol worship and built the Kaba as a temple for the worship of the One God. Pilgrims run between the two ancient hillocks, for example, just as Abraham's wife Hagar once ran between them in desperation after Abraham had left her and their son Ishmael there, and returned to his other wife, Sarah. The sacrifice of the sheep at Mina commemorates the alternative sacrifice allowed by God to Abraham in place of the sacrifice of his son. Throwing pebbles at the pillars represents the abnegation and stoning of Satan. The widely admired medieval commentator Muhamamd al-Ghazali, however, explained that what was really important about the throwing of pebbles at the pillars was that in fact it had no significance—and that to perform an act of worship that had no apparent rhyme or reason to it was an ultimate test of, and so an ultimate strengthening of, one's faith. Following al-Ghazali, one might say that one of the main points of the Hajj rituals is that they are entirely special, and so they make the whole Hajj entirely special—the most special experience in the entire life of nearly all pilgrims.

This entirely special nature of the pilgrimage is often commented on. The Kaba itself is frequently described as "like nothing else on earth"—something that seems to belong to an altogether different dimension from those we are used to, a protrusion from another reality. The afternoon spent on Arafat in a vast crowd of other pilgrims, identical in their ritual robes, is also an experience of a different reality. Few Muslims are unchanged by their experience of the Hajj: on their return to their homes and their normal lives, the religious element of life remains in the foreground, more real than the visible realities of normal life. Forever after, a photograph of the Kaba reminds the former pilgrim of the intensity of the experience of Hajj, rather as a photograph of a small child warms the heart of its grandparent.

The Hajj, as was said earlier, must be performed "if possible." It is expensive, though not as expensive as it used to be before mass air travel. It is still arduous and dangerous, though far less arduous and dangerous than it once was. Only Muslims who have the necessary financial means and can perform the pilgrimage without risking hardship for anyone who is dependent on them are obliged to go on Hajj. In practice, this usually means older people whose children are able to look after themselves, and younger people who have money but no dependents. Increasingly, however, Muslims who can afford an air ticket go on Hajj even when they are not strictly obliged to, and some return many times, even though they have fulfilled their duty with their first Hajj.

Even so, many Muslims never manage to go on Hajj. They instead participate from a distance, since the day on which the pilgrims gather on the plain of Arafat is the beginning of a long public holiday throughout the Muslim world, and the day on which the pilgrims at Mina slaughter a sheep is marked in the same way elsewhere. Even Muslims who remain at home usually buy a sheep or smaller animal (a chicken will do if that is all the household budget can allow) and slaughter it or have it slaughtered for them. For some, this brings back memories of a past pilgrimage; for others, it is a public holiday and festival with religious implications. To many Western observers, it is a strange festival, most notable for blood in the streets, since that is where many urban Muslims slaughter their sheep. In some European countries, this has become a major issue, with Muslims insisting on public slaughtering and non-Muslims (most of whom have never seen an animal slaughtered, and do not want to) remaining aghast. This conflict is really cultural, however, since there is no religious reason why a suitable slaughterhouse should not be used, or even—according to some—why meat should not just be bought in a shop. Non-Muslims generally have great difficulty in associating blood running in the streets with celebration. That excited Muslim children should be allowed to join in the fun of slaughtering a sheep, just as excited Christian children are allowed to join in decorating a Christmas tree, shocks many Westerners—unless, perhaps, they have grown up on a farm.

As well as the Hajj pilgrimage just described, many Muslims also perform a lesser pilgrimage, called the *umra*. This is not a requirement, and can be done at any time of year. It consists of visiting Mecca and performing the rituals of the pilgrimage in and around the Kaba. There is no assembly on Arafat, and no throwing of pebbles. There are no vast crowds, and the Kaba can be contemplated more at leisure.

Shi'i Muslims also perform a special category of pilgrimage, called *ziyara*, to the tombs of descendants of the Prophet, especially those of the Imams. *Ziyara* may be performed at any time of year, and is far less codified than the Hajj or *umra*, though books of recommended procedure (mostly collections of *dua* prayers) exist and are often used. The most popular tombs for these *ziyara* pilgrimages are that of Husayn at Karbala in Iraq, followed by the tombs of Ali at Najaf (Iraq) and of Reda at Mashhad (Iran), as well as other tombs in Medina and Damascus. Some Shi'a calculate that more individuals perform *ziyara* each year than Hajj. *Ziyara* to the tomb of the Imams has no significance for Sunni Muslims.

The term *ziyara* is used by Sunnis to describe visits to any notable tomb—that of a woman or a man regarded as in some way holy, for example a companion or a relation of the Prophet or a great saint from former centuries. These Sunni *ziyaras* can be short and quite casual. A traditional Sunni walking down a street with a few minutes to spare may notice that he or she is passing a mosque with a notable tomb, and may go inside to stand for a few minutes to say a *dua*. This is a practice on which modern Sunni Muslims frown, as they see something of polytheism in it. In Saudi Arabia, such *ziyara* is absolutely prohibited, and many tombs have been bulldozed to prevent it.

Sunni *ziyara* can however be much more elaborate, especially on the annual anniversary of a saint's birth (or death). Anniversary celebrations, called *mawlids* or *urs*, may last up to a week, and be the major annual event in a locality. Once again, they are both religious and secular occasions. For the devout traditional Muslims sitting in prayer in the saint's tomb chamber, the occasion is purely religious. For those outside the mosque following a procession, or simple drinking free tea, talking to each other and occasionally listening to reciters of religious poetry, the occasion is a celebration with religious overtones. For those further away trying their skill at fairground stalls that have been set up, the secular element is uppermost. For the disapproving modern Muslim walking past, the whole occasion is not just secular, but actively anti-religious. Modern Muslims, however, generally keep away. Traditional Muslims, in contrast, may travel from miles around to attend such anniversaries. The annual anniversary of Sayyid al-Badawi in Egypt, for example, attracts at least a million people. Some claim that it attracts more than Hajj.

Umra and the Shi'i *ziyara* are performed mostly by the devout, and are less notable experiences that the Hajj. They act as a sort of spiritual refreshment, a drinking at a stream of *baraka*. Sunni *ziyara* operates in a similar way for the devout, though it is less intense; for the less devout, it may be less of a spiritual experience than a way of collecting *baraka* for a very specific need, such as passing an exam or the healthy recovery of a sick farm animal. Even in these cases, however, there is a spiritual element produced by the turning to God, just as there is when a Christian prays to God or a saint for help regarding a specific need.

Reading the Koran

Reading and listening to the Koran is a lesser but important element of Muslim worship. Unlike the other acts of worship considered so far, it is not obligatory, and it is not one of the five pillars. To perform the *sala* it is necessary to know a few short passages from the Koran by heart, but that is all. In practice, though, devout and even somewhat devout Muslims spend time reading the Koran aloud to themselves, or listening to it read by others on the radio or on cassette tapes or an iPod. A shopkeeper may keep the radio in his store tuned to a station broadcasting the Koran for several hours each morning, and a truck driver may play tapes of the Koran for much of his journey.

Reading the Koran aloud is not the same as studying the Koran. The meaning of short passages of the Koran is examined during religion classes in schools, and students and scholars of religion spend much longer periods in this way, but for most Muslims the text matters more than the meaning. As we saw in an earlier chapter, the text of the Koran—as a direct manifestation of God in the world—has a very special significance for Muslims, irrespective of its meaning. The majority of Muslims do not even know more than a few words of Arabic, and so can only study the meaning of the Koran in their own language. Even so, they listen to it in the original Arabic (never in translation), and often read it to themselves in Arabic, although they do not understand the language that they are reading. Reading or listening to the Koran in this way is for a Muslim rather as singing or listening to a hymn is for a Western Christian. The sense of the words is not the main point, and is often not even given much thought.

It is easier for an Indonesian Muslim who knows no Arabic to read the Koran aloud than it would be for an American Christian who knows no Hebrew to recite the book of Genesis in the original, since there are very precise rules about how the text of the Koran should be read—where to put the emphasis, where to raise the tone of the voice and where to lower it, where to pause and where to speed up a little. Some learn these rules at school, while others rely on texts transliterated into their own language, with the emphases and tones marked in a variety of ingenious fashions. The Koran, when read according to these rules (as it always is), sounds to most Westerners as if it is being sung. It is not, however, being "sung," since "singing" the Koran is forbidden. It is, in English terms, being "chanted."

Traditional Muslims, unless they are scholars, will usually read or listen to the Koran for its own sake rather than study it for its meaning. Devout modern Muslims, in contrast, frequently read it for its meaning, often assisted by commentaries explaining that meaning (which is often far from obvious even to those who know Arabic). A modern non-Arab Muslim may have before him or her a page which contains the original text of the Koran, a transcription from Arabic into another script, a translation, and notes explaining the meaning of the text.

Remembering God

Zikr—"Remembering God"—is the specialty of the Sufis, the traditional and devout seekers of a more direct experience of God. As we have seen, Sufis may be Shi'i or Sunni, but most are Sunni.

The Sufi *zikr* comes in two forms. The daily spiritual exercises of most active Sufis, usually assigned them by their Shaykh or spiritual director, include a major element of repetitive prayer. Short formulas such as "there is no God save He" or "God, pray for our lord Muhammad, his people and companions" are repeated anywhere from a hundred to a thousand times, with a string of beads usually being used to keep count of the repetitions. Repetitive prayer was once familiar to Catholics in the form of the rosary, but is less common now; it is, however, a standard devotional technique of most religions.

The second form of Sufi *zikr* takes place usually once a week, when the followers of a particular Shaykh gather, either in a mosque or a house, to perform repetitive prayer together. Such a meeting is generally called a *hadra*. Depending on the Shaykh and the number of Sufis present, they may sit in a circle or stand in lines. At all such gatherings, *zikr* is performed together and simultaneously. The manner in which this communal *zikr* is performed varies from order to order and from Shaykh to Shaykh; sometimes it is very restrained, even entirely silent, but more often the prayers are repeated aloud, with special breathing patterns and rhythmic movements of the upper body. Often, these breathing patterns and movements are very pronounced; the worshiper sways or turns almost as far as is possible without falling over. In the unusual case of the Mevleviyya, the followers of Shaykhs connected with a particular order that was once widespread in Turkey, the worshiper actually turns full circles—these are the famous, but untypical, "whirling dervishes."

Communal *zikr* has something in common with individual *zikr*, but has different effects. Like other aspects of Muslim worship, it is a door into a different reality. At the least, the worshiper feels transported from the everyday into a calmer and more contemplative state. At the most, everyday reality vanishes altogether, and is replaced by an experience of the divine. This experience is sometimes so intense that a Sufi falls into something rather like a mild epileptic fit. This is not regarded as desirable by most Shaykhs, but is welcomed by some ordinary Sufis. A powerful reaction such as this is a very visible indication of the power of their rituals.

Active Sufis all perform both forms of *zikr*. Communal *zikr* also attracts casual participants, who may sometimes later become full and formal followers of the Shaykh, but often just join in for the experience. These worshippers will invariably be traditional Muslims, though not always only notably devout ones. Modern Muslims, in contrast, look on communal *zikr* with extreme distaste, regarding it as an importation into Islam from alien sources. The Wahhabis are especially hostile to communal *zikr*, which, in Saudi Arabia, can only be performed in complete secrecy.

Sufi orders were once found all over the Muslim world, but in many Muslim countries today they are found mostly in traditional, often rural areas. Some Sufi orders are "popular," with members who are mostly peasant farmers, while some are "elite," with members who are engineers, university professors, and Ulema. Sufism was once as common in elite circles as in popular circles, and Ulema were often Sufis as well. For such Ulema, formal scholarship and the Sharia were the external aspects of Islam, and Sufism was the internal aspect. The Sharia, it is sometimes said, is the cup which is needed to hold the greater truths that Sufism can access. In recent years, for reasons discussed in chapter 3, Sufism has almost vanished from elite circles in many Arab countries, though not in other parts of the Muslim world, especially West Africa. Iranian Sufism is alive and well, but takes somewhat different forms from Sufism in the Sunni world.

Most Sufis differ from other Muslims primarily in being more devout. There are of course plenty of non-Sufi Muslims who are also devout, but what most Sufi orders require in terms of religious practice makes the requirements of the Sharia seem light. Hence, few members of these orders are not devout. Some orders, however, require much less in terms of religious practice than most do. A few, especially in Iran, are known for their consumption of marijuana and opium.

There are also non-religious reasons for being a Sufi, then. Sometimes it is simply customary in an area or a family. Sufism is also a bit like Freemasonry in its social and business implications—indeed, the first Muslims to encounter Freemasonry thought that they had found a Western Sufi order. As well as being a religious organization, a Sufi order is also a sort of social club. Members of an order know and trust each other, which can be very useful in business. In the days when there were still trade guilds in the Muslim world, membership of a guild and of a particular Sufi order often overlapped.

Sufism exists in the West as well as in the Muslim world, and is probably the form of Islam that Westerners are most likely to appreciate. Some of the Sufi orders in the West are no different from those in the Muslim world, but some have adjusted to their new environment. These adjustments are generally a matter of increased liberalism, of emphasizing inner truth and putting less emphasis on the Sharia. This reflects the fact that the average Westerner is much more interested in inner truth than in the Sharia. Usually, these orders only accept Muslims, so a Westerner who wishes to join one has to become Muslim (and this is one of the main reasons for Westerners becoming Muslim). Sometimes an order will accept non-Muslims on the basis that they are likely to become Muslim sooner or later. Sometimes, however, a so-called Sufi order in the West consists mostly of non-Muslims and pays little or no attention to the Sharia. These "de-Islamized" Sufi orders have existed in the West since the start of the twentieth century, and generally have more to do with "alternative religion" in the West than with Islam. They may provide spiritual benefits to their members, but they have little, if anything, to do with "real" Sufism. They fall outside the scope of this book.

Summary

Worship is the essence of the religious experience of devout Muslims, and is present in the lives of all Muslims, whether as something they encounter on a daily basis or as something that they might one day turn to. The first of the five "pillars" of Islam is accepting that God alone is god, and that Muhammad is His Prophet. The other four pillars are acts of worship that must be performed at specific times and in specific ways. Prayer in the sense of *sala* is incumbent on almost all, though not all perform it on a regular basis, or even at all. Almsgiving in the sense of *zakat* is incumbent only on the rich, not all of whom perform this obligation. Ramadan is fasted by almost everyone, and mixes worship with festival. The Hajj pilgrimage is the major event in the lifetime of many millions, but still remains beyond the means of many; only the devout go on the Hajj, but even the least devout join in some way in the accompanying public holiday in their own countries. Traditional Muslims also perform *ziyara* at the tombs of saints, and Shi'i Muslims perform *ziyara* to the tombs of the Imams.

In addition to these general acts of worship, there is also reading aloud or listening to the Koran, recordings or broadcasts of which will be heard many times a day by anyone living in a large Muslim city. Sufis specialize in "remembering God" through individual and communal repetitive prayer, called *zikr* and *hadra*.

6

Inside the Harem

The Family

Apart from politics, nothing about Islam is more controversial in the West than the status of women. Most Westerners see Muslim women as victims, trapped in head-scarves and veils. "Whenever I see a head-scarf," wrote a reader to a popular French women's magazine, "I feel I want to seize it and pull it off." "Imagine!" roared a preacher in a Cairo mosque one Friday when the French government was about to ban head-scarves in public schools. "Imagine that it is *your* wives and daughters that the French want to drive naked into the streets!"

This chapter considers wives, daughters, and other women in Islam, but in the context in which the topic makes most sense to Muslims: the context of the family. I will consider head-scarves and other aspects of clothing in the following chapter.

The family is of enormous significance in Islam, and the Sharia regulates most aspects of family life. In practice, local custom and state laws are also important. While the laws of some Muslim states codify the provisions of the Sharia, the laws of other states contradict them on certain points, usually following modern Western practice. Local custom sometimes contradicts both the Sharia and state law, preventing women from taking advantage of rights that the Sharia or state law gives them. Muslims in the West are of course subject to Western laws, and these laws and Western custom also have an impact on them.

There are important differences between Western and Muslim views on the family and on gender roles. This is not just because of Islam. Economic conditions and local culture also produce differences between Western and Muslim views on family and gender. The Muslim world today contains many megacities, and Muslims are increasingly urbanized, but until very recently the vast majority of Muslims lived in villages where there was little or no education, no reliable contraception, and few if any opportunities for work outside the peasant household. Such conditions encourage family patterns very different from those encouraged by the conditions that became established in the West in the aftermath of the industrial revolution. The lifestyle of an illiterate woman who starts work in a peasant household at the age of nine and gets pregnant at fifteen can hardly be the same as that of a well-paid Western university graduate with access to reliable contraception.

Men and Women

Most Muslims' conceptions of gender are very different from those of contemporary progressive Westerners, and more like Western conceptions from a hundred years ago. Adult men are conceived of primarily as fathers, and adult women primarily as mothers. An unmarried man or woman of whatever age is seen in most Muslim societies (though not in the Sharia) as still in some sense a child. The Sharia and nearly all Muslims are agreed in regarding marriage and parenthood as the natural state of adult life.

This is very different from contemporary Western views. Western societies today see a single person as a full member of society—in fact, novels, movies, and television tend to focus more on unmarried men and women than on married ones. The idea of seeing men and women primarily in terms of their reproductive roles ("biological destiny") is regarded by many Westerners as abhorrent. Most Muslims, however, see the biological determination of certain destinies as a self-evident truth (though they do not use these terms). In poor rural communities, both men and women tend to marry young, and children follow quickly upon marriage, as is the case in heavily Christian areas of the American South. This pattern is changing fast in the growing cities of the Muslim world, and even faster for Muslims in the West, but norms always take some time to catch up with reality.

Islam takes it as axiomatic that men are stronger than women, not only physically but also mentally and morally, and that women are therefore in need of male protection and guidance. In this, Islam differs little from the classic view of women found in other monotheistic religions, at least in their older and more traditional forms. Such views have been challenged and to some extent overturned in contemporary Western societies, but in most Muslim societies they have not yet even been seriously challenged, though a small feminist movement exists, as I will discuss later in this chapter.

Despite this view of men and women as essentially different, women are conceived of in Islam as independent human beings with rights that must be respected and can be enforced. A century and a half ago, the rights of women under Islam were greater than those enjoyed by women in the West. The West has changed a lot over the last 150 years, but the Muslim world has changed less in this respect.

Sex and Segregation

The stories in *1,001 Nights* have left some Westerners with a view of Muslims as particularly devoted to sex. Many of the stories in *1,001 Nights* derive from a genre of mild pornography that has always been popular in the storytelling of the Muslim world, but is not at all representative of general practice. It is perhaps worth mentioning that many Muslims, having watched American soap operas but never having traveled to the West, have very strange views about Western devotion to sex.

Islam does not object to sex as such, either for men or for women. Like eating and drinking, it is a need that should be satisfied. A married person is expected to have sex with his or her spouse, and a marriage without sex can be dissolved. Unmarried persons are expected to marry or, if still young after divorce or the death of a partner, to remarry. Celibacy is regarded as unnatural. Like eating and drinking, sex is forbidden in the daylight hours while fasting. Otherwise, it is encouraged.

Sex outside marriage, however, is strictly forbidden in Islam, though fornication between unmarried partners is in theory viewed more leniently than sex between married adulterers. The logic of this distinction is that a married adulterer could have had sex with his or her spouse; an unmarried person has no such outlet, though a minority view in Sunni Islam permits masturbation, and Shi'i Islam permits a form of temporary marriage (discussed below). In practice, however, the distinction between fornication and adultery is often ignored.

Muslims, then, are not expected to repress their sexual instincts. Instead they are expected to avoid circumstances in which these instincts might be unduly and illegitimately aroused. Sex within marriage is fine; it is sex outside marriage that is not allowed. And if someone never sees a member of the opposite sex outside his or her immediate family (other than his or her spouse, if any), it is hardly possible to be tempted into extramarital sex. This is the basic logic of Islam's segregation of the sexes. It is expressed in the well-known *hadith*: "When a man and a woman are alone together, Satan is with them."

The degree to which segregation of the sexes is enforced in practice varies from society to society and family to family, as does the degree to which it is enforced equally on men and women. There is a general tendency toward emphasizing the segregation of women rather than the segregation of men. In theory, men are no more entitled to mix with women than women are with men, but in practice parents are usually far stricter with daughters than with sons, and husbands are usually stricter with wives than wives are with husbands. There are practical as well as attitudinal reasons for this. An unmarried son who is suspected of having made someone pregnant has damaged his marriage prospects to some extent, while an unmarried daughter who has been made pregnant has destroyed hers (unless the father of the baby will marry her). A wife can hardly object to her husband going to work, and usually has no way of knowing who her husband meets at work; a husband can easily object to a wife who does not go out to work (some do, of course) receiving male visitors at home.

The most severe variety of segregation forbids women to leave their houses at all save on rare occasions and with the specific permission of their husbands (or their closest male relatives, if unmarried), and forbids any visits at all by men unless they are close relatives. This variety of segregation is supported by many classic Sharia texts. An alternative variety of segregation, which can also be supported from the Sharia, allows women much the same freedom of movement as men, but insists on separate facilities for all purposes. Houses have two sets of reception rooms, one for men and one for women. At a celebration, the women will party and dance together in one place, and men will party (and sometimes dance) together in another place.

In Iran, houses once had two sets of door-knockers making different sounds, one low-pitched and one high-pitched. The low-pitched knocker was for a male visitor to summon a man to open the door, and the high-pitched knocker was for a female visitor woman to summon a woman. A third, more liberal variety of segregation allows women and men to mix in a more or less normal Western fashion in the immediate neighborhood of their homes and at work and school, but does not allow mixing in other contexts. It is fine for a young man and a young woman to chat in a group situation in a university cafeteria, but not to chat as a couple in the MacDonald's across the road, and certainly not to go out together in the evening. This variety of segregation is not explicitly recommended by the Sharia, but neither is it incompatible with the Sharia.

All three varieties of segregation are often found in the same country, though the more liberal variety is not found at all in countries such as Yemen and Saudi Arabia, where the mixing of the sexes at work and school is prohibited by law. In Saudi Arabia women are even forbidden to drive cars, an interpretation of the Sharia unknown anywhere else, and regarded by most non-Saudi Muslims (and by some Saudi Muslims) as ridiculous.

In general, the more severe varieties of segregation are not found in major cities; they are more characteristic of remote rural communities in countries such as Afghanistan. Devout modern and Wahhabi Muslims everywhere, however, often observe varieties of segregation that are more severe than their local norms, even when they are in the West.

Segregation can also extend outside the house, to a male refusal to look at a woman if it can be avoided (there is no objection to women looking at men). It may also extend to a refusal to touch a person of the opposite sex unless that person is a close relative. Devout Muslims of all varieties do not generally shake hands with persons of the opposite sex, partly because some interpretations of the Sharia hold that physical contact of any sort with a member of the opposite sex breaks a state of ritual purity. Other interpretations of the Sharia hold that the state of ritual purity is broken only by contact that involves an element of physical desire.

The more liberal varieties of segregation are characteristic of the elites in most Muslim countries, and are usually correlated more with class than with piety. Total absence of segregation is extremely rare everywhere in the Muslim world. Even in countries such as Turkey, where Islam is often quite absent from public life, some degree of segregation still exists. Turkish restaurants often have "family rooms" from which single men are excluded. This and similar arrangements elsewhere are often welcomed by women because they provide a degree of privacy. Unless devout, young Muslim men who are not used to social contact with women outside their own families often treat female strangers with little respect—unwelcome groping is a real problem in some cities. Young Muslim women therefore welcome protection from such young men for practical rather than religious reasons.

Whatever form of segregation exists, a younger woman going out at night or traveling is generally expected to be accompanied by a male chaperone, who should either be her husband or a close male relative. This, like the "family room" of Turkish restaurants, is partly for the protection of the woman, but it is also to ensure that the woman is protected from herself. Liberal families—usually the more elite or those living in Turkey or the West—often regard it as quite normal for a woman to travel on her own, but such families are few in number.

Despite segregation and the Sharia, extramarital sex does take place in the Muslim world. In a very small number of very Westernized households where little attention is paid to Islam, extramarital sex is treated much as it is treated in the West today, and some Muslims conform to standard Western dating patterns, especially when living in the West. But even liberal and non-observant Muslim households generally treat extramarital sex as it was treated in the West a hundred years ago—as a dreadful transgression, never to be repeated, especially by women.

Some Muslims distinguish between casual and serious partners in extramarital sex, a distinction not made by Islam. A serious partner is one whom one hopes to marry from the beginning; a casual partner is one with whom one has fun, and has no intention of marrying. Those Muslim women who practice extramarital sex do so in total secrecy, and only very rarely take casual partners, but Muslim men who practice extramarital sex are as likely to take casual partners as are men anywhere. The main difference between Muslim and Western societies in this respect is that in Muslim societies a casual partner almost never becomes a serious one. The sort of woman who willingly becomes a casual partner is by definition not a woman one would want to marry. Unfortunately for Western women in the

Muslim world, a non-Muslim woman who engages in extramarital sex is almost by definition a casual partner.

In Shi'i Islam, there is one legitimate form of what is in effect extramarital sex: temporary marriage. From a legal point of view, this differs from regular marriage (discussed below) only in that it is agreed in advance that the "marriage" is to last only for a specified period, whether a few hours or a few months. Since the woman is required to wait three months between marriages (just as after divorce, as is discussed below), the paternity of any child born of such a "marriage" is established, as is paternal responsibility for it. Most Shi'i marriages, of course, are regular ones, intended to last until death, and Shi'i society regards the regular marriage as the norm. Temporary marriage is sometimes used by couples who are engaged to be married in a regular marriage, usually with an agreement that sex (but not kissing) will wait until after the regular marriage. The couple can then associate during their engagement without the constraints that the Sharia imposes on unmarried persons. It is also sometimes used by devout university students studying abroad. In general, Shi'is frown on temporary marriages that are merely for the purpose of sexual enjoyment, even though they accept that the Sharia allows temporary marriages for this purpose.

Sunni Islam does not accept the Shi'i concept of temporary marriage, insisting that an intention to end a marriage after a specified period means that no real marriage actually takes place. Intentions are known only to God, however, and can also sometimes be disguised by humans. A rich Sunni Muslim man on vacation abroad may marry a local woman, aware at the time that there is a risk of divorce when he goes home. When he is about to go home, he may find himself divorcing, just as he thought might happen. Many Westerners would see this as little different in substance from a brief, casual, vacation romance.

There is also one curious justification of extramarital sex that is used by a small number of Muslim men, usually Wahhabis. There is no requirement in the Sharia for Muslim men to segregate themselves from their slaves, and men are in fact allowed by the Sharia to have sex with their female slaves. This was once the legal basis on which the very rich collected concubines, the famed "harem"—the Arabic word *hareem* actually means "private," and denoted the private apartments of the female members of a large family. Slavery is extinct in the Muslim world today (with one or two very untypical exceptions), and so this provision of the Sharia is regarded by most Muslims as no longer applicable. Some Muslim men, however, apply the provision very loosely, not to female slaves (which they do not have) but to all females who might once have become slaves. The argument holds that enemies captured in war were then enslaved; that non-Muslims in non-Muslim states are potential enemies; and so that non-Muslim females in non-Muslim states may be deemed slaves. It is therefore permitted to have sex with them. It must be stressed that this argument is seen by most Muslims as dubious in the extreme, if not as totally ridiculous. It is, however, sometimes used by somewhat devout Muslims to justify to themselves their amorous exploits while on vacation in the West.

Marriage

The segregation of the sexes raises obvious problems when it comes to marriage. If one never meets a member of the opposite sex, how can one get married? Increasingly, and for those with access to it, the internet provides a perfect solution to this dilemma. For others, the general solution is to rely on one's relatives' contacts. Marriages arranged in this way remain common throughout the Muslim world. An arranged marriage need not be the same thing as a forced marriage, though it may sometimes amount to the same thing. In very traditional communities, future spouses often meet for the first time on the day of their marriage. A more liberal variety of arranged marriage is more common, however, and is more like what Westerners call a blind date. A man and a woman are introduced and left to see how they get on with each other. If they do not get on, they part ways.

Marriages in rural communities are often arranged between first cousins. When such a marriage occurs, everyone concerned can be confident that they know all about both bride and groom, but there is also a practical side: the rules of inheritance (discussed later) encourage this sort of marriage as a way of keeping property together.

"Love marriages" between partners who choose each other independently are becoming increasingly common in the Muslim world, and have always taken place to some degree. But they have also always been somewhat controversial, because of their apparently random nature. In all but the most severe systems of segregation, men and women do sometimes meet each other, and when they meet, they sometimes fall in love. Even with love marriages, however, it often happens that the man and woman concerned never meet alone until after their engagement. Because of the limited number of contexts in which men and women usually meet, there are more love marriages to colleagues at work and to relatives in the Muslim world than in the West.

Muslims should marry Muslims, but Islam allows a Muslim man to marry a Christian or Jewish woman (though not a follower of a non-monotheistic religion such as Hinduism). A Muslim woman, in contrast, is allowed only to marry a Muslim man, the assumption being that the religion of the husband will prevail (which is, ironically, the opposite of the assumption made by Judaism). This rule of the Sharia is reflected in the laws of most Muslim states, which do not allow Muslim women to marry non-Muslim men. If a Muslim woman marries a non-Muslim man under the law of a Western state, this "marriage" will simply be regarded as having not taken place by the Sharia, and by most Muslims. Until quite recently, the laws of certain Western states returned the compliment with a vengeance, not recognizing any sort of marriage between Muslims performed in the Muslim world. The main consequence of this was to make it impossible for Muslims living in the West to divorce each other, as no court would dissolve a marriage that it did not recognize as having happened in the first place.

In practice, a Muslim woman wishing to marry a non-Muslim man may sometimes persuade him to convert to Islam; even a nominal conversion will be accepted by most Muslim families, and by Muslim society as a whole. Such a conversion is not a major problem for many Western Christians, who may well only be nominal Christians in the first place. It can be a problem for an Arab Christian, however. In most parts of the Arab world, conversion to Islam by a Christian will never really be accepted by other Arab Christians, including the convert's immediate family. Similarly, it is not accepted by Muslims for a Muslim woman to convert to the religion of the man she wishes to marry; she will simply be considered an apostate, and liable to the death penalty under the Sharia (as an apostate, not because of the marriage). This penalty is only enforceable today in countries such as Iran and Saudi Arabia, and is very rare even there. A man or woman who converts from Islam to another religion, though, will usually be rejected by his or her own family, and certainly by Muslim society as a whole.

One result of this rule of the Sharia is that female Muslims in the West often face major problems in finding a spouse. Muslim men can, and do, marry Western women who are nominally Christian; marriages between Muslim women and Western men who convert to Islam are less frequent. There are thus fewer unmarried Muslim men to marry Muslim women than there are unmarried Muslim women to marry Muslim men. Some Muslim families attempt to solve this problem by sending a daughter back to their country of origin to find a husband.

A problem facing any Muslim considering marriage with a Westerner is that contemporary Western custom normally requires a closer relationship before marriage than many Muslims regard as permissible. Many Westerners would not dream of marrying someone they had not previously had sex with. Another problem, which really needs a book to itself, is that of cultural differences—not only between Muslim and non-Muslim, but even between a Muslim woman raised in the West and a Muslim man raised in the Muslim world. Religion is only one element in cultural differences. Sadly, cultural differences often cause marriages to fail. Marriages between a Muslim woman and a non-Muslim man who has sincerely converted to Islam and become a devout Muslim, however, seem to do better than most "mixed" marriages.

Islam sees marriage as a contract, to which there are two parts. The first part relates to getting married. To get married, the groom must give the bride a sum of money which has been agreed upon in advance—the opposite of the old Western practice of a dowry being given to the groom. Sometimes this sum is paid in full, but more usually only part of the full sum is paid immediately. The remainder (often half) is due to the wife on the death of her husband or on divorce. Local custom varies. In the West and in some Muslim countries, a nominal sum such as $5 may suffice. In other countries, substantial sums of money may be involved. In the Muslim world, sometimes gold jewelry replaces money or forms an important part of the payment, as can furniture and other household goods. Sometimes the bride is expected to contribute something as well in the form of furniture or household goods, though there is no requirement for this in the Sharia. Occasionally, some or all of the sum goes to the bride's family, though the Sharia does not allow this. Negotiations over these matters may be prolonged, and almost always involve the families of the two future parties. The Sharia requires that the woman be represented by her closest male relative, who is deemed more likely to protect her interests effectively. Although marriage is between two individuals, the arrangements are generally made between two families, which will also remain more involved after the wedding than is normal in the West.

Once negotiations have been concluded, payment and moving in together may either happen immediately or follow after an interval. This is a also question of local custom. In many Muslim societies, the interval between negotiation and moving in is a kind of cooling-off period: the two parties can get to know each other better and in a different context, and if they do not get on well, they can stop proceedings altogether. A marriage is only complete when the payment has been made and when the couple has moved in together (or, technically, had sex for the first time). This may not happen for months, or sometimes even for years.

Getting married, then, is a two-stage affair, neither stage of which involves any religious ritual or takes place in a mosque (save sometimes in the West, when the mosque has a second role as a community center, and where the example of the Christian church marriage encourages Muslims to use mosques for similar purposes). What the Sharia requires is not ritual, but celebration. Sometimes separate parties are held for each of the two stages, and sometimes the two stages are combined and celebrated with one party. If only one stage is to be celebrated, it is normally the final stage, of moving in. The logic behind the requirement for a celebration is that a marriage must be public, and a party makes public the private arrangement reached by two individuals.

The second part of the contract of marriage as seen by Islam relates to the state of being married. The husband is obliged to support his wife financially so that she can live in appropriate comfort, what is "appropriate" being a function of her standard of living before marriage. In return, the wife is obliged to obey her husband, and also to have sex with him unless she has a valid excuse (such as a headache—though according to the Sharia no headache may last longer than three days). She may be beaten (though not badly beaten up) in the event of disobedience (a point I will discuss further in chapter 8).

The wife, then, is entitled to a share in her husband's income, but he is not entitled to any share in hers. In practice, however, wives often work and contribute to the household budget, for reasons of economics. In peasant households everywhere, everyone except very small children shares in agricultural work, and housework is not rigidly separate from agricultural work. In poor families in large Muslim cities, a single income is often not enough. Sometimes, especially in large cities with high unemployment rates, reality is the diametric opposite of the Islamic contract: unemployed husbands are maintained by working wives, since women can often find work (for example as domestic servants) more easily than men. Wives sometimes also run small businesses, often from their homes. All this gives them real economic power, since the income generated is their income, even if (like their husbands' income, if any) it goes mostly on daily household expenses. Even when wives work and couples operate a single household budget, wives usually keep some separate savings of their own, often in the form of gold jewelry.

Although a wife is not explicitly obliged under the Sharia to serve her husband by—for example—cooking for him, in practice she is always expected to "look after" her husband as well as her house and children, whether or not she is also working outside the house. Only the very rarest of extremely Westernized Muslim husbands would think for a second of doing any housework, even though the Sharia is silent on this topic. Since Muslim men in the Muslim world almost invariably live with their parents until marriage and boys are not usually given household tasks, few Muslim men have even the most basic idea about what to do in a kitchen or how to approach a pile of dirty washing.

In wealthier families, there is often a choice as to whether a wife works or not, since the husband's income alone is adequate to support the family. In such cases, it is generally agreed that the wife's duties as a mother take precedence over all else. Since wealthy families in the Muslim world generally employ maids and nannies, however, even small children need not be an obstacle to combining work with domestic duties. When the household's views on segregation do not present an obstacle, wives often work for the sake of intellectual and social stimulation, though this varies from country to country, and is nowhere as frequent as in the West. There are, however, reasonable numbers of female Muslim bankers, journalists, doctors, professors and fashion designers, as well as female Muslim maids and peasants.

The part of the marriage contract that requires the wife to obey her husband is generally kept, at least formally: the husband instructs, while the wife persuades. A Muslim wife is unlikely to openly defy her husband, but may well persuade him to change his mind. A Muslim husband may try to openly defy his wife, but will not always succeed. As in non-Muslim societies, it ultimately depends on the characters involved—whether the wife does what her husband wants, whether the husband does what his wife wants, or whether both come to amicable agreement.

What has been said so far may suggest a limited and rather physical conception of marriage. That is the bottom line of Islam's approach, but there are other understandings too. Marriage, it is often said, is "half of religion"—by which is meant that it is a very important part of religion. This view has little to do with sex; though one great medieval Islamic scholar, Ibn Hazm al-Andalusi, argued that human love is the closest one can come to heaven, since when two humans love each other they weaken the barriers that creation and the flesh place between their individual souls. These are the same barriers that creation and the flesh place between humans and God. Human love, then, is a foretaste of heaven. The observation that marriage is "half of religion," however, has more to do with the way in which marriage is an antidote to selfishness, producing for both men and women an absolute requirement to compromise with, and care for, another person.

Children

The expected consequence of marriage is children, and children form the core of Muslim family life. Among Muslims, it if often said that a marriage without children is like a garden without flowers, and that heaven lies at the feet of mothers—a slightly different point.

Islam does not oblige people to have large families, however. Contraception is permitted by the Sharia, so long as both parties agree, and is accepted by nearly all Muslim societies. Abortion is also regarded by many as permitted, again with the consent of both parties, so long as the fetus has not reached the age at which it is deemed to have acquired a soul (four months). In practice, Muslim women sometimes use contraception without the knowledge of their husbands.

Family size in Muslim societies varies much as it does everywhere. Peasants tend to have large families, partly because their children represent a labor resource more than a financial burden, and partly because of the expectation of children dying in infancy. Despite improvements in healthcare and education, infant mortality in poor rural areas of the Muslim world remains relatively high. At the other end of the scale, urban professionals who will pay large sums for their children's education, and who also tend to marry later anyway, have smaller families.

When a child is born, it is deemed to be Muslim, since its soul has come directly from God and (as we have seen) it still remembers God. Children born to Muslims are automatically Muslim; children born to followers of other religions will be brought up into these other religions by their parents, who thus unintentionally lead them astray. It makes no difference if the child's mother is a Christian or a Jew; to bring the child up as a Christian or a Jew would be to convert it to another religion. The child's father, of course, can only be Muslim, since a Muslim woman cannot marry a non-Muslim man. No rite of entry into Islam therefore exists,[1] though it is *sunna* to welcome a child into the world by repeating the Call to Prayer into each ear as soon as possible after birth.

Male children are often preferred to females, and the Sharia assumes that this will be the case. In poor societies, from Arabia at the time of the Prophet to rural parts of most Muslim countries today, males are likely to contribute more to the family budget than females. Males are also seen as less trouble when it comes to marriage, and cannot get pregnant in irregular circumstances. It is a maxim of Islam that heaven is the reward of parents who bring up three daughters properly—which implies some sort

---

[1] An adult who has been brought up in another religion can convert to Islam (or, technically, return to Islam) very easily, simply by recognizing and accepting two truths that he or she once knew anyhow: that there is no god (*ilah*) save God (Allah), and that Muhammad is the (final) Prophet of God. An adult has to announce this recognition in front of witnesses, but no such public announcement is required of someone who has never followed any other religion.

of compensation for a shortage of sons. In the end, however, female children are generally loved by their parents as much as male children, if not more so.

A newborn child needs a name. Local customs vary, but in general the child is named by its parents, sometimes reusing the name of a grandparent or a name from a grandparent's family. The involvement of relatives in family life is such that disputes between those who want a name from the mother's family and those who want a name from the father's family sometimes leave the newborn child un-named for several days. Normally, only one name is given; in exceptional cases, a child gets two names.

Male names tend to be more traditional, as in many cultures; parents are more adventurous with female names. Females may be called almost anything, so long as the name is not specifically identified in the society in question as belonging to another religion. The wife of President Hosni Mubarak of Egypt is Suzanne, for example. Males tend to be called after one of the prophets (including Jesus); a first-born male child is often called Muhammad. Sometimes, strange names are given to ward off envy; a male child may sometimes be named after the day of the week he was born on, or even given a female name. This is then normally replaced with a more usual name if the boy survives infancy. Many males are named with one of the 99 names of God, prefaced with *Abdul*, "slave of." Abdul Rahman is thus the slave of the Merciful, and Abd Allah is the slave of God. The two parts of the name cannot be separated, any more than the O of O'Connor can be separated. Westerners, however, frequently separate them. The Pakistani wife of a physician called Abd Allah was unsure how to react when repeatedly addressed by an American hospital director as "Mrs. Allah" (Mrs. God).

In non-Arab parts of the Muslim world, local pre-Islamic or non-Islamic names are sometimes given to boys, often in addition to an Islamic name. The Islamic name is then used in public, and the local name is used at home and by close friends. Non-Islamic names for boys were once occasionally given to boys in the Arab world also, though it is unusual today. The disappearance of non-Islamic boy names is mainly a function of the general increase in religiosity, but also has other advantages. In later life, the senior Egyptian general Hitler Tantawi presumably found his father's 1940s-era anti-British political enthusiasm[2] embarrassing; the Egyptian playwright Lenin Ramli was probably a bit less embarrassed by his first name.

The naming of children is often an issue for Muslim parents in the West, and for non-Muslims and nominal converts married to Muslims. Many possible Islamic names are excluded because Westerners will not be able to pronounce them properly. Familiar Western names are also generally excluded, because they represent almost an abnegation of Islam. There is no reason in the Sharia why a Muslim boy should not be called William, but his grandparents would tend to think that this would imply that he was not going to be brought up as a Muslim. The non-Muslim or nominally Muslim spouse of even a non-observant Muslim will often be surprised by their partner's insistence on a Muslim name.

Once a baby has lived for seven days, it is *sunna* to perform a ceremony of thanksgiving (in earlier centuries, many babies did not survive for long, as is still the case in the poorest parts of the Muslim world today). The thanksgiving ceremony has many local variations, but normally includes the sacrifice of a sheep or goat, most of the meat of which is then distributed to the poor. Sometimes the baby's head is also shaved, and the weight of the baby's hair in gold is then distributed to the poor. These two elements come from Islam. Local custom often adds other touches, involving candles, coins, or candy.

The Sharia has little to say about the early upbringing of a small child, except that it should be looked after properly. Much has been written about Muslim childcare and its implications, but childcare practices in fact vary considerably from society to society, and have almost nothing to do with Islam.

Muslim children are generally circumcised around the age of four or five, with differences according to sex. A boy will have his foreskin removed, an event that is celebrated by a party at which he is the star guest. The details of the party vary from region to region and class to class. Male circumcision is an uncontroversial practice, followed also by Jews and many

---

[2]During the Second World War, most Egyptians knew almost nothing of Hitler beyond the fact that his armies were trying to end the British occupation of Egypt. Had he succeeded, his plans for Egypt would have speedily made him a lot more unpopular than the British, of course.

Christians. The circumcision of girls, in contrast, is much more controversial, especially for Westerners. There is disagreement among Muslims both over what exactly should be done, and over whether female circumcision is required, *sunna*, customary, unnecessary, or deplorable. Practice also varies from country to country. In general, the severest forms of female circumcision are found in Africa (where similar procedures are practiced by non-Muslims as well). The clitoris and labia are commonly removed, and the vagina is then sewed almost shut. Less severe forms of female circumcision, involving the total or partial removal of the clitoris, are found in parts of the Arab world, though rarely among the elites. Circumcised mothers tend to have their daughters circumcised as a matter of course, arguing (if asked) either that it is necessary or *sunna*, or that it is essential to make daughters manageable and obedient (an argument that the Sharia does not make). Female circumcision was until recently unknown in countries outside the African continent, but some reports suggest that the practice may be becoming more common. At the same time, however, the Ulema in most countries are increasingly arguing against female circumcision. It is not yet clear how much impact this is having.

Once children reach about seven, they are considered to have reached the age of reason, and their religious education should begin (though in practice it may well have started earlier). Children this age were once sent out to work—this is still the case in the poorest areas of the Muslim world, but seven-year-olds elsewhere are now generally found in school. Eldest daughters of poor families are least likely to be sent to school, since their mothers often require their help at home. Some poor families are reluctant to educate any daughters, either because they think it is not necessary, or because they think it is easier to find husbands for uneducated women, since men may be reluctant to marry women who are more educated than they are.

Some Muslims argue that a child should start to pray at seven, while others argue that prayer does not become obligatory until puberty. Prepubescent children are not generally taken to pray in mosques, though there is no reason why they should not be, and sometimes they are taken on a visit. All agree that a child aged over seven should be taught the basic elements of Islam, including proper manners. The child also normally learns several sections of the Koran by heart.

Muslim children learn about Islam from their parents, just as most children generally start to learn about life from their parents. When parents pray, small children are generally delighted to find their parents at floor level, and often join them. More formal education takes place at school (*madrasa* in Arabic). The quality and approach of schools varies widely across the Muslim world. In many countries, schools are run by the state and the school system differs little from that found in the West, except that "religion" classes concentrate on Islam, and that the quality of education is often a lot worse than in the West, because the schools are badly run and short of resources, and the classes are vast. Sometimes teachers are so badly paid that they have to take second jobs as taxi drivers or café waiters to make ends meet. In the richer and better governed countries of the Muslim world, public schools may be of much higher quality. In other countries, there are still private religious schools, where the quality of education is usually higher than in the worst public schools. Some are traditional schools where the syllabus is entirely religious, while others teach a full modern syllabus, but with greater than usual emphasis on religious subjects and proper behavior.

In all types of school, the basis of religious education always has been, and remains today, the memorization of the Koran—as much of it as possible, and sometimes the whole of it. Starting with the memorization of the Koran is partly for practical reasons: everyone who prays needs to know some sections of the Koran by heart to include in the *sala* prayer. It is also because memorization is often the standard technique for teaching anything, including biology and civics. How else does an underpaid and undereducated teacher with three textbooks cope with a class of eighty children? From an educational point of view, memorization is not in itself a problem. What matters is what is then done with the material that has been memorized. In the best schools, whether the occasional well-funded and well-staffed public school or a private religious school with motivated and dedicated teachers, understanding is then achieved through illustration and discussion. In the worst schools, memorization becomes an end in itself, and that is all there is to education. Children then learn to reproduce texts, whether the Koran or a biology textbook, that they do not understand. It is quite possible that their teacher does not understand them either. This has nothing to do with Islam; it is a function of poverty and bad administration. Such children may come to understand something of the sections of the Koran they have learned later in life; the same is unlikely to be true of the sections of the biology textbook, which they will quickly forget.

Where classes do move beyond memorization to interpretation, the interpretation depends on the school's administration. A school run by Wahhabis will teach Wahhabi views on everything from the Koran to biology, while a school run by sophisticated and cosmopolitan Muslims will encourage children to reach more sophisticated and cosmopolitan conclusions.

Muslim children are generally expected to treat their parents with respect, which in the most traditional societies may extend to remaining standing while in the presence of their father. Discipline in traditional societies is in general old-fashioned, and often involves beating (I will discuss violence further in chapter 8). Complete strangers may deliver verbal admonitions to children, an aspect of Islam's views on the general duty of virtue promotion and vice prevention, and of the nature of Muslim communities.

For the Sharia, childhood ends at puberty, defined as a woman's first period or a man's first nocturnal emission. Islam then considers the former child an adult, with all the legal powers and religious duties of any other adult. For women, this occasion is marked in Iran by a party at which the woman is formally given objects such as a Koran, a prayer mat, and a scarf. In practice, most Muslim states today ignore the Sharia and use either 18 or 21 as the age of majority, at which a person become legally competent. In any case, adulthood does not end the duty of respect and obedience to one's parents. Adolescent rebellion is generally not tolerated in Muslim societies, and does not usually occur. It is certainly not regarded as a normal stage of development. Neither is it normal in any Muslim society for unmarried children to leave their family home and live on their own before marriage. In the West and some other countries where Muslims are a minority, however, adolescence follows the local pattern.

Children of whatever age are expected to defer to their parents' judgment and wishes until marriage, and families continue to be involved after marriage. This of course assumes that children remain living close to their parents, which tends to be the case in poorer and more traditional communities. When children travel far away, such links are inevitably weakened.

Islam places great emphasis on the proper treatment of orphans, who are regarded as the most deserving recipients of all forms of charity. To bring up an orphan in one's own household is an excellent thing to do, and will be rewarded at the day of judgment. Orphanages in the Muslim world are among the best funded charities. This has one negative consequence, according to many child development experts: money might sometimes be better spent on helping a child's relatives to look after that child themselves, but instead goes to institutions that, however well run, are less in children's interests. Orphans are generally taken good care of, whether in orphanages or in other families, but there are "street children" in some large Muslim cities—sometimes, the sheer magnitude of the problem overwhelms the resources of private charity, and the state administration is also unable to cope. This problem, however, is nowhere anything like as serious as it is in some large, poor cities outside the Muslim world

Adoption as often practiced in the West, in contrast, is forbidden by Islam, which regards it as a form of deceit. To bring up a needy child is noble; to pretend that a child is your own if it is not, in contrast, is dishonest.

Polygamy and Divorce

Islam allows for two disturbances of the standard family: divorce and polygamy. Muslims today generally agree on their views of divorce, but not of polygamy. Divorce is regarded by Islam as a misfortune, to be avoided if at all possible. It is said that of all the things God has allowed, divorce is what He most hates. It is still necessary at times, however. Polygamy, in contrast, is regarded as normal in more traditional societies, but rejected as an aspect of Islam that belongs to the past (much as slavery does) by some less traditional societies and individuals.

Divorce in Islam is simpler than marriage. If both spouses have agreed to it before they married, either spouse can simply declare the other divorced, and it's done. Such an arrangement is, however, unusual, for cultural rather than religious reasons. It is more likely that the husband declares his wife divorced, which he may do by mutual consent, or against his wife's will. The husband's right to unilateral instant divorce under the Sharia, however, is now restricted in practice by the national laws of many Muslim countries, which often require divorce cases to be brought to court. Social pressure also acts as a restraint on a husband who is thinking of divorcing his wife against her will, as does the need to pay her the remainder of the sum agreed upon when they married (as a form of alimony). A wife, however, has difficulty in divorcing her husband against his will. She has to show good reason and get an outside authority to intervene. Typically, a wife has to prove insanity, neglect, abandonment, or very severe abuse. The Sharia does not consider adultery as a ground for divorce, since an adulterer is (at least in theory) liable to execution. Divorce, at that point, is not a concern. All in all, the Sharia clearly favors the husband in the decision to divorce or not, since he is deemed to be the more rational of the two parties, though the laws of many Muslim countries redress this balance to some extent. In practice, wives in failed marriages are more likely to face difficulties in trying to divorce their husbands than they are likely to find themselves abandoned after being unilaterally divorced by their husbands, though this does sometimes happen.

A man who divorces his wife without her consent is obliged to give her the remainder of the total sum agreed upon when they married, but the Sharia makes no other provision for maintenance payments in the event of divorce. There is no division of joint money or possessions, since money and possessions are considered to belong either to the husband or the wife — not to both—depending on their original source. A man may even recover the sum he paid to his wife on marriage as a condition of divorcing her, but only with her consent. Once again, these basic rules are often modified in some way by the laws of many Muslim states, which may for example require the payment of child support, or even alimony.

The Sharia provides that in the event of divorce, children generally remain with their mother. A child who has reached the age of seven, however, can choose to remain with its father, or to return to the father if it has previously been with its mother. Some interpretations specify different ages for boys and girls. A mother who is a notorious reprobate may lose custody of her children to her own mother or grandmother if they are righteous people, or to her ex-husband's mother (or her ex-husband) if she (or he) is a righteous person and her mother and grandmother are not, or are dead. If all parents and grandparents are notorious reprobates, custody passes to righteous sisters and brothers and cousins. "Reprobate" is defined in terms of religious practice, but a mother with a major character flaw (for example, a drunkard) would generally be considered a reprobate.

The Sharia allows remarriage after divorce—immediately for men, and after a woman is sure she is not pregnant (defined as after having had three periods). If she is pregnant at the time of her divorce, she can only remarry after she has given birth. A mother who remarries, however, loses custody of her children from an earlier marriage, to her own mother if alive and righteous and to her ex-husband otherwise. Once again, these Sharia rules are often modified by the laws of contemporary Muslim states.

An alternative to divorce and remarriage for men, though not for women, is polygamy. This option is not available for women; one reason is that until the arrival of DNA testing it was not possible to establish the paternity of a child born to a woman with several husbands, and polyandry (the female equivalent of polygamy) is found in very few human societies. Men are allowed by the Sharia to marry up to four wives. This right has been removed by legislation in some Muslim countries, and cannot be exercised in the West for the same reason. It is also sometimes removed by a stipulation in a first marriage contract that grants the first wife the right of divorce in the event of her husband marrying a second wife, though it is sometimes argued that such a stipulation is invalid, since it contradicts the intention of the Sharia. A husband's right to several wives is also removed, in the view of some Muslims, by a modern interpretation of the Sharia, which relies on the Sharia's requirement that all wives be treated equally. Since it is impossible in practice to treat all wives absolutely equally, it is argued, polygamy is actually forbidden. This interpretation is accepted by some modern Muslims, but is rejected by most traditional Muslims.

In practice, polygamy is now found only in those Muslim countries that have not banned it, and even then only occasionally. In traditional societies, polygamy is regarded as entirely acceptable, but is found rarely for the simple reason that it is expensive—each new wife needs a new marriage payment, and the cost of maintaining two families is twice the cost of maintaining one. Polygamy is only an option for the rich, and few Muslims in traditional societies are rich, though Saudi Arabia is both rich and (in this respect) traditional. In less traditional societies in other countries where polygamy is not prohibited by law, it is encountered rarely, both for financial reasons and because society is often somewhat reluctant to accept it. Polygamy is as illegal in Tunisia as it is in America, but it remains legal in Egypt. One well-known Egyptian industrialist has two wives, one of whom is his own age, and one of whom is rather younger—and who was previously his secretary. While a Tunisian industrialist who fell in love with his secretary might have divorced his existing wife before remarrying, the Egyptian industrialist has another option.

When polygamy does occur, there is a range of possible outcomes. At one extreme, all the wives and children concerned live in a state of permanent rivalry and unhappiness. The Sharia requires a husband to provide separate and equal facilities for all wives and to treat them all equally and fairly, but in practice more than one wife often has to share the same house, and the most recent wife is either treated better than the other(s) by her loving husband, or used as a variety of servant by the senior wife or wives. At another extreme, an older wife may be a lot happier about her older husband's relationship with a younger woman than she would have been if he had divorced her to marry again, and the younger woman may be a lot happier to have the legal protection and social recognition conferred by marriage than she would have been if she had merely been someone's secret lover.

Polygamy is a living feature of many Muslim societies, but of relatively few Muslim families. Some Muslims regard it with abhorrence, as something that has no more place in the modern world than slavery; some regard it as perfectly normal; some are not quite sure what they think about it.

Death and Inheritance

When Muslims die, they are buried within a short period, usually 24 hours. The funeral is not the focus of mourning, and is generally purely functional. The corpse is washed, wrapped in cloth, and taken on a bier into a mosque for the funeral prayer, performed after one of the regular *sala* prayers. The funeral prayer takes only a few minutes, and many of those present are unconnected worshipers who know no more of the person for whom they are praying than that person's gender—which they are told before the funeral prayer starts because they need to know whether to pray for God's mercy on "her" or on "him." After the funeral prayer, the corpse is buried, without a coffin, on its right side and facing toward Mecca, the direction of the *sala* prayer. Cremation is not acceptable. In some countries, the dead are buried in crypts, and in others in cemeteries. In the latter case, a tombstone is generally erected somewhat later, or in Iran placed horizontally over the grave. What is inscribed on the tombstone varies from place to place. Sometimes there is nothing other than an appropriate quotation from the Koran, or perhaps a few lines of poetry, and the date of death. In this case, tombs can only be identified by those who know their exact location. In some parts of the Muslim world, the name of the deceased is also recorded on the tombstone, and in Iran there also may be an etching of the deceased's likeness. Tombstones even without names, let alone with etchings, are discouraged by Wahhabis.

The focus of mourning is not the funeral, but the paying of visits of condolence to the family of the deceased by more distant relatives, friends, and acquaintances. Such visits are generally paid within two days of death to the family's home, though men sometimes give their condolences at a local mosque instead. Visitors first speak a few words of condolence to the relatives of the deceased, using a single short phrase such as "We come from God, and to Him we return," a Koranic quotation. The visitors then usually stay for a period anywhere between twenty minutes and two hours, listening to the Koran, occasionally talking a little, and remembering the deceased. If they have traveled from far away, they may stay for several days as the guests of the deceased's family. This kind of visit happens in villages, but not as much in cities. Crying is discouraged, and dramatic acts of grief such as tearing one's clothing are forbidden, though in some societies they are still the norm.

Once the burial and condolences are complete, life should return to normal as soon as possible. Excessive periods of mourning are forbidden — in general, three days is thought to be enough, though a widow may mourn her husband for four months. The deceased is not forgotten, however, and his or her grave is visited regularly, often on the anniversary of death.

Inheritance is governed strictly by the Sharia. The general principle is that no more than one third of the deceased's estate may be disposed of freely by Will, though this one third can be increased with the agreement of all the other heirs, which does sometimes happen. The remainder is allotted to the deceased's relatives in fixed shares, irrespective of the deceased's wishes. Blood relatives are favored over relatives by marriage; when there are children, a widow receives only one-eighth of her deceased husband's estate; widowers, in contrast, receive one-fourth.

Once widows or widowers have received their share, the children then share the remainder, with sons taking twice as much as daughters, but only after giving specified (usually small) shares to other more distant relatives, such as their grandparents, uncles, aunts, and first cousins. This rule of inheritance is one reason why marriage to first cousins is often found in the Muslim world, as mentioned earlier. The precise rules of inheritance are extremely complex, and can normally be applied only by someone who has made a special study of them.

The Islamic rules of inheritance clearly discriminate against women. This is generally justified on the grounds that women are not obliged to maintain men, but men are obliged to maintain women. A husband who inherits a $20,000 share in a $100,000 estate has to share the income from his $20,000 with his wife and children, and possibly also with his unmarried sisters; a wife who inherits a smaller $10,000 share in a similar $100,000 estate does not have to share the income from her $10,000 with anyone.

The two main effects of these rules are to leave widows with less than they would normally receive in the West (unless their husbands provide more out of the one-third that they can dispose of freely), and to break up accumulations of wealth, which is spread around more widely than would probably be the case otherwise. One indirect consequence of this is that few Islamic societies have ever developed anything resembling a hereditary aristocracy, since large fortunes can rarely be kept together for more than a generation or two. Another indirect effect is the fragmentation of peasant land-holdings, with a small field sometimes being broken up into tiny plots that are of little use to anyone. This was less of a problem in the past, when village land was often held communally and so was not subject to inheritance rules, but has become more of a problem as Western-inspired systems of individual landownership have replaced communal systems.

Unless all the heirs agree to allow more than one-third of an estate to be disposed of freely, the rules on inheritance can only be circumvented by means of gifts made before death (but not on one's deathbed). Whether or not this is done varies from family to family, and also according to family circumstances. The educated father of a sensible unmarried daughter and an unreliable spendthrift son is unlikely to rely on his son to look after his daughter after his death. The rules can also be circumvented by someone who is rich and less devout: they can move property to a Western country with laws which do not specify shares due to various relatives, and make a Will under the laws of that country. The laws of many European countries do specify such shares, however, though they spread inheritance less widely and more equally than the Sharia does.

Feminism

Two varieties of feminism are found in the Muslim world, one very similar to Western feminism, and one more Islamic. Western-style feminism generally has limited impact, with its exponents sometimes being better known in the West than in their own countries. Western-style feminists are seen by most other Muslims as irreligious representatives of an alien culture. In reality, few such feminists are devout Muslims, which immediately undermines their arguments. These arguments are generally grounded in conceptions borrowed from contemporary Western discourse, conceptions which are incomprehensible to most Muslims. Western-style feminists are normally non-observant members of Westernized elites, and are listened to only by other non-observant members of Westernized elites.

Islamic feminists, in contrast, ground their arguments in Islam and the Sharia rather than in abstract conceptions derived from the West. They do not dispute that men and women are intrinsically different, but call for women to be granted in practice the rights that they are given by Islam in theory. They call for fairer treatment of women, and for better protection. They argue for speedier divorce proceedings, for childcare facilities, and other such practical improvements in women's lives. They are generally devout modern Muslims, and although their impact has so far been limited, it has been greater than the impact of Western-style feminists. Their arguments are much more comprehensible to the average Muslim, and their basis in Islam makes it harder to contradict or ignore what they say. In Singapore, Islamic feminists from the Muslim minority have already succeeded in making various useful amendments to the Administration of Muslim Law Act, but Singapore is unusual.

Many Westerners conceive of Muslim women as being uniformly ignored and miserable. There are, of course, ignored and miserable women in the Muslim world, especially in the large cities, where the expectations of younger women most often clash with those of their husbands. Older women, in contrast, are often more socially and religiously conservative than their husbands. Restrictions that a young woman's grandmother in the village accepted as entirely normal are less easy for her granddaughter to accept, aware—as she is—that some others live differently. An educated woman will also often resent the dismissive way in which most Muslim men will treat her views on topics other than cooking, washing and babies (though she may nonetheless find ways to make her views count).

The lives of many Muslim women are undoubtedly hard as a result of the economic and political circumstances of the countries in which they live, and as a result of their own lack of education. These circumstances make the lives of men hard, too. Perhaps the lives of poor urban Muslim women are sometimes harder, though, because hard-working women in the poorer classes are frequently exposed to the demands of unemployed and often feckless sons and brothers, and on occasion even husbands or fathers, who need money for cigarettes and entertainment. These are demands which the women in question find hard to refuse, but which they cannot afford, and which they resent as unjust.

On the whole, however, it is wrong to see Muslim women as miserable. From the perspective of Western understandings of life it is hard to explain why, but most Muslim women are not remotely miserable. Perhaps they take comfort in the fact that, at least when their brothers and sons are not unemployed and feckless, a Muslim woman can rely on them in a way that actually places her in a position of real power. Perhaps they appreciate the way older women are generally respected by younger relations of both genders, and by the outside world. Perhaps they are simply proficient at creating for themselves the sort of social space they want to occupy.

Summary

Islamic conceptions of the two sexes are very different from contemporary Western ones. Men and women are understood by both the Sharia and most Muslim societies primarily in terms of their reproductive roles, an understanding that makes more sense in poor villages than it does in today's large cities. Women are seen as inferior to men and in need of male guidance and protection. Both men and women are expected to avoid circumstances where sexual desire might be unduly and illegitimately aroused, though in practice the rules of segregation affect women more than men. Unmarried men, however, are as short of female company as unmarried women are short of male company.

Marriages are often arranged, though one or both parties may be given a say in the matter, and sometimes even a veto. Love matches also exist, especially among the elites. Marriage contracts are carefully negotiated, and marriage itself is seen by the Sharia as a contractual arrangement, though in practice most marriages develop as emotional relationships.

Divorce is easy for a man and difficult for a woman, who always risks losing custody of her children. Polygamy is rare, but still exists. The Sharia rules of inheritance are generally observed, and again favor men over women, on the basis that the financial responsibilities of men are greater than those of women.

Some Muslim feminists regard the position of women in Islam much as most Westerners do, though they cannot always admit this in front of Westerners. Such feminists have no significant following outside Westernized elites. Feminists who call for women to receive such rights as they are given by Islam gain more of a hearing, but even so have had little impact on social and legal practice in the Muslim world. Although Westerners might expect Muslim women to be uniformly miserable, this is plainly not the case.

7

Food, Frocks, and Funds

Daily Life

Unveiling Islam, a best-selling book for Evangelical Christians hoping to convert American Muslims, starts off by suggesting social visits. This is a smart move, as a lot of the scientific literature on conversions stresses that social contacts play a much greater part than many would expect. But the well-intentioned Evangelicals face a hard task. On visiting a Muslim household, they must be prepared to remove their shoes. They must be very careful not to shake hands using the left hand. They should eat whatever is put in front of them, whether or not they have any idea what it is. When Muslims visit them, on the other hand, they should explain carefully with each course that its preparation has not involved lard or shellfish. Women should not speak emphatically to men. And that's just the beginning.

I myself have never tried shaking hands with anyone using my left hand. I expect it would cause confusion, even in Evangelical circles. And I suspect that if my dinner host explained carefully the preparation of each dish I was served, I would begin to suspect that someone was trying to poison me. On the other hand, while most Muslims eat shellfish perfectly happily, some do not. Islam does have an impact on most aspects of Muslims' daily lives—it does not stop with worship. It also lays down rules far more comprehensive and complicated than those found in Christianity, though less complicated than those found in orthodox Judaism.

The daily life of Muslims is not just about Islam; it is also about individuals and families, about local customs and cultures, and about economics and politics. We did not need to pay much attention to these factors while considering the Islamic world view or Muslim worship, even though they play some part in world view and can also even play a part in worship. Local customs and cultures are more important in Muslim daily life, however, and vary considerably from place to place. Over the centuries, peoples from very different cultural and historical backgrounds have become Muslim. If we consider even a selection of the major cultures concerned, it is immediately obvious that the pre-Islamic Arabs, the pre-Islamic Persians, the pre-Islamic Indonesians, and the pre-Islamic Africans had absolutely nothing in common with each other. They do have a lot in common now—Islam—but many differences still remain between these cultures.

Islam and local culture have a complicated relationship. Islam modifies local culture, and local culture modifies the local understanding of Islam. In the end, it is sometimes impossible to say where the culture stops and religion starts. It is easy to say what is religion and what is culture when it comes to ways of performing the *sala* prayer—nearly all is religion. When it comes to family and gender, it is also easy to see what is religion and what is culture. If something is not mentioned in the Sharia, or even contradicts the Sharia, then it must be culture (or perhaps economics). When it comes to aspects of daily life like ways of treating guests, however, culture and religion merge.

This chapter concentrates on what different parts of the Muslim world have in common, which is largely of religious origin, rather than on local cultures, in which many differences divide one part of the Muslim world from another. The chapter thus covers those aspects of daily life where religion is most significant, and ignores those where religion is less important and where local customs and cultures matter more.

General Principles

Ritual purity is the topic that classic Muslim scholars' manuals usually start with, and this chapter follows their example. Ritual purity is a concept that is more familiar to Jews than to Christians, but on a day to day level, purity and impurity are familiar to all of us. The idea of water from a mountain spring is more attractive than that of water from a city reservoir. Purity and impurity have little religious significance for Christians, though spring water might be preferred to water from a puddle for conducting a baptism, and most Christians would prefer to change a diaper at home rather than in a church. In Islam, however, as in Judaism, the concept of purity is fully articulated in religious terms. The pure is associated with the good, and the impure with the bad.

Spring water is not only by definition pure but is also "purifying," and may be used in an act of worship. Water from a puddle is not purifying, and may not be used in an act of worship, but is not actually impure. The contents of a diaper are by definition impure, and their presence would invalidate an act of worship. Tears are pure; blood is not. Meat from a properly slaughtered sheep is pure and may be eaten; meat from an animal that died of disease is not pure and may not be eaten, and the pig is defined as impure, as is the dog (though some disagree about dogs). Money earned from honest labor is pure; money earned from the sale of illegal narcotics, alcohol, or stolen goods is not. The former may be used to pay for a Hajj pilgrimage, but if the latter is used for this purpose, the pilgrimage is invalidated. Of course, in the West, money laundering attempts to turn dirty money into clean money. Though not often articulated in modern Western life, the basic idea of purity and impurity is still there.

Most things encountered in daily life are neither purifying nor actively impure. A tomato is a tomato, and a telephone is a telephone. Even these things, however, may become impure through contact with something that is impure, though purity may be restored by washing off the impure contaminant with something purifying. Exactly the same is true of human beings—blood may be washed off the skin. Judaism specifies particular rites for removing impurity in this way, but Islam does not. There are some guidelines (for example, naturally running water can always be considered purifying), but basically it is a question of whether or not something is clean in the normal, everyday sense. The only ritual required to establish purity is that which we looked at in chapter 5, when looking at preparations for performing the *sala*. A Muslim butcher about to pray first removes physical impurity in a practical fashion by taking off his blood-stained apron, and then removes ritual impurity through ritual ablutions.

Substances defined by Islam as impure are always avoided. In many Muslim countries, shoes (which are unlikely to be clean) are left at the door, as are dogs. Even in countries where treatment of shoes and dogs is closer to the Western norm, more traditional and more devout Muslims will still keep them outside. Muslims generally wash their bodies and their clothes more frequently than might be expected given their general economic standard. Poor Muslims whose houses do not even have running water are generally remarkably well washed. On the other hand, what a Westerner might see as dirtiness is not always so defined by Islam, and so may be worried about less. A Westerner who bathes only once or twice a week may be shocked by the amount of trash in the streets of a Muslim city; few Muslims are unduly worried about torn cardboard boxes and empty plastic wrappers in the street, but all Muslims would regard the well-dressed but un-bathed Westerner as dirty.

One of the areas of daily life in which Islamic conceptions of purity create the most misunderstanding among Westerners is the use of the bathroom. For a Muslim, it is essential to remove any peripheral residue of urine or feces from the body using water. This is the requirement of the Sharia, but it translates into general conceptions of hygiene as well. Wiping with paper is simply not good enough, just as wiping dirty dishes with paper would not strike a Westerner as an acceptable alternative to using detergent and hot water. Muslims who know Western bathroom habits regard them fundamentally as rather disgusting. Most Westerners who think they know Muslim bathroom habits also think them disgusting. The misunderstanding is over how the water is applied. In the days before piped water, Muslims generally poured water from a jug into one hand, and then projected the water toward the area of the body that needed to be washed. The Western understanding concentrated on the hand, not the water, and so imagined Muslim hands as filthy. These days, where piped water has arrived, Muslims normally use devices such as short lengths of hose pipe attached to an extra faucet, or just an ordinary bidet. This keeps the hand well away from the area to be washed.[1] Similar but more elaborate devices are becoming popular in non-Muslim Japan for purely hygienic reasons.

Just as the categories of pure and impure carry over from the obvious to the less obvious, so does another dichotomy, that of left and right. Right is preferred to left, as it once was in the West, where the left-handed were thought sinister (*sinister* being Latin for "left"). It is *sunna* to put your right foot first

---

[1]Some Shi'i Ulema, however, maintain that physical contact as well as water is required to ensure cleanliness. Contact is required with the area to be washed, not the substance to be washed off it.

on entering a mosque, and your left foot first on leaving it. It is *sunna* to put the right sock on before the left sock. It is *sunna* to give and receive with the right hand, whether presents or money. If a Koran is placed on the same table as another lesser book, the Koran should be to the right. It is also, and perhaps most importantly, *sunna to eat and drink with the right hand.*

Such rules strike many Westerners as bizarre and pointless. Many Muslims ignore them too, except when eating, when the use of the left hand would be very bad table manners. The most devout Muslims, however, will observe such *sunna* recommendations scrupulously. This has two major consequences for them. First, God reaches in some sense into the most prosaic recesses of their lives, and the act of getting dressed or of paying in a shop assumes a religious or ritual significance. In Sufi terms, God is remembered even more often.

The second consequence might be called "mindfulness." Much of what we all do every day is mindless, in the sense that if we try to remember exactly how we got to or from work or school only a few hours ago, the details are generally hazy or absent. Such routine journeys are made almost automatically, or—in other terms—mindlessly. Whatever was in charge during them, it was not the conscious "me" that is meant to be in charge; it was some lower "me." The need to think about which foot to put first, then, potentially transforms the act of entering or leaving a mosque (for example) from a mindless, automatic act into a conscious one. And the dominance of the conscious "me" over the lower "me" is regarded by many Muslim commentators on spirituality as being almost an end in itself. In practice, though, which foot is put first may easily become entirely automatic too.

Food and Drink

Islam has many rules relating to food and drink. Most of these rules are in the recommended or *sunna* category, but some are in the forbidden or obligatory categories. Pig meat is as forbidden as carrion, for example. It is obligatory to slaughter animals in the way prescribed by the Sharia, which requires that an animal be slaughtered quickly and cleanly, with a single cut of a sharp knife. The blood should be allowed to flow away freely (blood is impure), and at least one of the animal's legs should be left untied, to allow the animal some freedom and reduce its suffering. Ideally, a chicken should be slaughtered by having its neck quickly and cleanly broken. Shellfish and prawns, according to some, are *makruh*. Since different views on such questions dominate in different regions, this produces differences of practice: prawns are eaten happily in countries such as Morocco, while more devout Turks will avoid them. Evangelicals, then, should not serve them to devout Turks.

The major exception to these food rules derives from the general principle that necessity justifies that which is otherwise forbidden. Hence, a Muslim can eat pork (or indeed anything else, save human flesh) if the alternative is starving to death.

None of these rules is much of an issue in the Muslim world, since pigs are not kept, and all animals are routinely slaughtered as described above. These rules are an issue, however, for devout or somewhat devout Muslims in the West. Pork is widespread, and all animals are routinely slaughtered in ways that may seem quick and clean to Westerners, but that clearly depart from the letter of the Sharia. Knives are not used, and an animal stunned before being slaughtered is thought by some Muslims to be technically dead in Sharia terms before being killed and so, actually, to be carrion.

Muslim responses to these difficulties vary, as ever. Even a declared atheist who was brought up as a Muslim is unlikely to eat a pork rib, as even the least devout Muslim has grown up thinking of pork as being in much the same category as dog-meat. Few Westerners order dog on visits to Korea (where it is regarded as a delicacy)—not for religious reasons, but simply because of deeply ingrained conceptions of what is and what is not eatable. What about a beef steak from a regular Western slaughterhouse? The least devout Muslims do not worry, and some other Muslims rely on a *hadith* report that the Prophet allowed Muslims to deem the food of the Jews and Christians to be clean unless they knew it to be otherwise. Many devout Muslims in the West reject the accuracy and applicability of this *hadith*, though, and will only eat meat slaughtered in the Islamic or—if necessary— Jewish fashion (according to some, *kosher* slaughtering satisfies the most important requirements of the Sharia). The shops in which so-called *halal* meat is sold sometimes develop into centers of Muslim community life in the West.

The next problem for devout Muslims in the West is what to do about other food products, such as cookies. What does "animal fat" mean in a list of ingredients? Might it be pig fat? Even if not, how was the animal in question slaughtered? What about gelatin — how is that manufactured? Iron supplement tablets? Responses vary from those who avert their eyes from the lists of ingredients and just eat the cookies, to those who go shopping with lists of all the standard food additives, classified as allowed or forbidden. Some Muslims in the West just give up and become vegetarians. Although Jews have rules for vegetables, Muslims do not.

For devout Muslims in the West or the Muslim world, there are all sorts of *sunna* recommendations relating to food. Some of these have passed into the general culture of most Muslim countries. It is *sunna* to wash one's hands before and after eating, and to drink after rather than during the meal. It is also *sunna* to be generous with one's food, so it is good to offer to share one's food with anyone nearby. Such offers are routinely made in the Muslim world, and are not just to avoid envy (as I mentioned in chapter 4). They are considered an important aspect of good manners; it would be extremely rude to eat a packet of potato chips on a train, for example, without first offering them to nearby passengers. It is also good manners to refuse such an offer, at least once or twice. As a rule of thumb, if an offer is made three times, it is serious; to accept on the first offer is not polite, unless all that is being offered is a single potato chip or a cigarette. This leads to numerous misunderstandings between Muslims and Westerners, since a Westerner may take a visitor's first polite refusal of a coffee as final (it is not), or unhesitatingly accept a Muslim's polite offer to share part of his or her meal (which may leave a hungry Muslim reflecting on Western greed). In the West, Muslims generally learn to follow Western practice — to accept a coffee at the first offering, and not to give their lunches away to strangers.

Being generous with one's food also means pressing it on one's guest, and refusing to take no for an answer, since "no thanks" is assumed to be mere politeness. This has also led to difficulties for Westerners in the Muslim world, when initial appreciation of local hospitality turns to dismay as an ever fuller stomach protests at yet another spoonful being placed on the protesting Westerner's already full plate. Such difficulties can usually be solved by expressing one's thanks to God ("al-hamdu li'Llah"), standing up and going to wash one's hands, indicating that one has really finished eating, but local practice differs. In Turkey, one's glass will continue to be refilled with tea indefinitely whatever one says, until one places one's spoon in a particular way over the glass. In other Muslim countries, the position of one's spoon has no more significance than it does in the West.

Kindness to strangers is generally considered a great virtue by Muslims, and many Western visitors in the Muslim world are astonished by the kindnesses they receive. Some Westerners, in contrast, go to the Muslim world expecting to be received hospitably, and are disappointed. It depends on individuals, as always, and also on the place. The Muslim countries in which Western tourism is best established are Egypt and Morocco, and in both countries there is a class of semi-criminals who prey on defenseless tourists. My own first visit to the Muslim world was to Tangier in Morocco, and it was very nearly my last. Every time I left my hotel I immediately collected a retinue of unsavory-looking men offering to be my guide, to sell me a carpet or brasswork, to provide me with marijuana, or even find me a girl. When I remonstrated that I did not want a girl, I was frequently offered a boy instead. Whatever I said or did, I could not get rid of these pests. I was finally reduced to reading novels in my hotel room. I certainly did not leave Morocco impressed by Muslim kindness to strangers.

Some years later, I was doing fieldwork in rural Sudan. The Nile had flooded, and transport was disrupted. At one point I found myself with no alternative but to walk several miles during the hottest part of the day. After a while, exhausted, I stopped to rest in the shade provided by the wall of an isolated house. After a few minutes, a small girl came out of the house with a stool for me to sit on. A few minutes later, this was followed by a glass of water. Sweet tea followed. Then some dates. After a while, restored and grateful, I went into the house to thank my nameless benefactors. They were so poor that their only furniture was a few stools and some beds, homemade out of palm branches; yet, they would not let me leave without pressing on me a bag of dried dates to sustain me through the remainder of my journey.

Anyone who has traveled in poor and remote areas of the Muslim world has similar tales to tell. Such kindness to strangers is less common in large cities, but is still encountered there. A Swedish friend of mine who was living in an apartment in central Cairo was once visited by a friend, a fellow Swede. As a result of some misunderstanding, the visitor arrived from the airport at my friend's apartment while my friend was out. The neighbors from the floor above found the visitor waiting on the stairs with her suitcase, and invited her in. They gave her tea, then lunch, then a bed for the night. In fact, by the time that my Swedish friend returned, her visitor was so comfortably installed with the neighbors that she stayed with them for a week.

This sort of hospitality has to be treated carefully. It can easily be abused, and of course should not be. It can even be abused accidentally. Poor rural families should not generally be visited at mealtimes, since they will happily and even enthusiastically give away food that they badly need themselves, only to go hungry later. It should also be remembered that Muslim conceptions of politeness require offers of hospitality to be made under all circumstances, and that not all of them should be accepted. I suspect that the family in Cairo that offered a bed to the Swedish visitor were secretly a little surprised when the offer was accepted, though in that case the cultural misunderstanding turned out well as all became the best of friends.

Dress

How a Muslim dresses is partly conditioned by Islam, especially by the understanding of gender discussed in chapter 6. It is also conditioned by local custom, and—increasingly—by global fashion as well: Nike is as popular in the Muslim world as elsewhere. The Sharia sets certain minimum requirements for dress, however, by its definition of nakedness, and these are very influential. There are two definitions: one for men, and one for women. The definition for women is the more controversial one.

A man is deemed to be naked if any part of his body is visible below the belly-button or above the knees. In this state he cannot perform the *sala* prayer, and should not appear in public. This definition is said to provide a prudent margin of safety around the genitals, which should not be seen under any circumstances whatsoever (though some interpretations allow spouses to see each others' genitals). In addition, the Sharia insists that clothing be thick enough for the color of the skin underneath not to be discernable, and that men do not wear gold or silk, which is ostentatious and effeminate.

In practice, the prohibition on gold is often ignored by the less devout, and the prohibition on silk is often ignored too, especially by those who wear smart Western business suits (which look best with silk ties). The definition of male nakedness is also often ignored, especially on the beach, where Muslim men frequently wear normal swimming trunks. So-called "Islamic" swimming trunks that stretch from the knees to the navel exist, but are rarely actually seen. Soccer shorts are also in general use in the Muslim world, though serious objections to them have been raised in Saudi Arabia. Otherwise, other types of shorts which would violate this rule are much less used in the Muslim world than elsewhere, and most Muslim men prefer to keep themselves well covered—which also makes sense in climates where the sun is strong and burning.

The use of a piece of cloth to cover the head also makes sense in hot weather, and some European soldiers fighting in the North African desert during the Second World War ended up adopting "Arab" head-dress—though normally with white or khaki cloths rather than the red-and-white checked cloths favored in Saudi Arabia and the Gulf. Many devout Muslims, however, also cover their heads even in cities in the winter, because it is *sunna* to do so. The form of head covering varies from a cloth to a cap, but is rarely a hat with a brim. The Sharia says nothing about brims on hats, but during the nineteenth century the idea grew up that a Muslim should not wear a hat with a brim because it meant that he could not touch the ground with his forehead while praying. The fashion for wearing baseball caps backwards is thus a great boon for trend-conscious male Muslim adolescents.

The use of traditional garments such as the full-length gown sometimes called a caftan may have various significances. As well as satisfying the requirements of the Sharia, the caftan is a very practical garment in hot weather, especially in the desert. In the cities of some Muslim countries, such as Egypt, it is the dress of manual laborers—the better-off wear much the same clothes as are worn in the West. In other countries, such as the Emirates, it is the dress of the "citizen": it serves to distinguish the privileged Emirati national from lesser types of being such as Indian immigrant laborers (Muslim or non-Muslim). In Sudan and some parts of Pakistan, almost all males now wear traditional dress, without exception, whatever their class. In Pakistan and Afghanistan, the *shalwar kameez* (a very long shirt worn over very baggy pants, also called the *kurta pajama*) replaces the caftan that is the traditional garment of men in the Arab world.

In all Muslim countries, and sometimes even in the West, traditional dress also has the virtue of not being Western. Those who wish to make a cultural or religious statement of a nationalist variety will therefore often insist on wearing traditional dress rather than jeans—not because jeans are forbidden by the Sharia, but because jeans are seen as alien to Islam and to their culture. The tie disappeared from Iran after the Islamic revolution for exactly this reason. An Arab man wearing a caftan in Chicago, then, might be a rich Saudi wearing clothes that confer higher status at home, a politically radical Moroccan demonstrating his rejection of Western norms, or an Egyptian laborer brought over to do building work in his country's consulate.

The definition of nakedness for women is different from the definition of nakedness for men. A woman is deemed to be naked if any part of her body is visible except for her hands and face, and in such a naked state cannot perform the *sala* prayer. In addition, the Sharia insists that female clothing be sufficiently loose so as not to reveal the contours of the body, as well as being sufficiently thick for the color of the skin underneath not to be discernable. Some maintain that even the hands and face cannot be revealed in public, though all agree that the prayer can be performed in private with hands and face visible.

Almost no devout Muslim woman disputes this definition of nakedness when it comes to performing the *sala* prayer. A Muslim woman wearing a strapless dress may well carry a shawl in her backpack which she uses to cover her hair and shoulders when praying. There is a great variety of individual and social interpretation when it comes to public appearance, however. What is meant by "social interpretation" is the general view in a particular place at a particular time. In general, social interpretation has become more strict in most parts of the Muslim world since the 1970s. In Egypt in the 1960s, for example, women in the cities (though not in the countryside) often wore tight skirts ending above the knee, and scarves covering the head were almost unknown (save, again, in the countryside). By 2000, tight skirts and female knees were nowhere to be seen, and headscarves had become the general rule. Such a change took place almost everywhere in the Middle East except in countries like Saudi Arabia, where the original social interpretation was already so strict that it could not get any stricter. In Turkey, by contrast, female dress in the cities has remained almost unchanged, because the Turkish state has worked hard to prevent the spread of head-scarves, seeing this as part of the defense of secular values. Social interpretations of male dress, however, remained everywhere much as before.

Individual interpretation today varies more than social interpretation. Some devout modern Muslim women apply the more restrictive definition of nakedness, and cover their hair and ankles, and perhaps their face and hands, before going into the streets. Equally devout women may however insist on keeping to older definitions, going out with their hair and forearms showing. Such women may also wear normal bathing suits at the beach, and think that their fully dressed sisters look ridiculous as they wade into the sea wearing almost exactly the same clothes they would wear on the street. On the other hand, less devout women in the Muslim world may cover their hair because it makes them look respectable one month, and uncover their hair because it makes them look more attractive another month. Devout Muslim women in the West may leave their hair uncovered because they do not want to stand out. Less devout Muslim women in the West may cover their hair to show pride in their ethnic identity. The possibilities and motivations are almost endless—and always need to be considered in the context of local social interpretations.

Feminism has had little impact on hair covering. Some Muslim feminists regard pressure to cover themselves as an oppression that must be resisted, while other Muslim feminists (including all those who base their feminism in Islam) regard pressure to expose their bodies as an oppression that must be resisted. Unlikely as it may seem to most Westerners, the fully covered women whose hands and face are invisible may be a committed feminist, though of a variety largely unfamiliar in the West. In that case, she regards her scantily dressed Western sisters as the unfortunate victims of male exploitation, much as certain Western feminists regard certain varieties of advertising.

Sometimes, individual interpretation collides with social interpretation, or even with the law. In Iran or Saudi Arabia, any woman—even a non-Muslim foreigner—who does not cover her hair is breaking the law. In Egypt, a women who does not cover her hair is more likely to attract obscene comments from construction workers than one who does—but is also more likely to get a job in certain internationally oriented companies. In Tunisia, a female academic who covers her hair is far less likely to be taken seriously by her colleagues. In Turkey, any woman who covers her hair will not be allowed onto university premises, or be able to work in a government office.

Some women whose individual interpretation differs from the local social norm accept the restrictions they disagree with, and some try to get around them. An Iranian woman may wear her obligatory head covering so far back on her head that much of her hair is clearly visible, and may wear a loose-fitting dress slit up the side to display tight jeans underneath. A Turkish woman may cover her hair, but with a wig, which is not objectionable to the authorities. An Egyptian woman may combine a head-scarf, which satisfies local norms, with tight jeans, which she likes. Sometimes, however, individual women openly defy the system. No woman is known ever to have walked through an Iranian or Saudi city in hot pants, but a female Turkish parliamentary deputy, Merve Kavakci, once entered the Turkish parliament in a head-scarf. This act created such outrage among the other deputies that Ms. Kavakci ended up losing not only her parliamentary seat but even her Turkish citizenship. Fortunately for her, she was also an American citizen.[2] Her act of open defiance of Turkish social norms probably owed more to her time in Texas than to Anatolia.

Head-scarves, then, are a major issue in the Muslim world, and also in parts of Europe. Some European countries regard what people choose to wear on their hair as a private matter, but others are concerned about what they see as the need to defend secularism, or perhaps their own local culture. When a few Muslim high school students turned up at a French high school wearing head-scarves and were sent home by the school principal, the resulting uproar lasted for months, and occupied the attention of several ministers and even of the president himself. Finally, a law was passed to ban the wearing of head-scarves in schools.

Some thoughtful Muslims regret all this, complaining that the head-scarf seems to have become more important than prayer, which they regard

[2]The legal basis for removing her Turkish citizenship was that, although private persons might hold two citizenships, those holding public office or in parliament might not.

as a self-evidently ridiculous development. Others welcome more restrictive norms as a public sign of growing general piety. Whatever one's view, the head-scarf has clearly become the major symbolic focus of several different struggles.

Other than requiring it be covered, the Sharia has nothing to say about female hair. It is *sunna*, however, for a male Muslim to have a beard. The Taliban regime in Afghanistan is the only regime known to have made the growing of a beard a legal requirement, but devout Muslims everywhere—especially modern ones—attach much importance to beards. The beard is the male equivalent of the head-scarf, almost as important symbolically, but less vexed.

In principle, devout modern Muslims wear beards; in practice, however, they may not, if only to keep clear of the police. As we will see in chapter 11, in many countries in the Muslim world political "Islamists" are the only serious alternative to regimes that are perceived as corrupt and despotic. The security forces of such countries thus make it their business to disrupt Islamists' activities. To the extent that a large beard is often a sign of Islamist sympathies, it also becomes a signal for the police to act. A non-observant Egyptian Muslim actor who was growing a beard for a part he was rehearsing gave up and shaved after his briefcase was searched by the police three times in one afternoon. Less secular Muslims in the Muslim world have often followed suit.

The Arts

Across the Sunni world, the pictorial arts do not play an important part in either worship or life. This is a dramatic contrast to their role in Catholic and—especially—Orthodox Christianity. To Sunni Muslims, the Christian use of images and statues seems indistinguishable from idol worship. Shi'i Muslims, though, have a different view, which I will consider later in this chapter.

The Sunni Sharia is uncompromising when it comes to images and statues. Anyone who creates an image or statue of a living thing is imitating the Creator, and will be damned as a result. It is also forbidden to possess images or statues of living things. The only exception to this is necessity. If it is legally required to include a photograph in a driver's license, then the blame attaches to the authorities who make such a requirement, not to the Muslim who complies with it. The Ulema also argue that it is allowed to buy material that includes pictures, such as a newspaper, so long as the main objective is to read the text, not to look at the pictures. Similarly, it is allowed to eat cookies made in animal shapes, if the main objective is to satisfy hunger. No exception, however, is made for children's toys, dolls, etc. The radio is acceptable, but movies and television are not.

This strict interpretation of the Sharia is in practice ignored by almost all Muslims, who make a pragmatic distinction between photographs and other forms of image making. Particularly strict Wahhabis and a few modern Muslims still object to television and even to passport photographs, but nearly all other Muslims—including devout ones—allow them. Family snaps are ubiquitous in the Muslim world as everywhere else, and when there are objections to television, the problem is usually what is shown on it rather than the medium itself. Painting and statues, however, are still generally rejected by the devout, and any representation of a prophet is out of the question. This presents problems for television programs about the life of the Prophet Muhammad—it is usually handled by making sure that the Prophet stays off screen. No pictures, including pictures of animals, will be found in a mosque.

The Shi'a take a different view, and are quite happy with pictorial representation—except of God. There is some disagreement over pictures of the Prophet, who is occasionally painted with a white veil obscuring his features. Paintings of Ali, the first infallible Imam, are very popular, sold in the streets and hung in mosques. Since painters' conceptions of human spirituality all tend to have something in common, an uninformed Westerner might be forgiven for mistaking one of the standard portraits of Ali for a portrait of Jesus.

Except among the Shi'a and in courts where rulers were more interested in dignity and display than in following the Sharia, the pictorial arts have rarely flourished in the Islamic world. Today, however, most Muslim countries have art schools, if only to produce commercial artists and illustrators, and there are also art galleries and exhibitions. These activities are frowned upon by the devout, though, and ignored by the majority of the population. Their products are rarely of very high quality, perhaps because the related aesthetic senses are given little scope for development.

The decorative arts, in contrast, have never been subject to any variety of ban. Muslim societies have as a consequence excelled at the decorative arts, possibly more than the West. The arts of geometric decoration, binding, tile making, and fabric design, once highly developed in Muslim societies, have all recently suffered somewhat as a result of industrialization, but the training of professional writers is still taken very seriously. The art of calligraphy is much appreciated, and provides the standard decoration in a mosque or in a private house. The texts used are usually of Koranic verses. Ancient mosques may display particularly superb pieces, and the work of the best calligraphers commands high prices. The houses of poorer Muslims display cheap and rather tacky calligraphy, often in plastic and now frequently mass produced in China.

Architecture was once an art in which Muslims took great pride and often excelled, but over the last century, distinctively Islamic architecture has almost disappeared. Save in remote places where traditional techniques persist, most "Islamic" architecture today is exactly the same as would be found anywhere else in the world, with the addition of a few "Islamic" or "oriental" features—an occasional arch or dome.[3]

A further art that has always flourished in the Muslim world is poetry. Much of the poetry of Muslims remains religious, now composed mostly by traditional Muslims. Poems in praise of the Prophet are a favorite genre. There was once also a strong tradition of secular poetry, often celebrating entirely forbidden activities such as drinking wine and conducting romantic affairs. That tradition has vanished, though some fine secular poetry on a more contemporary model is still written for a small market (the market for poetry is now small everywhere, of course). The most interesting Muslim poetry is that which is both religious and secular, and makes use of the tension between these two genres. The Muslim poet best known in the West is Rumi, who wrote (in Persian) of love and intoxication—leaving it to

---

[3]There have been some more serious attempts to develop a modern form of Islamic architecture, notably by the Egyptian Hasan Fathi and by several Iranian architects, but none of these has become widespread.

his audience to decide whether the love was human love or love of God, and whether the intoxicating wine was of the variety that can be bought in bottles or the invisible variety that is in the gift of God alone. Although Rumi left the decision to his audience, it is clear from what we know about him from other sources that his poetry was, in fact, religious.

> That moon, which the sky ne'er saw even in dreams, has returned
> And brought a fire no water can quench.
> See the body's house, and see my soul,
> This made drunken and that desolate by the cup of his love.
> When the host of the tavern became my heart-mate,
> My blood turned to wine and my heart to kabab.[4]

Prose literature is a recent development in the Muslim world. Although there is no more objection to prose in the Sharia than there is to poetry, prose literature in Arabic is now generally produced and consumed in much the same circles as painting is, and is usually of a similarly low quality. Turkey and Iran are exceptions, producing fine prose literature that is widely appreciated. This exception can have little to do with religion, since Turkey is secular and Sunni, while Iran is publicly Islamic and Shi'i. It may have something to do with the fact that the two greatest Muslim empires of later premodern times, the Ottoman and Safavid empires, were based in what is now Turkey and Iran, respectively. The influence of vanished imperial court cultures may explain greater artistic sophistication today.

Theater is a recent arrival in the Sunni world, found in the same circles as painting and prose literature, and regarded by most Muslims as alien, irrelevant, or both. In the Shi'i world, however, there is a long tradition of passion plays, which I will discuss in chapter 10. Although these plays serve primarily religious ends, they are often artistic triumphs in their own right — heavily formalized by modern Western standards, but including fine writing and acting.

Though there has never been much religious objection to poetry, there are serious objections to its associated arts — singing, music, and dancing. Again, the Sharia is uncompromising: no musical instrument save the tam-

---

[4]Rumi, from the *diwan* of Shams of Tabriz, trans. R. A. Nicholson.

bourine is permitted. There is disagreement about drums and bells, but it is clear that making any string or wind instrument, playing such an instrument, or listening to it, are all forbidden. Singing is allowed only by some of the Ulema, and then only at wedding parties, so long as no string or wind instruments are used, and so long as no man hears a female voice. Dancing is likewise allowed by some Ulema at weddings, in the absence of string or wind instruments, and so long as the movements of the dance are not "languid or effeminate," and—of course—so long as men and women do not mix.

Like the prohibition on images, the prohibition on singing, music and dance is generally ignored, except by hard-core Wahhabis and to a limited extent in post-revolutionary Iran, where the Ministry of Guidance forbids female soloists, though it sometimes allows a female chorus. The Muslim world has several distinct musical traditions, some religious and some secular, and several quite as sophisticated as the tradition of Western classical music. Tapes of music and singing are to be heard all over the Muslim world, and female singers are as popular as they are in the West. Just as most objections to television by the devout relate to the content rather than the medium, most objections to female singers by the devout stem from the associations rather than the singing—to the subject matter of the songs, to the revealing dress of the singer, and to her presumed private life. Islam makes no connection between singing and prostitution, but the two activities are firmly associated in the mind of most Muslims, and, to some extent, in the practice of most Muslim countries.

Dancing is also found almost universally, though the more devout will often not dance, even though they will attend celebrations where others are dancing. The two sexes generally dance alone, however—men with and in front of men, and women with women and out of sight of men. Discos where the sexes mix and dance together and alcohol is served exist in some Muslim countries, but are seen by most Muslims—and even by not especially devout ones—as little different from brothels.

Singing, music, and dancing differ from painting in that, although sternly forbidden by the Sharia, an ancient tradition in these arts has developed and survived. While painting produced in most of the Muslim world is rarely of much quality, music can often be of high quality, though using unfamiliar keys and idioms that at first sound awful to the differently trained ear of most Westerners. Muslim music is now making its way in the World Music scene, and even into mainstream music. "Belly-dancing" (also called "Eastern dance") is also becoming ever more popular outside the Muslim world. These two contributions to the global culture are probably the only significant elements other than poetry to come from the Muslim world, and have nothing to do with Islam. The other major arts of the Muslim world — calligraphy and decoration — are more closely connected to the religion of Islam, and have not been exported.

Business

Much of the Sharia covers commercial law. Its rules generally relate to simple agricultural economies, and are often followed scrupulously by devout Muslims living in such economies. In more complex economies, however, they are hard or even impossible to apply. Although there is provision for partnerships, for example, there is no concept of the corporation or of limited liability. For this reason, the Sharia rules have generally been replaced by codes of commercial law on the Western model, and most business arrangements in the Muslim world today ignore the Sharia. As always, however, the Sharia rules are influential in determining the attitudes of individual Muslims. That businessmen ignore the Sharia is one reason why many less sophisticated Muslims tend to regard businessmen as corrupt by definition.

The two most basic principles of the Sharia's commercial regulations are that dealings must be fair and open, and that although it is fine to profit from one's work, it is wrong to take advantage of someone else's misfortune, i.e. of one's position in relation to theirs. A third principle is that it is wrong to cut off someone's source of income.

Few Westerners would disagree with these general principles, but many of the detailed regulations that relate to them produce major difficulties for anyone trying to do business in modern Western ways. Not taking advantage of one's position means that "speculation" is forbidden. If a trader buys some flour and the price goes up, he or she should sell it at the purchase price plus a reasonable profit margin, not at the new price. This would put most commodity traders and even many wholesalers out of business. That it is wrong to cut off someone's source of income means, for example, that no one should drive a competitor out of business, and no one should fire an employee unless there is no alternative.

Sharia rules also make most contemporary financial transactions impossible. To lend money to someone in need is encouraged as an act of charity. Once someone is no longer in need, they should return the money they have borrowed. To charge interest on a loan is completely forbidden, since that is taking advantage of someone else's unfortunate position. Under the Sharia, then, a Muslim cannot borrow money to buy a house—partly because he or she does not actually *need* the money (houses can be rented), and partly because he or she cannot pay interest on the loan.

Some (but not very many) Muslims interpret the Sharia's prohibitions on unnecessary loans and interest so strictly that they conclude that paper money is sinful. A dollar bill, in this view, is a receipt for my money lent to the US government—which is forbidden, since the US government does not actually need my money. Even worse, fluctuations in the price of gold mean that the value in gold of my dollar bill varies. The difference between the value of my dollar bill in gold at the time when I receive it and when I exchange it for something else is a form of interest. The only legitimate currency is thus gold or silver. One particular group of Muslims has therefore privately relaunched the gold dinar, which at the time of writing can be used for transactions over the internet in the form of an e-dinar.

Needless to say, the devotees of the e-dinar form a tiny minority of Muslims, and Muslims in general accept the use of paper money. Many devout Muslims, however, will not take out bank loans or deposit money in interest-bearing bank accounts. Various techniques have been evolved to get around this, and a major industry of "Islamic banking" has grown. This industry is based in countries such as Saudi Arabia where the Sharia is the main form of state law, and where there are also a significant number of rich Muslims whose potential deposits make the business worthwhile. The worldwide market for "Islamic" financial instruments was estimated in 2002, perhaps a bit optimistically, to be worth some $200 billion.

In essence, all Islamic banking is an attempt to dress up standard international banking practices in Sharia clothes—that is, an attempt to ignore the spirit of the law while respecting the letter. Interest paid to depositors thus appears as a share in the bank's profits that just happens to be about the same amount as a normal bank would have paid in interest over the same period. Interest charges appear as transaction charges, which again mysteriously resemble what another bank might have charged in interest. A significant number of modern and Wahhabi Muslims find these arrangements satisfactory, but many Muslims are happy just to use the normal banking system. Most traditional Muslims do not have enough money to use any sort of banking system in the first place.

The Sharia not only prohibits most contemporary banking transactions, but also almost any financial transaction one can think of. Insurance is technically a form of gambling (and so forbidden). If horse number 15 wins, I get some money, but not otherwise; if my house burns down I get some money, but not otherwise. It's all a gamble. As with deposits and loans, some Muslims resort to Islamic banks and insurance companies that dress up their operations in Sharia clothes, but again, most simply ignore the Sharia and use the same financial instruments as Westerners do. Most Muslims, it should be noted, have never thought of taking out insurance, which is not widely available outside major cities, and do not know what futures trading is.

There is disagreement over the extent to which the Sharia applies to dealings with non-Muslims. Some Ulema have argued that non-Muslim business partners should be treated in exactly the same way as Muslim business partners, while others have argued that only non-Muslims in the Muslim world are protected by the Sharia, and that non-Muslims outside the Muslim world may legitimately be cheated. Some have even gone so far as to argue that non-Muslims anywhere may legitimately be cheated. In practice, Muslims who deal honestly with Muslim business partners will deal honestly with all their business partners, and dishonest (and therefore not especially devout) Muslims will be dishonest with everyone—perhaps consoling themselves with an argument that it is acceptable to cheat non-Muslims.

Western visitors to the Muslim world sometimes consider the bargaining practices they encounter there to be dishonest. In the West, it is considered acceptable to ask whatever price one thinks one can get for a used car, but not acceptable for a shopkeeper to ask whatever price he thinks he can get from an individual customer for a bath towel. A shopper who discovers that the towel he or she paid twenty-five dollars for is normally sold in the same shop for five dollars will think he or she has been cheated. In the Muslim world, a bath towel is generally thought to be worth whatever someone is prepared to pay for it, just as a used car is. A shopkeeper who sells a wealthy customer a towel for twenty-five dollars instead of the normal five dollars considers himself a good businessman, not in any way dishonest. A Western shopper will not agree. This leads to much irritation, but really has nothing to do with religion.

Summary

The daily life of Muslims is guided by local custom (which varies widely) and by Islam, but common themes can be found everywhere, including such abstract concepts as purity and the superiority of the right over the left. The Sharia provides detailed rules on food and drink that reflect some of these general principles. The rules on food are not an issue in the Muslim world, but can be a major issue for Muslims in the West or in other countries where they are a minority.

The Sharia provides rules on clothing for both sexes, but it is the rules on women's clothing that are most controversial. Actual practice varies from country to country, and from woman to woman. The issue is extremely complex. The use or absence of a head-scarf by a woman, like the use of traditional or modern Western clothing by a man, can mean totally different things in different places and with different people.

Muslim kindness to strangers often goes to extraordinary lengths. Care must be taken not to abuse the hospitality of poor Muslims, even accidentally.

The arts in the Muslim world are affected by Islam to the extent that those condemned by the Sharia—especially painting—rarely flourish, while those which have religious applications—especially calligraphy, poetry, and architecture—are those in which Muslims have achieved most.

The detailed rules of the Sharia relating to business are generally ignored, though they have given rise to an important market for "Islamic" financial instruments. General ethical principles relating to business can be derived from the Sharia, but local practice is, again, generally more important.

8

In and Out

Community Life

ccording to *In the Name of Allah*, a cheap novel I once bought at a
rail station, Muslims regard those outside their own communities
as barely human. "For Moustapha Ali," explained the novel about
its chief villain, "cutting the throat of a stranger was of no more consequence than cutting the throat of a sheep."

The fictional Moustapha Ali would have been regarded as a psycho-
path by any sane Muslim, whether he was a stranger or not, but the community does matter to Muslims—or rather, communities matter. There are
several different ones: there is the worldwide community of all Muslims,
the *umma*; there are individual Muslim states; there are communities of
mazhab (I will explain exactly what these are later); most important of all,
there is the local community. It is within the context of the local community that "virtue promotion and vice suppression" takes place. When reform
of reprobates and criminals fails at this local level, the Sharia imposes harsh
penalties—which still matter, even though most Muslim states now have
legal systems that are not very different from Western ones.

This chapter deals with all of these Muslim communities, and with
what goes on within them, except for politics. Islam and politics is a large
and separate subject, which I will consider in chapter 11.

The *Umma*

The most important Islamic community, in theory, is the *umma*, the worldwide community of all Muslims. All Muslims learn that all other Muslims

are their brothers and sisters, and most would accept in principle that this is more important than loyalty to any other group, including tribe or nation. In practice, however, the *umma* is normally remote. In those Arab and African countries where the tribal system still operates, loyalty to tribe still matters more than any other loyalty. Elsewhere one of the major objectives of the state's school system is to convince everyone that they are all members of a single nation, and owe their primary loyalty to that nation, and so to its representative, the government. In countries such as Egypt, this has been successful: most Egyptian Muslims feel closer to an Egyptian Christian than to a Malaysian Muslim. In countries such as Iraq, riven by ethnic and denominational cleavages, loyalty to the nation never became more important than loyalty to the ethnic or denominational community.

The place where the supra-national *umma* matters most today is, paradoxically, in the West. In America, Muslims might see themselves as Arab-Americans or Turkish-Americans, or after a few generations might see themselves just as plain Americans. In this they would follow earlier waves of "hyphenated" Americans. But regardless of how they see themselves, immigrants from Muslim countries (and their descendants) are increasingly labeled not on the basis of geography but of religion, and treated by others in the West as Muslims. Sometimes the label "Muslim" is applied with hostility, especially since the terrorist attacks of September 11, 2001. Sometimes it is applied out of the best of motives, by believers in multiculturalism who are careful to be sensitive to different cultures. It may be as unwelcome in the second case as it is in the first. Dounia Bouzar, a liberal French intellectual, rails against the way so many Westerners try to understand all those of Muslim origin in terms of Islam. She prefers to be a French intellectual who is Muslim, not a Muslim intellectual who is French.

Whatever the reason for its use, the use of the label "Muslim" has an impact on those to whom it is applied. Minorities everywhere tend to accept the labels applied to them, to the extent that even some Americans living in Arab countries may end up thinking of themselves as "foreigners" first and Americans second. Unless he or she is actually Christian, even a secular Arab-American who is repeatedly labeled "Muslim" may end up thinking of himself or herself as Muslim rather than as Arab or as American, and identifying primarily with the global *umma*. The alienation of Western

Muslims from their surrounding societies is a problem, though more of a problem in Europe than in America. I will consider this in chapter 12.

Mazhabs and Muftis

A second, somewhat theoretical, community to which any Muslim belongs is that of the *mazhab,* a term for which there is really no satisfactory translation into English. It is sometimes translated as "school," in the same sense as when that word is used in talking about the "impressionist school" of painting.

When interpreting Islam or deciding on the finer points of the Sharia, the Ulema cannot just come to any arbitrary conclusion. They have to pay attention to the work and conclusions of the Ulema who came before them, just as an American judge has to take precedents into account—though what matters is not so much the precedent as the evidence and logic behind it. These precedents were formalized many centuries ago into accumulated bodies of former decisions, and these are called the *mazhabs*. At first there were many rival accumulated bodies of decisions, but as time passed, some of these became less popular, until only four Sunni *mazhabs* and one Shi'i one were left. These five remain in existence today. Any one member of the Ulema studies the analytical methods and former decisions of one particular *mazhab*, though reference may sometimes be made to the others for comparative purposes. Likewise, an ordinary Muslim follows the decisions of one particular *mazhab*. Some Western scholars see the Wahhabi movement as a new, fifth *mazhab,* though it does not itself accept that label. What I call "modern" Islam is also, perhaps, a new and separate *mazhab.*

The four Sunni *mazhabs* agree on most points, but disagree on details, rather as the legal systems of different American states do. One *mazhab,* for example, holds that it is acceptable to keep dogs as pets, while the others hold that they can only be kept for a specific purpose, such as for hunting or as guard dogs. One *mazhab* maintains that it is necessary to raise both hands in salutation several times during the *sala* prayer, while another holds that it is enough to do this once, at the beginning of the prayer. One holds that prawns are *makruh,* and another sees no problem with them.

Rather than attempt to resolve these differences, a very pragmatic compromise was reached: even when they disagree, all four *mazhabs* are accepted to be equally right. There may thus be up to four acceptable, though different, answers to any given question.

In practice, the differences between the Sunni *mazhabs* have only minor significance today, though the differences between the Sunni *mazhabs* and the single Shi'i *mazhab*, the Ja'fari *mazhab*, are more important. As we have seen, the Ja'fari *mazhab* permits temporary marriage and the making of pictures of the Prophet, for example, neither of which are acceptable to any Sunni *mazhab*.

In many countries, there is only one *mazhab* with any real following. Turks and Indians, for example, almost without exception follow the Hanafi *mazhab* named after Abu Hanifa, that *mazhab*'s greatest scholar (and so do not, for example, generally eat prawns), while Malaysians almost all follow the Shafi'i *mazhab*, Moroccans the Maliki *mazhab*, and Saudis the Hanbali *mazhab*. Shi'i Muslims all follow the Ja'fari *mazhab*, named after the infallible Imam who founded it. In those countries, the rulings of other *mazhabs* are little known and of no real importance. Moroccans, however, are more likely to look favorably on people who keep dogs as pets, since it is the Maliki *mazhab* that maintains that this is an acceptable thing to do. In some other countries, such as Egypt, there are two or more *mazhabs*. In this case, somebody may occasionally switch from one *mazhab* to another—if they cannot resist the appeal of a particular puppy, for example. This is regarded as legitimate, so long as it only happens once or twice in a lifetime. Most Muslims would consider a puppy as a frivolous reason for taking a serious step, but that really was the reason that family lore gives for the change of *mazhab* by the grandmother of an Egyptian friend of mine.

Each *mazhab* in each major city (or sometimes each country) has a senior official, called a Mufti—literally, a "giver of opinions." Any member of a *mazhab* with a difficult question about the proper interpretation of the Sharia may go to ask the opinion of his or her Mufti. In theory, a Mufti is a senior member of the Ulema, respected by all for his scholarship and wisdom, and selected by his colleagues for those reasons. In practice, the position of Mufti is so important that in most Muslim countries the government has taken over the task of appointing him, so that political skill is now required, as well as—and perhaps even more than—scholarship and wisdom.

When a Mufti is asked a question, he will (if he thinks the question deserves it) consider it and then deliver as an answer a formal opinion, known as a Fatwa. The world's most famous Fatwa was that given in 1989 by Ayatollah Khomeini of Iran, condemning the British writer Salman Rushdie to death for causing grievous mischief[1] and insulting the Prophet. That was, however, a very unusual Fatwa, if only because it was given by a head of state. Khomeini is the only known Mufti also to have been a head of state. Muftis normally have no control of any sort over political power. At the most, they sometimes issue Fatwas which end with a statement that the state should take steps to encourage or discourage something, or issue Fatwas that legitimize some view of the state in which the Mufti lives. Fatwas that act as final sentences of death on persons who have not been tried in a court are not known outside post-revolutionary Iran.

Fatwas now, more typically, either address big questions such as the legitimacy of organ transplants or stem cell research, or the dilemma of a particular individual. As I noted in chapter 6, if a Muslim woman wants to marry a Christian, she cannot do so unless the Christian converts to Islam. In the Arab world, nominal Christians do from time to time convert to Islam for this reason. The father of a woman whose fiancé had converted in this way was worried that the conversion was not genuine. He discussed this problem with friends, with people whose opinions he respected, and with the Imam at his local mosque—and received contradictory advice. To resolve the question, he asked a Mufti, who told him that as long as he did not actually *know* that the conversion was not genuine, he could and should regard it as genuine.

It is not known how the father reacted to this Fatwa—probably with relief. A Fatwa, however, is only an opinion, even if it is the opinion of someone who should know what they are talking about. It is no more binding than advice from one's lawyer is. No one is obliged to follow a Fatwa, and in practice Fatwas are often widely ignored. In 2000, for example, the senior Mufti

---

[1]Technically, creating *fitna*. Creating *fitna* is acting in a way that disturbs the proper order of things, whether in politics (such as fomenting civil war) or in morals (such as a striptease).

in Egypt gave a Fatwa to the effect that smoking was forbidden because it damaged the health and was a waste of money. The Egyptians carried on smoking as enthusiastically as ever before—though a few dozen individuals probably quit.

Local Communities

The community that matters more in everyday life than the *umma* and the *mazhab* is the local community. The local community, of course, also matters in Christianity. Practicing Christians belong to a parish, and go to a particular church. They often take part in activities organized by their church, which may also become a major focus of their social life. The local Christian community both helps to reinforce people's belief and practice, and discourages backsliding. Similar Muslim communities based around a mosque and its Imam have come into being in the West, partly in unconscious imitation of the Christian model, and partly because Muslims living in the West need to create a community of fellow-believers, since such a community does not exist naturally. These "Islamic Community Centers," as they are often called, serve multiple purposes, from education to social welfare, as well as worship, and are of great importance in Western countries.

In the Muslim world, however, mosques are places to pray in, not centers of communities. As we have seen, there is no equivalent of the christening in Islam, and marriages are not performed in mosques. Funeral prayers are performed in mosques, but are brief and impersonal, not community occasions. In cities, most of the people who attend a given mosque have no idea of the name of the Imam, and have never spoken to him. In fact, most people simply go to whichever mosque is closest to them at any particular time. The choice of mosque to pray in during the week has no more significance than the choice of a bus stop to catch a bus. The choice of a mosque to pray the Friday prayer in has more significance, but most Muslims will still generally go to whichever mosque is closer. Some may avoid their closest mosque because they dislike the preacher there, or because his sermons are too long—or they may simply turn up at the end of the sermon, in time for the prayer. Some Muslims—especially devout modern ones—do choose a mosque for Friday prayers because they like the

preacher there, and get to know the preacher and each other. This, however, is unusual, and even in these cases, the local community never becomes as important as a Christian parish. The only religious community
that routinely functions like a Christian parish is the Sufi order, discussed
in chapter 2.

The basic local community of the Muslim world is the village or the
urban neighborhood. In a small village, everyone knows each other, and
everyone also knows the Imam, who occupies a respected position there. In
the smallest villages there may be no permanent Imam, and a local figure
will preach the Friday sermon, perhaps reading it out from a book of model
sermons. In either case, there is a distinct community which is in a sense
gathered around the mosque, but what matters in these cases is the village,
not the mosque.

Even in the cities of the Muslim world, something like the village community is often found. Many older cities were once accumulations of formally defined neighborhoods, each one with a single entrance which was
often closed at night. This architectural pattern disappeared over a century
ago, but something of the spirit behind it has survived. Even if not everyone
in a neighborhood knows everyone else, many people do know each other,
and news circulates quickly.

The neighborhood does not usually coincide with a single mosque, and
even if it does, the Imam of that mosque has no particular responsibility for
ensuring order or piety in the neighborhood. In the days of formally defined
neighborhoods with closed entrances, each neighborhood chose its own
"elder" for these (and other, non-religious) purposes, but in most of the
Muslim world that system vanished with formally defined neighborhoods
(though it still survives in Turkey). The responsibility for ensuring order and
piety is placed by the Sharia on each and every Muslim. According to the
Sharia, "vice prevention and virtue promotion" is a duty of every Muslim in
the same way that prayer is.

The best way of promoting virtue and preventing vice is offering advice
that will not give offense to the person advised; if this does not work, more
direct words can be used. If words fail, then actions are required. If argument has not persuaded an errant Muslim to stop drinking alcohol, the next
step is to pick up his or her glass and pour away its contents. There is disagreement about acting in ways that will lead to a fight (as the example just

given might). The general view is that only those given some authority by the state may use physical violence, but some hold that anyone may resort to force on their own responsibility if they decide this is necessary. No one is obliged to risk their physical safety or even to expose themselves to excessive abuse from a group of people in order to promote virtue and prevent vice, and under some circumstances it is enough to condemn an evil act to oneself. If one is convinced that one's words will do little good, it is

 less important to speak them, but still recommended.

Thus every Muslim who sees another Muslim drinking in a bar has the religious duty of remonstrating with him. In practice, Muslims in cities where bars exist can usually get on with their drinking in peace, if not in much comfort, partly because bars are rarely located within residential neighborhoods. Muslims who return home visibly inebriated, however, may well find that others in their communities will confront them, fulfilling their duty of vice prevention.

Devout Muslims are often adept at phrasing an admonition so as to cause minimum offense. If a man is wearing a gold chain, for example, another man may remark within his hearing that he is delighted that so few men nowadays wear gold. Less judicious condemnations are more common among groups such as the Wahhabis, who may well approach someone and simply remark that while some people do not realize it, the wearing of gold by a man is forbidden by Islam.

Virtue is sometimes promoted and vice suppressed through means not envisaged by the Sharia: charities, community centers offering everything from education to marital counseling, help-lines, and the like. These are usually found in the West, partly because it is in the West that Muslims are most conscious of the need to organize their community, and have before them the examples of Western "civil society"—all those voluntary activities that make such a difference to the way Western societies work. In many countries in the Muslim world, governments actively discourage "civil society" because they see it as a threat to their own monopoly of power. Under these circumstances, Muslims who want to give their time and energies for their fellows may operate health centers for the poor where charges are lower and treatment better that at government clinics, or establish free lending libraries of religious books, but they are usually unable to do much else.

Iran is something of an exception to this rule. A variety of organizations that receive some funding from the government but are more or less independent of it work on social welfare, education, and so on, and may serve as a focus for their local community. A similar role is played by the *hay'at,* organizations for the commemoration of the martyrdom of the Imam Husayn (a central figure for Shi'i Muslims, whom I will discuss in chapter 10). Such a role was once played in the Sunni world by some Sufi orders, but this is now only the case in traditional areas where Sufism remains strong.

Race

One question which arises in the context of the local community is that of race. Race is not dealt with in the Sharia, since Islam is in theory color-blind. But Muslims are not color-blind, whatever the Sharia says. There are two main approaches to race among Muslims, depending largely on their ancestors' experience of European imperialism.

By 1920 nearly the whole of the Muslim world had come under the imperial control of one or another of the European powers. Different European powers governed their various Muslim populations quite differently. At one extreme, the British administered the dirt-poor Trucial States on the eastern side of the Arabian peninsula (today the United Arab Emirates, and—since the discovery of oil—extraordinary rich) with the lightest of hands. Local rulers were obliged to sign treaties with the British promising to have relations with no foreign power save Britain, and to observe truces with each other (rather than fight each other from time to time, as had previously been the case). Apart from that, local rulers were left to their own devices. An Arabic-speaking British official would visit from time to time, usually just a junior official given the area's lack of importance, and that was it. British rule thus had little impact on local society, or on local conceptions of race.

At the other extreme, the British ruled India for centuries in a way that changed Indian society beyond recognition. After an initial period of relaxed relations, an informal system of apartheid grew up during the nineteenth century whereby the British and the "natives" were rigidly segregated, and it was made quite clear that the British were inherently superior. With rare exceptions, "natives" entered British households and clubs only as servants. At the same time, English became the official language of India, and a minority of Indians became more adept at various areas of British culture—from the law to literature and cricket—than the British themselves. And yet they remained "natives."

Muslim attitudes toward race in areas such as India which were exposed to long periods of European racism are complex, and are similar to attitudes toward race in the southern United States. Muslim attitudes toward race in areas that were never really exposed to European racism, in contrast, are much less complex. Skin color is not associated with superiority or inferiority, or with past injustice. In many countries, centuries of migration and intermarriage has left a variety in skin color that encompasses all shades from the Mediterranean European to the African—and nobody pays any real attention to it. This may be hard to many Westerners to believe, but it is the case—with a few notable exceptions.

Even Muslim societies that have not experienced European racism are not entirely color-blind. A light complexion is everywhere considered beautiful, especially in a woman, rather as blonde hair is in parts of the West. Light complexions are also associated with higher social class, where they are found more often—partly as a result of the tastes of generations of wealthy men looking for what were considered beautiful wives, and partly as a result of the fact that in centuries past such men were sometimes rich enough to afford white slaves for their harems.

The one notable exception to this otherwise idyllic picture of race relations concerns African features (not just a dark skin). For centuries, just as rare and expensive white slaves were the favored possession of the very rich, more easily available and cheaper black African slaves were the possessions of the somewhat rich. To some extent, the association between African features and slavery persists. African visitors and refugees in some Arab countries are sometimes subjected to the most appalling treatment—not by everyone, but by many. They may have great difficulty in getting served in shops and restaurants, and may even be subjected to physical violence by complete strangers in the street. African-Americans in the Arab world may be treated as Africans are. This treatment is in no way endorsed by the

Sharia or Islam, and is in fact condemned by all devout Muslims and by many others—but it still happens all the same.

Crime

The official system of criminal law in most Muslim countries today differs little from the system of criminal law in Western countries, but informal systems of criminal law may still be in place in remoter regions where the government has little impact. These informal systems are usually a mixture of Sharia and local custom, which may well contradict the Sharia. In some Muslim countries the Sharia is still the law, or the main source of criminal law. Even in places where non-Sharia systems of criminal law are in place, Sharia rules have an impact on what both Muslims and the local community people regard as just and as unjust.

The crimes punished in any Western legal system are generally also punished by the Sharia, though certain more "modern" crimes such as speeding or insider trading are not envisaged. Some more complex crimes such as credit card fraud are not defined by the Sharia, and so are hard if not impossible to prosecute under the Sharia. There are also acts not regarded as crimes by most modern Western legal systems that are defined as crimes by the Sharia. The most important of these are extramarital sex, the consumption of intoxicants, gambling, and homosexuality. As we saw in chapter 6, extramarital sex exists among Muslims, despite Islam and the attitudes of Muslim societies. Likewise, intoxicants, gambling, and homosexuality also play a part in the lives of some less devout Muslims. They are, however, condemned by all Muslim societies, and illegal in some Muslim countries.

The Sharia is very clear about alcohol: it is forbidden (except for medicinal uses, where necessity may justify the otherwise prohibited). The story is often told among devout Muslims of a man who was offered the choice between committing murder, committing adultery, and getting drunk. He chose to get drunk. While drunk, he committed adultery and murder. As we saw in chapter 4, many traditional Muslims understand the Sharia partly as a series of exercises to control the ego (*nafs*); alcohol may be regarded as the fastest and easiest way to remove control over the ego.

Not all Muslims observe the prohibition on alcohol, however. Someone who prays regularly is most unlikely to drink alcohol, if only because prayer when intoxicated is forbidden, but also because of the order in which devout Muslims commonly place their obligations. Even someone who does not pray will usually avoid alcohol, especially in the Muslim world outside Turkey. In some Muslim countries this is because alcohol is illegal. In others, although alcohol has remained legal since the days of European rule, it is still very clearly labeled in people's minds as sinful and dangerous. Again, the only partial exception to this is the major cities in Turkey.

Alcohol consumption is also little encouraged by circumstances in the Muslim world. In most of the West, alcohol is a normal part of social life. It can be bought in supermarkets, and is routinely offered to guests. In some Muslim countries, it is also available in supermarkets, but in others it can only be obtained from an illegal dealer in shady circumstances, rather like buying drugs in the West. Even in many Muslim countries where the sale of alcohol is allowed by law, it is not stocked in normal supermarkets, and bars (save in five-star hotels) are not usually attractive places. There are occasional exceptions (mostly in Turkey and Central Asia), but most bars are hidden in side streets, with windows of opaque glass. The interior of such a bar is generally dirty and smelly, and the tables are typically occupied by elderly single men with sad expressions on their faces. Some may well have fallen asleep at their tables. There is little to tempt anyone other than an alcoholic inside. Except in Turkey, even a restaurant that serves alcohol is not really a respectable place for a respectable person (especially a woman) to go. Restaurants that do serve alcohol do most of their business with Westerners.

Alcohol is sometimes consumed in other circumstances. The marketing of Scotch whisky has succeeded in making it an indispensable status symbol for certain types of wealthy Muslim men who like to regard themselves as well-traveled and cosmopolitan. Mysteriously, beer sales during the 1990s in Egypt made the leading local brewery one of the most attractive stocks on the local stock market, until it was finally taken over by a Dutch multinational. There were no visible signs of the consumption of all that beer, but it must have gone somewhere. Consumption never reached anything approaching Dutch or even Turkish levels, however.

Less devout Muslims in the West and Turkey often conform to local practice and join colleagues in a bar after work. Some have guilty consciences about this, but some do not. No Muslim in a Western bar can be described as devout, but many are not as far from their religion as one might think, and firmly intend to stop what they see as their bad habit one day (and some even do stop it one day).

All forms of narcotic are considered by most Muslims to fall into the same category as alcohol. Their medical use is allowed, but otherwise they are forbidden. This is not explicit in the Sharia, however, and so some Muslims argue that marijuana is discouraged (*makruh*) rather than forbidden. In many countries, the use of marijuana attracts less social stigma than the consumption of alcohol, and it is more likely that one will encounter a somewhat devout Muslim who uses marijuana than that one will encounter a somewhat devout Muslim who drinks alcohol. Some Ulema, especially in Iran, also argue that opium is not forbidden if used in moderation, though they recognize that opium's addictive nature causes problems. Nobody seriously suggests that narcotics such as heroin are anything other than forbidden.

Coffee and tobacco were once regarded by some of the most devout as varieties of narcotic and therefore as forbidden, and cafés (which commonly serve both coffee and tobacco) were seen as places of vice. Coffee is now accepted by almost all Muslims as allowed, and more Muslims today regard tobacco as discouraged (*makruh*) rather than forbidden. As the impact of smoking on health has slowly become known in the Muslim world, the argument is made more frequently that smoking is a form of intentional self-inflicted damage; intentional self-inflicted damage has always been forbidden, just as suicide has. Views are changing at the moment, but on the whole smoking is seen in many Muslim countries as entirely acceptable. The most devout, though, generally reject it, and in some areas smoking is regarded as being in almost the same category as the consumption of alcohol.

For Sunni Muslims, gambling, like alcohol, is entirely forbidden by the Sharia. The only exception to this occurs when the winner of a competition which serves some useful purpose, and does not depend principally on chance, receives a prize. Thus if someone wins a horse race or a Koran-reading competition, he or she may receive a prize—but no one else may bet on the outcome of the race or competition. Shi'i Muslims allow gambling on horse racing, however, so long as it is not excessive.

The Sunni Sharia's prohibition on gambling is very widely drawn. As we have seen, even transactions which would not strike the average Westerner as gambling (such an insurance) are forbidden by the Sharia. Despite this, most Muslim states require drivers to purchase liability insurance. In its narrowest sense, though, the prohibition on gambling is observed much as the prohibition on alcohol. In a country where alcohol is illegal, so will slot machines and casinos be illegal. In a country where a few bars exist, some five-star hotels may have a casino as well as a bar. In a country where alcohol is more widely available, so will gambling be more widely available, and there may even be a state lottery, as there is in Tunisia. Devout Sunni Muslims, however, will avoid the state lottery as much as they avoid beer.

Commercial promotion is a gray area in terms of gambling—buy ten packets of my product, collect ten tokens, and receive a prize if you can match them up in a certain way. While a strict interpretation of the Sharia might condemn such promotions as gambling, the executives who dream them up are often not used to thinking in terms of the Sharia, and many ordinary Muslims may not analyze the promotions in Sharia terms either.

Male homosexuality (defined as sodomy) is forbidden by the Sharia just as fornication is, and is subject to the same penalty (severe beating). Lesbianism is also forbidden, though the Sharia is less clear about its punishment. Homosexuality will therefore be avoided by devout Muslims, just as extramarital heterosexual activity is avoided. However, although segregation of the sexes may serve to make fornication and adultery difficult, it certainly does not prevent homosexuality—in fact, segregation of the sexes and the prevention of extramarital heterosexual activity inevitably constitute a sort of encouragement to homosexual activity.

Less devout and nonobservant Muslims sometimes regard homosexuality as an acceptable form of casual sex, and some aspects of homosexuality have on occasion achieved a form of public respectability in certain Muslim societies, despite homosexuality's condemnation by Islam. Homosexual activity is today condemned by all Muslim societies, however, and no variety of homosexual relationship is considered in any way similar to marriage. Just as in the West of a century ago, there is no widespread concept of homosexuality as the natural orientation of certain individuals. While some may be more drawn to homosexuality than others, so are some more drawn to murder and arson than others; that does not make murder and arson good for anyone. Even those who themselves engage in homosexual activity generally regard it as rather like masturbation, and see no contradiction between youthful homosexuality and a later (heterosexual) marriage. The unmarried gay Muslim who regards his or her sexual orientation as a valid personal lifestyle choice is rare in the extreme, save in the West.

Punishment

In any legal system, the punishment of criminals serves three possible purposes: retribution, reform of the criminal, and deterrence (of other potential criminals). It is generally accepted that deterrent impact is a joint function of the severity of the penalty and of the chances of getting caught—a point that most drivers will immediately appreciate. Many of us will exceed the speed limit if the chances of being caught seem low, unless the potential penalty is very high. Few drivers will speed past a highway patrol car, however low the penalty. Put differently, the more efficient the justice system, the more lenient the penalties can be.

Until modern police forces made detection of crime more likely, all criminal justice systems relied on savage and exemplary punishment to achieve deterrence. The reform of criminals by non-violent methods only became a concern of the courts somewhat recently. Much of the credit for this development goes to the Quakers, who opened the world's first modern prison in Pennsylvania in 1790. Until then, in the West as in the Islamic world, prisons were used either for holding people for interrogation or pending trial, or for keeping people out of circulation (especially the political opponents of a ruler).

The Quakers' idea was to transform the criminal into a penitent, finding God in his or her individual cell, just as monks once meditated in their cells. Over the fifty years following 1790, this non-violent approach to criminality spread across the Western world. Not only were penitentiaries to be found everywhere by the 1830s, but older varieties of corporal punishment disappeared, just as modern police forces were being introduced. Western legal systems had formerly used exactly the same penalties as the Sharia imposes (flogging, maiming, and execution), along with one punishment the Sharia does not impose (branding). Branding remained available as penalty for desertion from the US army until as late as 1872, but maiming had vanished everywhere in the West by 1840. The flogging of women was banned in Britain in 1820, and of men in 1948; the last US state to use the penalty was Delaware, in 1952. Execution was abolished in Tuscany in 1786, in 1846 in Michigan, and in most of the rest of the world after the Second World War (America is now the only country in the West which routinely carries out executions).

As in the West, some tension exists between Muslim criminal justice experts (who focus on reform) and the general Muslim public (which is often more interested in retribution and deterrence). The general public in most Western countries has less and less faith in the ability of penitentiaries to produce penitence. Few Muslims in the Muslim world ever expected penitence from the inhabitants of penitentiaries. They are more interested in deterrence and retribution, as is the criminal justice system of the Sharia, the development of which preceded modern police forces by more than a thousand years.

The punishments specified by the Sharia are old-fashioned corporal ones—flogging, maiming, and execution—rather than modern ones like prison. Compensation is achieved either through paying a fine to the injured person, or by ensuring that the harm inflicted on the criminal is the same as the harm that the criminal inflicted. The relatives of a person who has been murdered, for example, may chose between retribution by means of the convicted murderer's execution or by means of monetary compensation.

The Sharia combines savage and exemplary punishments with a high standard of proof. The classic example of this is the punishment for adultery, which is execution. To prove adultery, however, one must have four witnesses to the actual act of intercourse, who must be able to testify that penetration occurred. Alleging adultery without being able to prove it is considered slander, and the punishment for that particular variety of slander is the same as the punishment for adultery (execution). Thus, although the penalty for adultery is certainly savage and exemplary, the chances of being convicted under the Sharia are very low indeed. Only married persons can commit adultery; unmarried persons commit fornication. Thus an unmarried woman who becomes pregnant will easily be convicted, but of fornication (which is punished by flogging), not of adultery.

In practice, the Sharia penalty for adultery is today applied principally in Saudi Arabia. Social penalties for extra-marital sex, however, are severe by Western standards. Any woman suspected of unchastity will be treated with general disrespect within her neighborhood, and is unlikely to find a husband. A man, in contrast, will generally simply be regarded as a reprobate by the devout, and avoided by them. The woman thus suffers a more severe penalty, while the man more or less gets away with it. This is the practice of most Muslim societies—a variation on the practice of many other societies—and is not a consequence of Islam.

The Sharia prescribes maiming as the punishment for theft. "Theft," however, is very narrowly defined. Neither stealing jewelry left on a table nor snatching someone's bag on the street are theft, for example—though breaking into a locked container to steal jewelry is, and armed robbery on an out-of-town highway is a similarly serious offense.

The penalty for drinking alcohol is flogging, and the offense is fairly easy to prove (if someone is drunk, they have presumably been drinking). The penalty for apostasy is execution, so long as the apostasy is public and is not followed by repentance. Thus a Muslim who announces conversion to Christianity and refuses to recant will be executed, but a Muslim who becomes an atheist and does not tell anyone will not be punished, nor will a Muslim who publicly denies the divine origin of the Koran but then later admits that this was a mistake. Like executions for adultery, executions for apostasy have always been few and far between.

The Sharia is in practice often mixed with customary law—what an American lawyer might call "common law." Customary law has no theoretical standing at all under the Sharia, except in areas where the Sharia is silent—for example concerning penalties for failing to share in the maintenance work for a local communal irrigation system. Despite this, it was and in many areas still is applied. Customary tribal systems of retribution are harsh, often creating conflicts that tend to escalate. If an underaged child accidentally shoots someone else in the foot, the child's parents might be obliged by the Sharia to pay for medical treatment. Tribal custom might require that the child's father is shot, in which case the child's uncle is obliged to shoot the person who shot his brother. A vendetta then escalates. Traditional Yemeni houses, which are tall and well built, look very nice—but in fact are built like fortresses, with no windows on the ground floor, as a result of the prevalence of such vendettas.

Customary laws also provide penalties for extramarital sex, or anything approaching it, that are far harsher than those of the Sharia. In many parts of the Muslim world, especially in poorer and more remote areas, any woman caught in even mildly compromising circumstances, without the Sharia's exacting definitions and difficult standards of proof being satisfied, will be killed, often by her father or brother. Her presumed lover may also be killed by her relatives, but that is less important. Such societies have a strong concept of what is called "honor" that is accepted by all, in which honor depends principally on the chastity of unmarried females. When a woman has stained her entire family's honor by the appearance or reality of unchastity, there is only one way for that honor to be restored for the benefit of all: the death of the woman in question.

It can be argued that Islam views such honor killings as murder pure and simple, but the societies in which this concept of honor is entrenched generally regard such killings as required by religion, even though there is no justification for this view in any of the Ulema's interpretations of the Sharia. Even where such killings are regarded as murder by the Sharia and by national law, the local authorities may turn a blind eye to them.

These customary-law penalties have no more sanction in the Sharia than do speeding tickets, but are still regarded by many less educated traditional Muslims in rural areas as being somehow "Islamic." The logic is that the customs and traditions of Muslims are by definition Islamic. This logic may be quite false, but that usually makes little difference in practice.

The Sharia rules for court procedure are quite different from modern Western ones. Firstly, the "adversarial" system common in the West is unknown, and lawyers are not used (in fact, recourse to a lawyer is strictly speaking a form of corruption). Witnesses are under oath to tell the truth, and may be questioned by the judge, but are not cross-examined. The main test of a witness's veracity is character. A righteous adult man is assumed to be telling the truth; a man who is a reprobate is assumed to be lying. A man of dubious character is less reliable than a righteous man, as is a woman, even if righteous. Non-Muslims are assumed not to be righteous. A witness who has a personal stake in the outcome of a case or is known to be absent-minded will not be accepted, whatever their character. These procedural rules are little followed today, and would hardly work in a large city where people do not know each other. They might still work in a village.

The rules of procedure of customary law systems vary widely, and are generally even further from modern Western procedures. In the Arab world, for example, they still include "trial by ordeal" (unknown in the West since the Middle Ages, during which it was common everywhere in Europe). The accused swears that he or she is innocent of the crime he or she is accused of, and then places his or her tongue on red-hot metal. If the tongue burns, the accused has lied, is guilty, and may be executed. If not, the accused is acquitted. I myself have never seen a trial by ordeal, but a friend of mine has a servant who was once acquitted of murder after such a trial by ordeal. I have never dared to ask him about it.

There is probably nowhere in the world where the Sharia rules on crime and punishment are fully implemented today. Even in countries such as the Sudan or Saudi Arabia which claim to apply the Sharia, modern Western rules of court procedure and punishment have often been adopted—what usually remains is the more savage and exemplary punishments. In remote areas where state laws are not enforced, mixed Sharia and customary legal systems are the rule.

Outside such areas, the main impact of the Sharia's criminal law on most Muslims today is a conviction that crime should be punished in a way that provides effective retribution—but many Westerners are convinced of that also. Only those modern Muslims who favor the re-establishment of the Sharia as state law (a political stance I will discuss in chapter 11) are committed to reintroducing the system in full.

Violence

The Sharia provides for violent corporal punishment for criminals, and permits violence within the family: the beating of wives by husbands, and of children by those in authority over them. By contemporary Western standards, the Sharia is undoubtedly violent—though not by earlier Western standards. As we saw, Western criminal justice systems also used savage and exemplary penalties until after 1800, and British husbands (for example) were allowed to beat disobedient wives until 1891. The beating of children is currently illegal in some Western countries, and allowed in others.

Although few Muslims see any objection in principle to corporal punishment, regarding it as appropriate for children, wives, and suspects in police stations, most Muslims object to excessive violence in practice. A parent or teacher who is known to beat children mercilessly or without cause will be admonished, as will a husband who routinely beats his wife excessively or for no apparent reason. In the most extreme cases, the police may even get involved. Similarly, while the application of a little physical pressure to a suspect in a police station raises few eyebrows, severe torture is nowhere approved of. That police forces in nearly all Muslim countries use torture routinely is not the result of Islam, but of the absence of effective controls over police behavior, and also of the lack of the training and technical resources that the police would need to make effective use of more sophisticated methods of investigation. Torture in Muslim countries is probably no worse than in most other poor countries. Torture, of course, is practiced from time to time by Western states as well.

At an individual level, most Muslims today are probably less violent than Westerners were in 1800 or even 1850. Since there is little in Islam that actually condemns nonviolence so long as justice is also achieved, there is no reason in theory why a culture of nonviolence at a personal level might one day emerge in the Muslim world just as it did in the West during the nineteenth century. The rejection of slavery has become as general in the Muslim world as in the West, despite the absence of any condemnation of slavery in the Sharia. Although there is nothing in the Koran about turning the other cheek, there is a lot about the virtue of mercy.

There are movements for the promotion of nonviolence, usually defined as the prevention of domestic violence and human rights abuses, in various parts of the Muslim world, but the members of these movements are generally liberal Muslims motivated by values they have absorbed from the West. They rarely attract much popular support, partly because they do not express their messages in Islamic terms that make sense to the rest of the population. They are suspect partly because they seem so Western (and so alien), and partly because they often advocate causes with which there is no public sympathy, such as gay rights.

Summary

The worldwide community of Muslims is important in theory, but in practice other loyalties—to tribe or nation—take precedence, save sometimes in the West. The local community matters more. Except in the West, where the mosque has come to operate rather like a church, the local community is based not around mosques but around villages and urban neighborhoods. The responsibility for encouraging good and religious behavior lies not with Imams, but with all members of that local community.

Intoxicants, gambling, and homosexuality are all forbidden by Islam, but are present in Muslim societies and are to some extent tolerated. Less devout Muslims sometimes drink alcohol, or smoke marijuana; other narcotics are generally regarded exactly as in the West. Gambling is on the whole restricted to five-star hotels (though permitted in Iran), as is social drinking. Homosexuality is nowhere considered a valid lifestyle choice, but is sometimes seen as an understandable vice.

In the absence of any widespread movement advocating nonviolence, most Muslims see no objection in principle to corporal punishment, whether of children, wives or criminals. In practice, excessive violence is objected to, and the criminal justice systems of most Muslim countries are based around laws very similar to those in force in the West, and use prisons in the normal Western fashion.

9

Good Muslims, Bad Muslims

Ethics

"My father was a very good Muslim," said my friend Abdul-Karim, with real bitterness in his voice. "He always prayed, and gave lots of money to the poor. So much, in fact, that my mother, sister, and I were always short of money. And although he loved all the Muslims with all his heart, my mother, sister, and I never saw much love."

The relationship between religiosity and goodness is a complicated one, in Islam as in all other religions. Many people are alienated from religion for the reasons that Abdul-Karim was—by the example of someone who, while apparently very religious, never seemed like a truly good person to those closest to them. Of course, Abdul-Karim's father might have been an even less kind human being if he had not been religious. Or perhaps if he had not been religious, he would have been less sure of his own righteousness, and more inclined to address the shortcomings that were so obvious to his children.

Islam does concern itself with goodness as well as religiosity. The Sharia emphasizes worship and rules for daily living, in the family and in the community, but it also deals with more general questions, which might in the West be called "ethics." The Islamic concept of ethics is somewhat narrower than the Western one, since issues that can be dealt with by means of precise rules generally are regulated by those rules. That is one reason why this book's chapter on ethics is my shortest one.

The Sharia, however, does not attempt to regulate everything. Ethical virtues and vices are hard to prove in court, and so they often have to be left up to the individual. That is the other reason why this is such a short chapter: because ethics are so individual, relatively little can usefully be said about the ethical or unethical behavior of Muslims in practice.

Ethics are dealt with in many collections of *hadith*, and in Friday sermons, as is intention. Throughout the Sharia, much emphasis is placed on intention. Like Western criminal law, the Sharia generally does not consider an act a crime if it was not intended, if it was accidental. The Sharia then goes further: the intention to perform an act of worship is an integral part of that act. If I just happen not to eat or drink all day, I have not been fasting. If I just give away some money without thinking, it does not count as part of my obligatory alms (*zakat*), though it would count as voluntary alms (*sadaqa*). Not only is the appropriate intention required for an act to count, but in many ways the intention is more important than the act. If I intend to give *zakat* or *sadaqa* to someone I think is a deserving beggar but is in fact a swindler, that is not my problem, but rather the swindler's problem. It is said that "we will be judged on our intentions"—interestingly, the opposite of the English proverb, "the road to hell is paved with good intentions."

In fact, these two sayings are not incompatible. That we will be judged by our intentions does not mean that we need not give any thought to the likely consequences of our actions. There is a well-known cautionary tale in Iran of a bear that, intending to swat a mosquito on her friend's nose, actually broke her friend's nose. This tale makes almost the same point as the English proverb: consequences matter.

All Muslims are conscious of the importance of intentions (and some of the least devout even feel that good intentions somehow compensate for lack of observance in other areas). This focus on intention shifts the emphasis from the visible (worship and rules) to the invisible (spirituality). Sufis and similar traditional Muslims are even more conscious of intentions than others.

Slander and Hypocrisy

Islam is concerned not just with the individual, but also with society. This concern is visible in the Sharia, which sets rules not only for private life but also for public behavior. It is also visible in a general rule of Islam that the only thing worse than doing wrong is to also *advertise* doing wrong. To drink alcohol is wrong; to drink alcohol in public is doubly wrong. To tell everyone that someone else is drinking alcohol is also wrong, since, in a different way, this too is advertising the drinking of alcohol.

To tell a drinker of alcohol that he or she should not be drinking is not only right, but a duty—the duty of virtue promotion and vice prevention, as discussed in chapter 8. The fact that one sometimes drinks alcohol oneself does not relieve one of performing such duties. Thus a secret drinker who admonishes other drinkers is preferable to an open drinker who does not admonish others. Western norms (and some individual Muslims) would condemn the secret drinker who admonished others as the worst sort of hypocrite; Islam, at least in principle, condemns the secret drinker's drinking, but approves the admonition.

Islam, then, condemns slander—"slander" being defined not just as harmful statements about someone that are false, but as statements that have no good reason to be spread, whether they are false or true. A number of well-known *hadith* condemn gossip of all sorts. This is partly for the protection of individuals who might be slandered, partly for the protection of the general public atmosphere, and partly because slandering and gossiping are wrong in themselves, and damage those who practice them.

Very devout Muslims will scrupulously observe these rules, saying nothing about someone unless it is good, unless there is some pressing reason to do otherwise. If a known swindler is about to deceive you, a devout Muslim will not stand by. First he or she will quietly reprove the swindler if he or she can, and then he or she will warn you against the swindler. But in general a devout Muslim will say little to condemn others, though silence from such a person is its own form of condemnation.

Among ordinary Muslims, these rules are less carefully observed. Gossip is common, and wrong is sometimes allowed to happen. The principle of speaking only good of people may, in the hands of the less devout, become no more than a tendency toward empty platitudes of praise.

One consequence of these rules on slander and gossip is that in many Muslim societies there is a deep reluctance to discuss general social problems. Evils that everyone knows exist are publicly denied, not only to outsiders but also within Muslim societies. In many countries, everyone will assert—quite against the facts—that there is no problem of AIDS or prostitution. This not only skews perceptions, but also often means that action is not taken to address problems. Unless it is admitted that a problem exists, there is no need to do anything about it.

There is a positive side to what a Muslim would call discretion and what a Westerner might call hypocrisy. Since moral standards often appear to be higher than they actually are, people are encouraged to live up to higher standards than they might otherwise. The logic goes: if everyone else seems to be praying, I will be more inclined to pray myself; if everyone else seems to be fornicating, I and my potential partner may be more inclined to fornicate.

What a Muslim calls hypocrisy (*nifaq*) is closer to the English concept of "deception." *Nifaq* is pretending to be a devout Muslim in order to win praise and respect, while actually being quite a different sort of person. The dangerous consequences of praise and respect are well known, especially among Sufis. One group of Sufis, the Malamatis of tenth-century Iran, went so far as to deliberately attract blame in order to avoid this danger, by publicly breaking certain individual rules of the Sharia (while respecting all the others). There are obvious dangers to this approach, and it is also an offense against the basic principle of preserving a public atmosphere of conformity with the Sharia. Most importantly, it is against the even more fundamental principle that one does not pick and choose among Sharia rules, but follows them all. The unusual approach of the Malamatis was thus heavily criticized by other devout Muslims, and the Malamatis no longer exist.

Virtues and Vices

Virtues and vices tend to be the opposite of each other, as is well illustrated in the Catholic list of the seven "capital" virtues and vices, where each virtue is paired with a "deadly sin"—the virtue of humility is paired with the vice of pride, for example.

There are no definitive short lists of virtues and vices in Islam, but what are considered to be the major virtues and vices can be identified by looking at the space given to them in books and the time given to them by preachers. The greatest area of agreement between Islam and Christianity is over vices. All save one of the Catholic "deadly sins" are regarded as major vices in Islam, and both religions place most emphasis on pride. There is less agreement, however, over virtues.

Islam condemns two varieties of pride: pride in relation to God, which negates many of the principle religious virtues, and pride in relation to other humans. A distinction is made between the feeling of pride and its expression, with the feeling being the more problematic, but the expression being the more obvious. Pride may be expressed in different ways, notably in one's dress and in one's behavior toward others. This, it is suggested, is why the Sharia prohibits elaborate and showy dress for men (gold, silk, and the like),[1] and is one of the reasons why the Sharia requires women to hide their beauty (since it is generally women who take pride in their beauty). This is also why it is not a good sign if one likes to be followed around by a retinue, or if one does not treat the less fortunate as one's equals.

The emphasis on the evils of pride are one of the reasons why a deep strain of egalitarianism is to be found in many Muslim societies (another reason, having nothing to do with Islam, is the "flat" social structure of the nomadic Arab tribe). This strain of egalitarianism, however, is often combined with a sense of hierarchy that is not found in modern Western societies, partly because modern Western societies are actually fairly equal. They may not look equal from within, since there are obviously rich and powerful people, and poor and disadvantaged people. However, in comparison to most Muslim societies or even to Western societies of a few centuries ago, the differences between rich (though perhaps not a few super-rich) and poor (though not the destitute) are minor. Rich and poor in a modern Western society enjoy much the same rights under the law in practice as well as in theory, wear much the same clothes, and eat much the same food. This is not the case in most Muslim societies, though one day—with economic development—it might become the case. At present, the gulf between the lives of rich and poor in most Muslim countries is immense. At a material level, the lives of the rich are much the same as the lives of well-off Westerners; while the lives of the very poor have advanced little in a thousand years. That is perhaps one reason why it is considered so important for the rich to treat the poor as equals: because they are not equals. In practice, not all rich and powerful Muslims treat the poor with respect, but more devout Muslims do, and poor Muslims value this treatment.

---

[1] Since gold and silk are allowed for women, it is also argued that the prohibition is a prohibition of effeminacy.

After pride comes greed, of which there are three main varieties: greed for money, greed for food, and greed for the opposite sex. These match with three of Christianity's deadly sins: avarice, gluttony, and lust. Greed is regarded as one of the main ways in which Satan enters the human heart, releases the ego, and transforms the human into an animal. The Sharia is an antidote to greed: obligatory alms act against avarice, fasting acts against gluttony, and segregation of the sexes acts against lust. Obviously, there are avaricious, gluttonous, and lustful Muslims, just as there are avaricious, gluttonous, and lustful non-Muslims—but perhaps there are fewer of them in traditional Muslim societies than in modern Western cities. Lack of ambition in the modern West is a failing; in the Muslim world, it is still widely perceived as the absence of avarice, and so as a virtue.

Total abstention from the good things in life (including money, food, and love) is not required, however. The practice of the Christian monastery is specifically condemned, and the closest Islam comes to anything like it is the "retreat" (khalwa) of some Sufis. This hardly ever happens nowadays, and was always a rare occurrence. It generally lasted a maximum of 40 days, and was usually done once in a lifetime. The Sufi performing a "retreat" came from the world and returned to it. Most importantly, as we saw in chapter 6, marriage is a duty for any Muslim—not just socially but religiously: one learns all sorts of virtues from living with and looking after a spouse and children.

The last major vice in Islam is anger, the Christian deadly sin of wrath. Anger is again emphasized as a way in which Satan can enter the human heart, and is frequently compared to fire. The main problem with anger is that it is a form of intoxication: an angry person is not in control of themselves, but has rather surrendered to their ego. An angry person commits evil that he or she would otherwise avoid. There is no sympathy at all in Islam for the contemporary Western view that it is good to "let it out." "Letting it out" is surrendering to Satan.

Two of the Christian deadly sins are treated differently in Islam: envy and sloth. For Muslims, envy is not so much a vice as a destructive force (as we learned in chapter 4). Envying someone or something is an attack on that person or thing, and is condemned more as an attack than as a vice. Sloth, however, is little emphasized in Islam, as a vice or in any other way.

The Sharia requires Muslims to fulfill their duties to others, including their spouses and children, but views this more as contractual than moral. Christians often emphasize sloth as a way in which Satan can enter the human heart, but Muslims do not. To many Westerners, some Muslims may just seem plain lazy. To many Muslims, Western industriousness sometimes seems to be a mixture of avarice and the wasting of the time and energy that is necessary to enjoy and appreciate life, let alone to achieve anything spiritual. Some Westerners would not entirely disagree about the downside of Western industriousness, and some Muslims would not entirely disagree about the downside of the more relaxed approach common in the Muslim world. Of course, it is always possible that the reason a Muslim is doing nothing is simply that he has nothing to do—that he is unemployed.

The opposite of a vice is generally a virtue, in Islam as in Christianity, though Islam does not have an explicit list of "contrary" virtues as Christianity does. In addition to these, there are a number of other virtues that are much emphasized by Islam, and these differ in interesting ways from Christian. Tellingly, there is often no exact English translation of the Arabic word used to denote the virtue in question.

First among the virtues in Islam is *tawba*, which is close in meaning to "repentance," but is more practical and also carries the sense of turning toward God. All humans do wrong; the best of those who do wrong are those who do *tawba*. *Tawba* is more practical than repentance in the sense that its emotional aspect is less emphasized than in Christianity: what is required is not deep sorrow and self-criticism, but recognition that an act was wrong, and firm determination not to repeat it. As a rule of thumb, if a wrong act is repeated, *tawba* was insufficient, and if it is not repeated, *tawba* was sufficient. *Tawba* that does not involve a real determination not to repeat a wrong act is not real *tawba*. A guilty conscience is of no value in itself. As a result, Muslims and Muslim societies tend to value feelings of guilt and the admission of guilt less than Westerners generally do.

The second greatest virtue in Islam is *sabr*, a concept that mixes acceptance of God's will with patience and endurance. Since misfortune comes from God as everything else does, it must be accepted. In fact, misfortune should even be welcomed as a form of divine favor, since if it is endured with patience, the sufferer will after death receive a reward from God that is greater than the suffering on earth. To react to misfortune with anger is a form of anger against God, which must of course be avoided at all costs.

This does not mean that misfortune should be welcomed for any other reason, or that a Muslim should not take practical steps to avoid it, including prayer. Endurance of one's own misfortune is also different from endurance of another's: compassion is a virtue, though if someone else's suffering seems too great, it may be necessary to remind them of the importance of *sabr*.

Sabr is often a cause of misunderstanding between Westerners and Muslims. If a devout Muslim's car has broken down, the Muslim may react with *sabr*: it is the will of God and must be accepted as such. Hearing this, a Western passenger may be tempted to reply that it isn't the will of God, but rather the absence of proper maintenance of the engine, and that if the Muslim had checked the oil level before setting out instead of relying on God, the engine would still be running fine and he—and the Muslim— would not be sitting by the side of the road. In fact, the Muslim is not disputing that it would have been a good idea to check the oil level, and may even learn from experience and check it next time, but the immediate issue is how to react now that the engine has broken down. The Westerner's anger and irritation will seem to the Muslim to suggest a lack of piety, an almost childish lack of self-control, rather than a practical approach to motor maintenance.

In practice, most Muslims suffer from misfortune as much as anyone else, and a different Muslim driver may react by kicking a broken-down car in frustration. Public displays of anger or anguish are sympathized with rather less in Muslim societies, however, and self-restraint is the norm. If a Westerner who has just missed a connecting flight because of a delay feels justified in venting anger on the airline and the weather, most Westerners will sympathize; fewer Muslims will see the venting of anger as justified, though they may be as sympathetic regarding the missed connection.

The third major individual virtue in Islam is honesty and sincerity—in Arabic, *sidq*. *Sidq* is the opposite of lying and deceit, whether to others or to oneself. Devout Muslims ensure that all their acts and intentions, statements and motives, are straight and pure. Less devout Muslims are aware of the need for this, though less observant in practice, and may stress the intention rather more than the actual utterance. Devout Muslims will not lie unless for very good reason, but less devout Muslims sometimes value what they see as the underlying truth more than the actual form of words used to express it. The statement that AIDS does not exist in the Muslim world is, from one point of view, a lie; from another point of view, it is a confirmation that AIDS should not exist in the Muslim world, that Islam properly observed would certainly prevent its spread, and that the varieties of sexual behavior that spread AIDS are condemned by Islam.

The extent to which *sidq* is observed varies a lot from one Muslim country to another. In some areas, Muslims are famed for their straightforwardness, while in other areas straightforwardness is notable by its absence, and deceit seems to be a way of life. In such areas, the devout are less deceitful than the local norm, but are still not often exactly straightforward by Western standards. Quite how this particular virtue has come to be implemented so unevenly is a mystery.

The fourth major individual virtue is *taqwa*, respect for God bolstered by fear of God, resulting in piety. God is above all else merciful, but it is still proper and necessary to be aware that punishment does exist. We should act for God, but also out of fear of his displeasure. The story is told of a great saint who, on passing a blacksmith's and seeing the fire in his forge, fainted out of fear of hell. *Taqwa* is, among other things, the opposite of complacency.

These four major individual virtues have little in common with Christianity's "heavenly" virtues of faith, hope, and charity, fortitude, justice, temperance, and prudence. Faith in Islam is not so much a virtue, as what makes one a Muslim in the first place; as such, it is of course much emphasized. Nearly all Muslims are familiar with a three-fold division of faith into stages. The first and essential stage is acceptance of the central aspects of the Muslim worldview, discussed in chapter 4—that "There is no god but God, [and] Muhammad is the Prophet of God." This is what distinguishes the Muslim from the non-Muslim, and is the first step, since it is what leads to the Muslim following the requirements of the Sharia. The second step is a very real, deeply held belief (*iman*) in this, and the third step is excellence (*ihsan*), which could be defined as the full practicing of the four major individual virtues discussed above. Faith matters, then, and perhaps matters above all else, but is not treated as an ethical virtue.

The Christian virtue of hope, in the sense of "desire for the kingdom of heaven, and trust in Christ's promises," is less emphasized in Islam. There is an equivalent virtue, *tawakkul,* which is essentially trust in God. It is definitely in the second league in Islam, however, rather than in the first league as it is in Christianity. *Taqwa* in some senses stands in its place.

The Christian virtue of charity, in the Catholic sense of "love for God above all things for His own sake, and of our neighbor as ourselves for the love of God," is present in Islam, but expressed rather differently. There is an element of love of God in *taqwa,* but in general it is not so much love of God that is emphasized as love of His Prophet. The love of the Prophet is especially emphasized by Sufis and by many traditional Muslims, though less so by Wahhabis and modern Muslims, who see certain forms of love of the Prophet as close to idolatry. For those Muslims who do emphasize love of the Prophet, that love is not so much a virtue as a blessing—a means to an end. Love of one's neighbor takes the form of love of one's fellow Muslim, but it is less the love that is emphasized than the consequences of that love. One famous list of virtues starts off with faith in God, and ends up with removing a stone from the middle of a path in case another Muslim might trip over it. Such an action is a form of *sadaqa,* voluntary charity. *Sadaqa* may take the form of a gift of money or of time and effort, or of both. Preparing the "Table of the Merciful" at which the poor may eat for free during Ramadan (see chapter 4) is *sadaqa,* involving the gift of time, effort, and money. Such altruistic acts are sometimes called acts "in the cause of God."

Summary

Islam and the West differ on their understanding of hypocrisy, with Islam being more interested in the consequences for society, and the West being more interested in the interior state. Islam and Christianity, however, more or less agree on their definitions of vices, and agree that the contrary of a vice is a virtue. Islam recognizes virtues that Christianity does not emphasize in exactly the same terms: repentance as *tawba* in the sense of turning away from evil, steadfastness as *sabr* in the sense acceptance of God's will with patience and endurance, sincerity as *sidq* and respect for God as *taqwa.*

10

More Moors

Other Denominations

"He wasn't quite sure whether the Sunnis were the good ones and the Shi'a the bad ones, or whether it was the other way round!" marveled a colleague of mine, reporting on dinner with the ambassador of a small Western country that shall remain nameless in an Arab city that shall also remain nameless. That ambassador was not alone in his confusion. Even Winston Churchill, whose decisions had more impact on the shape of today's Muslim world than the nameless ambassador's, on occasion got Sunnis and Shi'is mixed up.

For some purposes, Sunnis and Shi'is are just "Muslims"; for other purposes, the difference between them matters a lot—for example when they go to war with each other. And there are other denominations of Islam, too—not just the Wahhabis, whom we have already met on several occasions, but groups whom outsiders see as Muslim, but whom most Muslims do not see as Muslim.

So far, I have dealt mostly with the Islam of Sunni Muslims, pointing out from time to time where this differs from the Islam of Shi'i Muslims (a separate denomination), and from the Islam of Wahhabi Muslims (a distinct group that is almost a separate denomination, or perhaps a separate *mazhab*). This chapter goes back to these groups to explain how they split off from the Sunni majority, and then goes on to discuss the other denominations of Islam. Some can properly be described as denominations; some may only be sects; and some are probably separate religions with Islamic origins.

Shi'ism

The earliest, most important, and longest lasting split in Islam was between Sunni and Shi'i, each of which considers the other to have deviated from the Islam of the Prophet. The origin of this split was more political than religious.

The Prophet was central to the early history of Islam, so after his death in 632 things began to fall apart. Competition broke out between the three main groups within the community: the Prophet's earliest followers and closest associates, the people of Medina, and the Meccans. A related dispute was over who should lead the community, which was then just beginning to extend beyond western Arabia: No one could fully take the Prophet's place, but someone was needed to exercise leadership. Some maintained that the Prophet had indicated that he wanted his son-in-law, Ali, to succeed him, as both the political and the religious leader of the Muslims—not as a new prophet, but as a continuation of the Prophet's religious mission. Most disagreed, and chose another of the Prophet's closest associates, Abu Bakr, as a primarily political leader.

Abu Bakr thus became the first successor of the Prophet—the Arabic word for "successor," *khalifa*, giving rise to the English title of Caliph. He led the Muslims for only two years, and was followed by Omar, who was disliked by the Meccans for appearing to favor the people of Medina. When Omar died after ten years as Caliph, he was succeeded by Osman, a Meccan of the Umayyad tribe, who was thought to favor the Meccans and his own relatives too much, and was murdered after twelve years as Caliph. None of these caliphs were recognized by the followers of Ali, who became known as the "party" or *shi'a* of Ali.

After the murder of Osman, Ali then took over as Caliph, as his followers maintained he should have done in the first place, but the political turbulence proved too much for him. Mu'awiya, a cousin of Ali's predecessor Osman, rebelled, and after five years of maneuvering and of occasional battles, Ali too was murdered. Mu'awiya then took over, establishing a more or less regular political dynasty, called the Umayyad dynasty after his tribe. This dynasty was the first to govern the Arab Muslim empire, which stretched from Central Asia to the Atlantic. Most Muslims accepted the Umayyad dynasty, but the *shi'a* of Ali did not.

From time to time, the Shi'a rebelled against what they saw as the illegitimate Umayyad dynasty. During one of these rebellions, Ali's son Husayn, the grandson of the Prophet, was killed at Karbala in Iraq, an event that the Shi'a never forgot. Husayn's death was a form of redemption, a voluntary sacrifice to rescue the Muslims from the deviation that had been brought about by the rejection of the continuation of Prophet's religious mission, and because of the denial that human reason could comprehend this mission. While Sunni Muslims stress revelation as the sole source of Islam, the Shi'a also stress that the Prophet's religious mission was continued by Ali and the other Imams, not in the sense that they brought a new revelation that replaced the original one, but in the sense that their explanations of the original revelation were "protected from error" by God. This is why the Shi'a refer to the Imams as "infallible." The Shi'a also stress that human reason has the ability to distinguish the most fundamental principles of justice independent of revelation. In Shi'i terms, God is just because He does what is just, in contrast to the Sunni position that what God does is by defi- nition just because He does it.

For Sunnis, the death of Husayn at Karbala has little significance. For the Shi'a, it is almost as significant as the crucifixion is for Christians. The small clay tablet that Shi'is place on the ground in front of them before performing the *sala* often contains a minuscule but very significant element of earth from Karbala. Husayn died on the tenth day of the month of Muharram, a day called Ashura, which is fasted by some Sunni Muslims for quite different reasons. For the Shi'a, Ashura is the climax of a series of commemorative rituals. Sermons are preached remembering the events leading up to Husayn's death, emphasizing Husayn's goodness and the voluntary nature of the sacrifice he made for God, truth and justice, and the villainy of his persecutors and murderers. These sermons go into great and sentimental detail—any parent's heart will react to the sweet little granddaughter who says to Husayn "please, can we go home now?" as the bloody climax approaches. "It won't be long now," replies Husayn, as he ruffles her curly hair, knowing full well what fate awaits them all. It is not only acceptable to cry in response to these sermons, but expected. Every worshiper takes along a handkerchief.

In addition to these commemorative sermons, there are also passion plays, performed over several days, portraying the same story in much the same way. These plays have definite artistic elements, but are religious rather than artistic events. The audience goes not to admire the performance of an actor or the cleverness of the symbolism, but to share in the suffering, to weep for the holy martyr.

A third variety of Ashura commemoration is somewhat controversial, and allows the participant to share not just in the emotional suffering, but also in the physical suffering of the martyrs. Mourners, usually in groups and often in procession, beat themselves with whips or chains, often drawing blood on their bare backs. To many contemporary observers, usually Western or Sunni but sometimes also Shi'i, these ceremonies are disturbing and distasteful, and several attempts have been made over the last 100 years to suppress them, both by rulers and by the Shi'i Ulema. Despite everything, however, they survive among Shi'is everywhere, and for their participants they are an important expression and strengthening of faith.

As well as having an important variety of worship unknown to Sunnis (the mourning of Husayn at Ashura), the Shia'a also have a community institution unknown to Sunni Islam, the *marja taqlid* or "model for emulation." The Shi'a believe that the last of the Imams vanished in 873, and will reappear as the Mahdi at the start of the final days before Judgment. In the absence of the Imams, they hold that every Muslim (in practice, of course, every Shi'i Muslim, since other Muslims ignore all of this) should select the most outstanding living member of the Ulema as their personal guide. This will be their *marja taqlid*. These Shi'i "models" are not Imams, and are not infallible, but have far greater authority than any Sunni does over other Sunni Muslims. Sometimes there is only one "model," acknowledged by all Shi'a as *the* outstanding member of the Ulema; at other times, such as at the present, there are up to a dozen alternative "models" to choose from. These "models" have an authority similar to that of the pope in Christianity. There is no formal procedure for deciding who they are; they just "emerge" as a result of the accumulated recognition of other members of the Ulema. Ayatollah Sistani in Iraq is a "model," but not all who bear the title "Ayatollah" are "models." It is a little known fact that while Ayatollah Khomeini was such a "model," his successor Ayatollah Khameini is not—and the attempts of his followers to persuade the Ulema to recognize him as a "model" have failed. This is one reason why the leadership of Khameini is challenged far more often than that of Khomeini was.

Wahhabism

As we have seen, the single most important variation within Sunni Islam to-day is what we have called "Wahhabism." Although this is how outsiders re-fer to the movement, its followers prefer other terms such as *muwahidun* (unitarians), or just plain "Muslims."

Wahhabism started more than 250 years ago as a small and very radical religious movement. In the 1730s, Muhammad ibn Abd al-Wahhab, a mi-nor member of the Ulema in the Najd (the sparsely populated interior of the Arabian peninsula), decided that the Islam of those around him was mostly *bida* (illegitimate innovation). It is hard to say to what extent he was right—there are no independent accounts of what was happening in the Najd at that time. Certainly, many of the inhabitants were nomads, and the nomadic lifestyle is one that makes any sort of learning or culture difficult. The Arab nomads of the time were regarded everywhere as being unusually ignorant and superstitious, as well as a threat to public order. On the other hand, many of the things that Ibn Abd al-Wahhab and his followers con-demned as *bida* were then regarded by all other Muslims as perfectly nor-mal—for example, using a string of beads to count certain prayers, or even listening to music.

Ibn Abd al-Wahhab favored the most literal possible interpretation of the Koran and *hadith*. In about 1740, he launched his mission by arranging for a woman who had committed adultery to be stoned to death. No one could dispute that stoning was the penalty prescribed for adultery in the Sharia, but it was a penalty that was hardly ever enforced, and the stoning generated considerable shock. Shock was also generated by Ibn Abd al-Wahhab's view that those who did not follow him in his narrow and literal understanding of Islam were not real Muslims. This had important implications, since the Sharia protects only Muslims and those under Muslim protection. The im-plication, then, was that the Wahhabis could legitimately kill other Muslims (people who regarded themselves as Muslims, even if the Wahhabis did not regard them as such) and help themselves to their property.

This is exactly what happened, though mostly after Ibn Abd al-Wahhab's death, in the early nineteenth century. The Wahhabis formed an alliance with an ambitious tribal chief, Muhammad ibn Saud, whose forces launched a series of raids and conquests in the name of "pure" (i.e. Wahhabi) Islam. They started off by attacking nearby Shi'i cities and plundering them, and ended up moving on to the western side of the Arabian peninsula and conquering Mecca and Medina. It is impossible to say to what extent they were genuinely motivated by Ibn Abd al-Wahhab's vision of pure Islam, and to what extent they were motivated by desire for plunder. Arab nomads have always fought and raided, and an additional justification for this behavior may have been very welcome.

The Saudi-Wahhabi conquests led to considerable loss of life and property. Once in control of Mecca and Medina, the Wahhabis proceeded to implement their views there. They held, for example, that domes were *bida*, so all domes were destroyed — including the one over the tomb of the Prophet Muhammad himself. For the rest of the Muslim world, these acts were intolerable. The Ottoman Sultan assembled an army in Egypt to rescue Mecca and Medina from the Wahhabis. The Wahhabis were defeated between 1812 and 1818, and before withdrawing in 1840, the Ottoman-Egyptian army attempted to extirpate Wahhabism for ever, destroying the Wahhabi base in the Najd and exiling key members of the Wahhabi Ulema and of the Saudi family.

What the defeat and persecution of Wahhabism achieved, however, was not the destruction of Wahhabism, but its transformation into something rather more moderate. Sixty years later, when the Saudi-Wahhabi alliance started on a second conquest of Arabia, the Wahhabi Ulema were prepared to concede that non-Wahhabis might be Muslims, if deluded ones. Also, the Saudi leadership was careful to avoid a repetition of the killing, plundering, and destruction that had marked the first, brief, conquest of Arabia. The more enthusiastic soldiers were camped outside the towns and cities that were conquered, and not allowed to enter them, for fear of a repeat of the bloodshed and plunder had marred the first Wahhabi conquest.

This time, the Saudi-Wahhabi conquest was more successful. There was no need to worry about the Ottomans, since the Ottoman empire had been destroyed in the First World War, and the Saudi leadership was careful to maintain good relations with the new power that mattered, Great Britain — a power that, unlike the Ottomans, did not have views on what constituted "pure" Islam. After making himself Sultan of Najd, his home region, the Saudi leader first conquered the Kingdom of the Hijaz (the western part of Arabia that contained Mecca and Medina) and then annexed the adjoining Emirate of Asir. These three realms were combined, in 1932, into the Kingdom of Saudi Arabia.

At first, Wahhabism was established only in Saudi Arabia. Teaching of any other version of Islam was banned there, and the Wahhabi Ulema, with the support of the Saudi leadership, transformed the country they had created into an "Islamic" state on Wahhabi lines. They strictly enforced the letter of their literalist understanding of the Sharia and of public morality in general, partly through the Virtue Promotion and Vice Prevention Committee (the people whose operatives in a story from chapter 3 chased an Arab Christian into a mosque at prayer time). Wahhabism acquired some following in the neighboring areas to the east of Saudi Arabia that later became the United Arab Emirates, but Muslims elsewhere remained generally hostile to the new form of Islam. Traditional Muslims condemned Wahhabism for much the same reasons they had at the time of the first (short-lived) Saudi-Wahhabi conquest—that it was violent and intolerant, and that its understandings of Islam were simplistic when not just plain wrong. Some modern Muslims, however, admired Wahhabism, partly because it seemed an ally in their own fight against what they saw as superstition, and partly for political reasons. Here, thought some, is a strong movement of renewal . . . just what the Muslim world needs.

The Wahhabi movement was a reform movement, just like the various movements that produced "modern" Islam, discussed in chapter 3, which this book contrasts with "traditional" Islam. At first, Wahhabism was a very different type of reform movement, however. Modern Islam came into existence in major cities such as Cairo, as a result of the Muslim world's encounter with the West and with modernity. Wahhabism had nothing to do with the West or modernity, since neither the West nor modernity had had any impact on the Najd at the time the Wahhabi movement started. The Cairo movement (as I will call it) objected to traditional Islam because it seemed to contain much that was superstitious and abhorrent to reason. The Wahhabi movement also objected to traditional Islam because it seemed to contain much that was superstitious, but not on the grounds that it was abhorrent to reason. For the Wahhabis, the problem was that it was abhorrent to their understanding of the original revelation. The Cairo movement wanted to purge Islam of much that was irrelevant or obstructive to life in the modern (or at least the nineteenth-century) world; the Wahhabi movement had no knowledge of, or interest in, the "modern" world.

In the period since the end of the Second World War, Wahhabi views have been spreading across the Sunni Muslim world, for three main reasons. Firstly, the literalism of the Wahhabi movement combines comfortably with some aspects of the Cairo movement, of modern Islam. Secondly, Saudi control of Mecca and Medina, cities which are visited on pilgrimage by millions of Muslims from across the whole world and are central to the early history of Islam, makes it easy for the Saudis to claim to be *the* Islamic regime, as they do. Thirdly, oil made Saudi Arabia rich, and the alliance with America that replaced the alliance with Britain made Saudi Arabia secure. Wealth has attracted migrant workers from elsewhere in the Arab world, and they often take Wahhabi views home with them when they leave. Also, a secure and rich country that wishes to spread its influence can often do so.

The Saudi-Wahhabi establishment has set up well-funded training institutions for future Ulema, and often pays the fees and expenses of students from other parts of the Muslim world as well. A Malaysian member of the Ulema who has been trained in Saudi Arabia, for example, will generally preach the Wahhabi views he has learned there when he goes home. The Saudi-Wahhabi establishment has also set up various sorts of missions abroad. After the breakup of Yugoslavia, for example, Saudi-funded Wahhabis established schools in Bosnia, a country where Wahhabism was previously unknown. Many parents did not like Wahhabi views, but they had few alternatives if they wanted their children to go to cheap but reasonably decent schools. Wahhabism will not be unknown in Bosnia for long. Similarly, there are Muslim Students' Associations at many universities in America. These were set up by Muslim students from a variety of countries and backgrounds, but most of the financial assistance that they receive comes from Saudi-Wahhabi sources. Wahhabism, then, first shifted its understanding of Islam toward that of the Sunni mainstream, and is now shifting the Sunni mainstream's understanding toward its own. Shi'i Muslims remain uniformly hostile to Wahhabism, if only because Wahhabism remains uniformly hostile to them.

Sunni resistance to Wahhabi views comes mostly from traditional Muslims, who are themselves one of the Wahhabis' main targets. The other source of opposition to the Wahhabi-Saudi establishment is from extreme Wahhabis, of whom the most famous is Osama bin Laden, who consider that official Wahhabism's alliance with the Saudi regime has cost too much. It is indeed more of an alliance of convenience than of conviction, with few members of the (now very extensive) Saudi ruling family fully sharing Wahhabi views, and some being close to non-observant. The operatives of the Virtue Promotion and Vice Prevention Committee have no power over what goes on in the palaces of the Saudi family, and while a guest worker from another Arab country risks a beating if he fails to show up for prayers, a Saudi prince can drink as much whiskey as he wants in the security of his own palace. And some Saudi princes do, and this is known and much disliked by some Wahhabis.

Smaller Denominations and Sects

There are also groups within Islam that can be regarded as denominations or even sects. These started off in Sunni or Shi'i Islam, but have since branched off. Arguably, they now differ so much from Sunni and Shi'i Islam that they are really separate religions rather than sects of Islam. Some still describe themselves as Muslim, which can lead to confusion, and some do not. All are regarded with hostility by most Muslims, especially modern ones.

Baha'ism
The former Islamic sect—now really a separate religion—that is best known in the West is Baha'ism, though Baha'ism is little known in the Muslim world outside Iran, where it started. Baha'is today do not regard themselves as Muslims, and are in many ways much more Western than Iranian, but have the misfortune to be regarded as apostates from Islam by the revolutionary regime in Iran, at whose hands they have suffered persecution. The Baha'is recognize Muhammad as a prophet, but unlike Muslims they accord him no higher a status than Jesus or Moses. They also recognize a fourth main prophet, their own Baha'ullah, a Persian who died in Ottoman detention in Palestine in 1892. Their theology and practices have little to do with Islam, and are closer to nineteenth-century humanism. Little that is said about Islam in this book has any relevance to Baha'ism.

Ahmadiyya

The other former sect of Islam that is somewhat well known in the West is the Qadiyani Ahmadiyya—if that name is not familiar, it may be because the Qadiyani Ahmadiyya describes itself as Muslim, and its activities can sometimes only be distinguished from regular Islam by those who know what to look for, such as a reference to the "Ahmadi missionary movement." Like Baha'ism, the Qadiyani Ahmadiyya is found primarily outside the Muslim world and in the Muslim country in which it originated, in this case Pakistan. Like Baha'ism, the Qadiyani Ahmadiyya is persecuted in its country of origin. It is in fact even a criminal offense in Pakistan (and in Singapore) for an Ahmadi to represent him or herself as a Muslim, or even to refer to an Ahmadi "place of worship" as a mosque. Despite this, the beliefs and practices of Ahmadis are not dramatically different from those of Sunni Muslims. In one or two respects, the Ahmadis are a little more liberal, but what really sets them apart is a number of unusual beliefs. These include the belief that Jesus was buried in Kashmir, and—most problematically from the Muslim point of view—that their founder, Ghulam Ahmad (who died in 1908) was a prophet, though a lesser one than Muhammad. Otherwise, most of what is said about Muslims in this book also holds true for Qadiyani Ahmadis.

Ismailis

In addition to these two sects (or perhaps formerly Islamic religions) that are sometimes found in the West, there are three offshoots of Shi'ism that are important in some parts of the Muslim world, but not often found in the West. One of these is the Ismailis, who initially differed from other Shi'is principally in believing that the line of infallible Imams stopped rather earlier than other Shi'is believe, and in emphasizing secret, esoteric aspects of Islam that are largely unknown elsewhere. The worldview of the Ismailis is very different from the mainstream Islamic worldview I described in chapter 4. Some Ismailis, for example, believe in reincarnation.

There are various sub-groups within Ismaili Islam, of whom the best known are the Fatimids and the Nizaris. Both of these at various points accepted one of their own leaders as the start of a new line of Imams, and in some cases accepted a new version of the Sharia given to them by their new Imam. As a result, their practices differ significantly from those of other

Muslims described in this book. The Imam of the main Ismaili group to-day is the Aga Khan; his followers are found mostly in Central Asia, India, and Iran.

Alawis and Druze

The Alawis and the Druze are also very different from other Muslims, though they often describe themselves as Muslims and are to some extent treated as Muslims by their neighbors. That they are more tolerated than the Baha'is are, despite being equally far from regular Islam, is probably because the details of their beliefs and practices are not widely known, and also because they have been around for much longer, so that people have become used to them.

The Alawis are found mostly in Syria and Turkey (where they are called Alevi, not Alawi). The Syrian and Turkish Alawis differ from each other in important ways, since Turkish Alawis have incorporated much more Christian doctrine in their beliefs. Both varieties of Alawi regard Ali as greater than Muhammad, and the Syrian Alawis compare the relationship between Ali and Muhammad to that between Jesus and John the Baptist. Not only did Muhammad merely come to prepare the way for Ali, as St John did for Jesus, but Ali—like Jesus—was God appearing in human form. Similar views are held by the Druze, who are found in Israel, Lebanon, and Syria. It is a little hard to say exactly what the Druze believe, since the full details of their beliefs are revealed only to an initiated elite, but among other things they consider al-Hakim bi Amr Allah, the ruler of Egypt from 996 to 1021, an incarnation of God.

Red Lines

The sects discussed thus far are regarded with some hostility, but are well established and are generally left in peace to get on with their own affairs (except in Iran and Pakistan). They have been around for some time. Newer and smaller sects, however, are often suppressed. The Islamic conception of religious tolerance covers people born into other religions, but not Muslims who leave Islam. There is no conception in the Sharia that equates exactly to "heresy," if only because there is no single source of "orthodox" doctrine. This gives Muslims a much greater latitude of interpretation than medieval Christians enjoyed. There are, however, certain red lines that cannot be crossed. The two most important ways of leaving Islam are denying the existence of God or the prophetic status of Muhammad. Anyone who denies the existence of God, or suggests that anyone or anything has power equal to or greater than God's, is defined by the Sharia as an apostate from Islam. Similarly, anyone who denies that Muhammad was God's prophet, or claims to be a prophet themselves, or accepts the claim of anyone after Muhammad to be a prophet, is also an apostate.

This is the red line that unusual new religious groups often cross, or are accused of crossing. The leaders of new religious groups, in the Muslim world as in the West, often claim to be in receipt of some sort of communication from God. This is not necessarily a problem—saints routinely receive such communications, and many Sufi shaykhs hint at them. Sometimes, however, announcing a divine communication appears to others as a claim to prophecy. This is especially true if the communication contradicts a well-known and uncontroversial aspect of the Sharia, such as the need to pray. Contradicting such fundamentals as this is in itself another red line that cannot be crossed.

If someone establishes a religious group and tells his or her followers that God wants them to concentrate hard on the inner meaning of prayer at a time of general spiritual decay, no one will object; similarly, there will be no real objection to someone who recommends yoga exercises for relaxation as a preliminary to prayer, even though most people will think this rather odd (and those who are aware of the origins of yoga in a non-monotheistic religion might condemn it for that reason). If the leader of the group tells its members to wear blue clothes to pray, once again no one will object very much, though outsiders may feel it their duty to stress that this teaching is wrong. If, however, the leader says that God has announced that yoga exercises performed in blue clothes are an acceptable alternative to prayer, then trouble will result. Many Muslim states have laws against "insulting a heavenly religion" that will be invoked, and prison sentences can result.

The Nation of Islam
One unusual group that might be regarded either as a sect of Islam or even as a separate religion is the Nation of Islam (also known as the Black Muslims). This is a purely American group, founded in Detroit in 1930, about which almost nothing is known in the Muslim world. The members of the

Nation of Islam regard their founder, Wali Farad Muhammad (born Wallace D. Fard) as an incarnation of God, and regard Farad's successor, Elijah Muhammad (born Elijah Poole) as a prophet. The Nation of Islam, which attracted some 400,000 black Americans to its "Million Man March" on Washington, DC, in 1995 under the leadership of Louis Farrakhan, is more of a black nationalist organization than a religious one. Political and social goals such as black separatism, economic independence, and moral reform are more important than religious goals. These goals are supported more often by reference to the Bible than to the Koran, and members of the Nation of Islam believe equally in all of "Allah's prophets." The Nation of Islam's original conviction that whites are a race of devils destined to be destroyed by blacks at the battle of Armageddon is now less emphasized, but remains current. It has no echo in mainstream Islam. Other beliefs, such as the interpretation of "resurrection" to mean "mental resurrection" in this life, are equally bizarre from a Muslim point of view.

Some former members of the Nation of Islam have converted to mainstream Sunni Islam, including Malcolm X (born Malcolm Little), after a pilgrimage to Mecca in 1964. Malcolm X was formerly the Nation of Islam's most popular "minister," and was murdered within months of his conversion to Sunni Islam. The son of the Nation of Islam's former leader Elijah Muhammad, Wallace Delaney Muhammad, also converted to Sunni Islam, becoming Imam Warith Deen Muhammad and losing much or even most of his father's following in the process. As Sunni Muslims, these former members of the Nation of Islam abandoned their earlier racist doctrines and adopted the normal practices of Islam. Many former members of the Nation of Islam, however, retain a separate identity, and maintain an emphasis on the struggle against white oppression and for economic independence, as well as some unusual beliefs. In 2003, W. Deen Muhammad was describing his leadership as a separate *mazhab* within Islam.

There are also a number of other small quasi-Islamic groups in America, including remnants of the original Moorish Science Temple of America, founded in 1929 by the "Noble Prophet Ali Drew," to which the Nation of Islam's founder, Fard, originally belonged. Such groups have little to do with Islam as discussed in this book.

Traditionalism

Just as the Nation of Islam is really American Black nationalism dressed up in Islamic clothes, there is also a movement called Traditionalism that is really Western anti-modernism dressed up in Islamic clothes. Unlike the Nation of Islam, it is not a mass movement, but rather an intellectual movement with a small number of followers. Traditionalism is still of importance, however, especially in the West. Any Westerner who reads more than one or two books about Islam will probably find themselves reading books written from the perspective of the Traditionalist movement, especially if they are pursuing an interest in Islamic spirituality or Sufism. These books are generally exceptionally well written and persuasive.

The Traditionalist movement started in Paris in the 1920s, with some books published by a French philosopher, René Guénon. Guénon was a former occultist who had repented of his involvement in what he had come to see as dangerously misleading fake religions, and who had turned instead to a search for the original, true religion of mankind. He called this "tradition," giving the movement he started its name, but meant by "tradition" something quite different from what most people mean by that word. He and his followers thought that the only important tradition was original religious tradition, and that this was best preserved in Hinduism.

They did not become Hindus, however. Guénon emigrated from France to Egypt and advised his followers to follow him in becoming Muslim and following Sufi paths. Many did, especially when a follower of Guénon established an accessible but secret Sufi order in Switzerland just before the Second World War. That order, now called the Maryamiyya, has since then spread across most of the world, though it is still strongest in Europe and America. Until the late 1990s, when word began to get out, it remained secret, so that its members could get on with their daily lives without disturbance. Most of its members are Western intellectuals, and sometimes prominent ones.

The religious practice of most Traditionalists is much the same as the religious practice of ordinary Sufis. In daily life, Traditionalists generally follow a mixture between a Muslim and a regular Western line. Their worldview, however, is often very different from the Muslim worldview described in this book, and comes much more from the works of Guénon and his followers than from Islam. They see civilization as inevitably declining from a high point in the distant past into spiritual chaos and corruption—what most people call the modern world. The struggle between tradition and modernity parallels the struggle between good and evil, and Satan is incarnated in modernity. Satan himself, as a result, is not referred to—the concept of modernity in effect takes his place.

Traditionalists also see religions other than Islam as containing much that is as true and as useful as Islam, since all contemporary religions are really just different expressions of the same original truth. This sometimes leads them to adopt elements from other religions into their own practice. Some contemplate icons of the Virgin Mary as well as performing Sufi *zikr*, and an important group in America incorporates elements of Native American religion. Some Maryamis even follow religions other than Islam; Greek Orthodoxy is a popular second choice.

Summary

The earliest split in Islam, between Sunni and Shi'i, started with a disagreement over the proper successor to the Prophet, and over the nature of that succession. The Sunnis followed political leaders, and stressed revelation as the sole source of Islam. The Shi'a followed religious leaders, only one of whom (Ali) had political power, and stressed not only the original revelation of Islam, but also the continuation of the Prophet's religious mission by the infallible Imams, and the autonomous power of human reason. Several differences between the Sunni and Shi'i versions of the Sharia have been indicated already in this book, of which the most dramatic is probably the Shi'i institution of temporary marriage (see chapter 6). In worship, the most important purely Shi'i practice is mourning; in structure, the most important purely Shi'i institution is the *marja*, the model for emulation.

The most important recent split is between Wahhabis and other Sunnis. Various differences between Wahhabi and other Sunni Muslims have been indicated in this book. The relationship between Wahhabi non-Wahhabi Islam is one that is still changing, with a tendency for modern Muslims worldwide to become more and more Wahhabi as time passes, even though the reform movement behind the development of modern Islam and that behind the Wahhabi movement arose independently of each other and were originally very different from each other. Whether this process will continue (in which case Sunni Islam would become entirely Wahhabi) remains to be seen.

Some other "Muslims" in fact belong to groups such as the Nation of Islam or the Druze, groups which are connected to mainstream Islam, but are not really recognized as Muslim by the vast majority of the world's other Muslims (if they know about them). The beliefs and practices of these groups are as different from the Islam discussed in this book as are the beliefs and practices of the Baha'is, who consider themselves a separate religion. There are also groups such as the Qadiyani Ahmadiyya, which is much closer to Sunni Islam. The Traditionalists are almost identical to regular Sufi Muslims in their practice, but are very different from other Muslims in their worldview.

With the exception of Shi'ism and Wahhabism, though obviously of great importance to their believers, these groups are of little importance for understanding Islam and Muslims, so long as they are not confused with regular Islam.

11

Murder in the Name of God
Islam and Politics

S
ome years ago, President Mubarak of Egypt introduced multi-party democracy. The only important condition was that no party other than his own should be allowed to grow to any real size, or win more than a handful of seats at election time. As a result, elections rarely interested anyone very much, since the result was a foregone conclusion. But the motions had to be gone through, and one of the motions was to make voting easier for the illiterate by allocating an easily recognizable symbol to each candidate.

An unknown official, blessed with an odd sense of humor, allocated a very recognizable symbol to an Islamist candidate in the constituency I was living in: a pistol. The candidate would have liked to reassure potential electors that he was a reasonable and peaceful person rather than a crazy revolutionary, but the symbol he had been allocated led to the spectacle of twenty-five of his most adamant supporters marching through the streets chanting:

> Islam's the way, Islam's the way:
> The pistol is the best today!

That candidate did not win.

Islamism and violence are closely associated in many people's minds, even without the help of an official with an odd sense of humor. In fact, many Westerners see Islam as being more about violence than about God. Even the most seasoned Western traveler in the Muslim world often cannot repress a slight shudder as he or she passes someone in the street with the full black beard that usually indicates a fundamentalist.

Readers of this book will by now have appreciated that Islam is more about God than about violence. But political questions cannot be avoided. Before we look at the "clash of civilizations"—relations between Muslims and the West—we will look at politics in the Muslim world, because that is where it all starts. The inhabitants of Western cities where Muslim terrorists have spread death and destruction can be forgiven for thinking that political Islam is primarily about attacking the West, but this is not the case. Political Islam is primarily about the Muslim world itself.

Islam today is very political. The only serious opposition to the established regimes in many countries of the Muslim world comes from groups that want to establish what they call "Islamic" states. These groups are important for Muslims who are or may be ruled by them, and also occupy much attention in the West. I will discuss the relationship between Islam and the West, however, in chapter 12.

For very different reasons, both Westerners and Muslims frequently assert that in Islam, politics and religion cannot be separated. For many Westerners, this is a sign of Islam's backward and medieval nature; for many Muslims, this is a sign of Islam's strength and greatness. As we will see in this chapter, those who say that politics and religion cannot be separated are wrong. For a thousand years or more, the two were separate. This point is not just of historical interest: it is central to an understanding of the relationship between Islam and politics today, because that relationship is a very modern one. For this reason, I will start with a discussion of the medieval Muslim state, which allows readers to see how different that state was from what today's Islamists want. Many Westerners see Islamism as a throwback to medieval times: an understanding of what medieval times were really like shows that this is not the case.

The Medieval Muslim State

As we saw in chapter 1, the ideal for all Muslims is the original community established by the Prophet. In political terms, however, this model was of little practical use once the Arab Muslims had expanded their control over territories that spread from the Atlantic to China. Vast empires could not be administered on the old informal model that had worked well for a few tribes in the Arabian desert. Bureaucracies were required and so were brought into being or adapted from the remains of the bureaucracies of the conquered empires. Although minimal by today's standards, the governments of the medieval Muslim empires and states were often highly sophisticated by the standards of the time.

An immediate problem was the relations between these medieval states, or at least their rulers, and the Ulema. On the one hand, the model of the first Muslim community suggested that political and religious leadership went together. On the other hand, few rulers after Ali had the education or other qualifications necessary to lead the Ulema. Many were soldiers above all else, and some were not even literate. After an unsuccessful attempt by an Abbasid ruler in the ninth century to command the Ulema (in fact, to assert his authority over an obscure doctrinal question), a practical solution was reached among Sunni Muslims. It was generally accepted that religious authority lay with the Ulema, and political authority with the ruler. Shi'i Muslims, in contrast, did not accept this solution, and—at least in principle—regarded all earthly political authority in the absence of the infallible Imams as entirely illegitimate.

In the Sunni world, the division of labor that developed was as follows: the Ulema concerned themselves with religious doctrine, worship, and education (though a generous ruler might sometimes make a gift to endow a school or a mosque); the ruler concerned himself with defense, public order, and taxes; justice was shared between them. Treachery, offenses against public order, and failure to pay taxes were punished by the ruler, within whose sphere of authority they lay. Other aspects of law were left to the Ulema. The Ulema established courts for dealing with family law (divorce, inheritance, and the like), criminal law when public order was not involved, and commercial law, though various commercial guilds often dealt with their members disputes internally, through a form of arbitration. There was some untidiness about this arrangement, of course. The Ulema courts had no real powers of enforcement, and had to rely on the ruler's soldiers to carry out arrests, executions, and so on. Some rulers, especially the Ottomans who dominated Turkey and the Arab world for centuries until 1918, intervened in Ulema appointments in a way that reduced the independence of the Ulema considerably. The basic pattern, however, remained intact for centuries, and was a practical example of the separation of politics and religion.

This separation was a practical solution to a practical problem, and one for which there was never much theoretical justification—as a result, it was never really formalized. Rulers continued to rule in the name of Islam, even though their religious role was minimal. An important principle that was formalized, however, was that the ruler was subject to the Sharia, just in the same way as anyone else was. If the ruler issued an ordinance that in some way contradicted the Sharia, it was the right and duty of the Ulema to point this out to him . . . if they dared. Some rulers, predictably, paid more attention to the Sharia and the views of the Ulema than others, and some of the Ulema were braver than others in confronting erring rulers.

Few rulers dared ignore the Ulema altogether, however. The Ulema had much more contact with and influence over the population than the ruler did, and the approval of the Ulema usefully bolstered the ruler's authority and perceived legitimacy. As a result, the Ulema often ended up playing the role of intermediaries between ruler and ruled. When a ruler made a regulation that the people found intolerable for whatever reason, it was generally the Ulema who were expected to present the people's case to the ruler, often couching their arguments in religious terms. This role of intermediary made the Ulema powerful, and their power was increased both by their prestige and by their control over institutions such as schools, and over the endowments that accumulated over the centuries to fund these institutions.

Religion and State Today

When modern states began to be established in the Muslim world in the nineteenth century, the old systems had to change. Government grew. Rulers were no longer content to restrict their activities to raising enough taxes to pay a few soldiers—they needed modern armies like the armies of Europe, and modern armies were so expensive that an overhaul of the whole machinery of the state was necessary to pay for them. Administration was centralized, standardized, and improved. Bureaucrats were trained. Army officers, too, needed to be trained in a new and modern way. They needed to understand mathematics to use modern artillery properly, and to study military textbooks. The Ulema were clearly incapable of instructing army officers using manuals written in French, just as they were incapable of training the officials needed by the new ministries. Their monopoly of education had to go.

Legal reform was also obviously necessary. Muslim states were becoming part of the world economy, and in order to trade effectively with the West, a system of commercial law on the Western model was needed. As we saw in chapter 7, the Sharia's rules on commercial law are so different from Western law that the two systems are in practice incompatible. It was also generally agreed that economic development required a complete reform of land law. Commercial and land law codes closely resembling Western models were therefore introduced, and lawyers and judges were trained on Western lines to staff them. The Ulema lost their monopoly over the legal system, with one area of law after another being transferred to Western-style courts, until all the Ulema had left was family law, principally divorce and inheritance. In many countries, they soon lost these areas, too. Except in wild and remote places such as the area that was later to become Saudi Arabia, the Sharia was in the end entirely replaced by legal codes and systems modeled on those of Europe. At the time, nobody much objected to what seemed a very necessary reform if Muslim states were to compete with the rest of the world. Although today many call for the return of the Sharia, few voices were raised during the nineteenth century while the Sharia legal system was being abolished.

As we saw in a chapter 2, the prestige, authority and incomes of the Ulema collapsed. As the state took over their endowments and paid them salaries as it did to other officials, their independence vanished as well. The Ulema had always been subject to political pressure, but had previously been better placed than almost any other group to resist it. Now they were in the worst possible position to resist it. For centuries, the sons of senior Ulema had made careers as Ulema themselves; toward the end of the nineteenth century they started going to the new secular law schools or training as engineers.

In most states in the Muslim world today, with the notable exceptions as ever of Saudi Arabia and Iran, the Ulema have become servants of the state. This does not mean, however, that the state has made Islam its servant. Because the Ulema are not priests, Islam is not dependent on the Ulema—as the Soviet regime found when it tried to cleanse the Soviet Union of "superstition" (as termed religion). Once Christian priests had been shot, sent to the camps or otherwise disposed of, and churches had been closed, knocked down, or converted to other uses, the practice of Christianity declined markedly. Shooting the Ulema and closing the mosques in the Muslim parts of the Soviet Union, however, was far less effective. People could pray the five prayers at home quite easily without mosques or Ulema. Control of the Ulema does not give control of Islam.

Most states in the Muslim world today are in effect secular states. The Ulema play no role whatsoever in government or administration, but are also not independent of it. Almost the only trace of the old Sharia in legal systems is in the area of family law, where norms and principles derived from the Sharia have often been inserted into Western-style codes, except in Turkey, where not even that trace of the old Sharia remains. The state still has to pay attention to Islamic norms, to which many people remain committed, but no more than it has to pay attention to any other aspect of public opinion. Where the Sharia and Western laws disagree, however, it is usually Western laws that have prevailed. The Sharia forbids alcohol and gambling, but the laws of most Muslim states permit both—though usually with more restrictions than is normal in the West. The Sharia allows slavery (subject to certain regulations) and regards marijuana as discouraged rather than forbidden, but no Muslim state today permits slavery or marijuana (though in practice some Muslim policemen worry less about marijuana than their Western equivalents would, and one or two Muslim states occasionally turn a blind eye to practices akin to slavery).

Religion and state, then, are separated even more today than they were in the medieval period—except, as usual, in Iran and Saudi Arabia. This, however, is a situation that many radical political activists, whom scholars call "Islamists," want to change. Across the Muslim world, there are calls for the replacement of today's states and regimes by "Islamic" governments and "Islamic" states. An Islamic state is defined by the Islamists as a state ruled by the Sharia, and Islamic states are normally contrasted with today's secular states—the ones with essentially Western legal systems. Islamists often suppose that all Muslim states were once Islamic states, and claim to be attempting only to return to the original system. In fact, their conception of the Islamic state is very different from the actual medieval Muslim state we considered earlier. It is not a return to a medieval model, but a new model based on the original community of Medina.

The people I am calling "Islamists" are often also called "fundamentalists." This term, however, means different things to different people, and so is not very precise. A "fundamentalist" might just be a devout, modern Muslim without any strong political views at all; or a devout traditional Muslim, or a radical political activist, or even someone happy to use violence in pursuit of their political aims. These "fundamentalists" are very different types of Muslim, and should not be confused.

The Origins of Political Islam

To understand the political movement known as Islamism or as "political Islam," we will have to investigate two related questions. First, where does the political movement come from? And second, why do so many people find it attractive? The answers given below are those that I find most convincing. The questions, however, are pressing ones, and there are many competing theories. To examine all these theories and their merits would take up more space than this book affords.

Islamism has two main sources, one very ancient and one very modern. The ancient source is Islam itself, with which the reader is already familiar. The modern source is more controversial. According to one of the more convincing theories, that modern source is what is sometimes called utopianism—the idea that it is possible and necessary to build a perfect society.

Utopianism really first developed in the West during the eighteenth century, though traces can be found even earlier. In its mildest form, utopianism has benefited all of us. Mild utopianism was behind the convictions of nineteenth-century reformers that it was possible and necessary to improve public health, education, and working conditions in factories. In its extreme form, however, utopianism has caused more suffering and death than anything else over the last hundred years. Hitler and Stalin were both inspired by their own visions of utopia—visions that we may not share, but that were very powerful for those who believed in them. Mao Zedong had his vision of utopia too, and it led to the tragedies of the Great Leap Forward and the Cultural Revolution. During the twentieth century, extreme utopianism may have killed as many as 100 million people.

The Muslim world discovered utopianism during the nineteenth century, when scholars and intellectuals from various Muslim countries learned European languages and went to Europe, usually to Paris, to study. In Europe they learned about reason and natural law, and about the dreams of progressive European intellectuals for the perfection of human societies by replacing tradition and superstition with systems based on reason and natural law. A century or more later, most Westerners are more cautious and perhaps more cynical about the chances of perfecting of human society, but in nineteenth-century Paris such dreams were still fresh and powerful.

Various Muslim intellectuals, inspired by these dreams, tried to apply similar principles to their own societies. The first problem they encountered was how to fit Islam into their dreams. Progressive intellectuals in Europe usually had little interest in religion; some ignored it as an entirely private matter, while others put it under the general heading of superstition. Progressive Muslim intellectuals, however, could not ignore religion in this way. Even in the nineteenth century, religion was more present in every aspect of life in the Muslim world than in France, and progressive Muslim intellectuals who ignored religion risked being dismissed as stooges of the French. Some Muslim intellectuals did follow French secular fashions, and in what was to become the Republic of Turkey they became the majority. Elsewhere, though, they were always marginalized, and became even more marginal during the twentieth century.

The way around the problem of how to keep religion in the equation was to proclaim that Islam, reason, and natural law were all one and the same thing. Anything that was against reason was not true Islam, and anything that was against Islam was not true reason. Utopia, then, might be built on the basis of Islam, of the Sharia. The Sharia, rightly understood, called for constitutional government, hygiene, popular education, and almost everything else that was progressive in the nineteenth century. For these intellectuals, all of whom were modern Muslims, Islam had become something closer to an ideology than to the religion we have been considering so far in this book (though an element of religion always remained).

Some of these intellectuals were liberals in our current terms, and some were not. Their writings were the origins of Islamism.

Islamism in its current form really emerged in Egypt during the 1930s. This was the high point of utopianism and ideology in Europe, with Hitler's brown shirts, Mussolini's black shirts, Stalin's Komsomol, and countless other similar movements—popular movements dedicated to one vision or another of utopia. Egypt followed Europe's example, with Communists and quasi-Fascists, and also with a movement called the Muslim Brothers. Like some European movements, the Muslim Brothers started off calling for the purification and renewal of society, and ended up seeking political power. At first it was all about Boy Scouts, clean living, and the "Islamic sports spirit." The Muslim Brothers was set up as a mass organization with local groups organized in a way that looked so much like the Communists' cell system that the comparison was immediately made, and fiercely denied by the Muslim Brothers themselves. Then came political ambition, though with little detailed discussion of what constitutional arrangements were desirable. Finally, in about 1940, came the foundation of a "Secret Organization" within the Muslim Brothers that looked after military training. In 1948, they carried out its first high-profile political assassination—of the Egyptian prime minister, who had begun to take measures against the Muslim Brothers, fearing (rightly or wrongly) that they were preparing a coup attempt.

Islamism Today

The Muslim Brothers never took political power in Egypt. When the old order was swept away by an army coup in 1952, two rival mass movements hoped to shape the new order—the Communists and the Muslim Brothers. Neither succeeded. The most ambitious of the army officers behind the coup, Gamal Abdul Nasser, rounded up the Communists and then, once that threat had been neutralized, also rounded up the Muslim Brothers. Many leading Communists and Muslim Brothers died in jail, sometimes tortured to death.

The Muslim Brothers continued to exist, however, as an illegal, underground organization. They also gave rise to many other groups, usually even more radical than they themselves had been, sometimes led by former Muslim Brothers and sometimes just inspired by them. With time and as government persecution declined, the Muslim Brothers became less radical. The other, newer groups became more prominent.

Islamists proclaim that "Islam is the solution"—the solution to all problems. They aim to establish Islamic utopia in the form of the "Sharia state," usually called the "Islamic state." A few such states have already been established, and none of them have been utopias in practice. The utopias promised by Fascists and Communists were also very far from perfect, of course. The most sophisticated Islamic state was that established in Iran after the revolution there; Iran, as a Shi'i country, is of course different from most Muslim countries, but still acted as an inspiration for Islamists elsewhere. Less sophisticated Islamic states were established in Pakistan and the Sudan, both on the backs of military coups.

All Islamic states have been a disappointment because, in practice, Islam has turned out not to be the solution—or at least not to be the solution to the pressing problems from which most Muslim countries suffer. Islam has little to say about how to relieve poverty and unemployment, or about how to build efficient and competitive industries and effective health-care systems. Islamic revolutionary regimes, like most revolutionary regimes, have found themselves immediately confronted with the problem of securing their own power, usually by rounding up their enemies. When the Sharia has been "restored," what has actually happened has been neither a return to the medieval system nor the creation of the utopia once dreamed of by progressive intellectuals; instead, there is an emphasis on the most lurid parts of the Sharia—the punishment of thieves and adulterers by amputation and stoning. Such punishments serve as a very visible demonstration that the Sharia—or at least something new and different—has been implemented. They do not, however, solve many problems.

Few Islamists realize that the Sharia as implemented in contemporary Islamic states has little to do with the Sharia as it was implemented in premodern Muslim states. Stoning of adulterers, for example, was always there as part of the Sharia, but its actual use as a penalty was extremely rare, partly because premodern rules of evidence made it almost impossible to prove adultery in court. In many contemporary Islamic states, however, what has been implemented is not the old system of Sharia courts, but rather mod-

ern Western legal systems with penalties drawn from the Sharia replacing
the penalties usual in the West. The result is quite different.

Political Islamist movements all aim at taking power—if they did not,
they would not be political Islamists, but merely non-political groups of
Muslims. The means Islamists use to this end vary widely from country to
country, depending on local circumstances. In Turkey, the main Islamist
movement formed a regular political party, which (like other Turkish political parties) has gone through several changes of name: Refah, Fazilet, and
then AK. After making alliances with various other groups, the Turkish Islamists began to win elections. This success was ascribed by many observers
to voters' disenchantment with the other parties, and to the Islamists' success in building effective grass-roots organizations, something no other party
had previously done. One result of the Turkish Islamists' skills in adjusting
to voters was that as time past, the Islamists became much less Islamist. In
fact, the first lasting "Islamist" government in Turkey looked very much like
any other elected reformist government; its emphasis was on clean hands
and new hands, not on Islam. Although many secular Turks remain afraid
that an anti-secularist and anti-democratic agenda is simply being con-
cealed, there is as yet no evidence of this.

Similarly, Malaysian Islamists also organized themselves into a regular
political party, the PAS (Pan-Malaysian Islamic Party), and won power in
two Malaysian states (though never at a national level) through elections.
PAS remained Islamist, but the changes it could make to the states where it
held power were limited by a system that grants most powers to the national
government.

Algerian Islamists organized themselves into a regular political party,
the FIS (Islamic Salvation Front), and looked set to win a national election
when it was canceled by the Algerian army. Both PAS and the Turkish Islamists accepted electoral defeat without complaint when it came their
way, but the FIS did not accept the cancellation of the election it would almost certainly have won. Groups within the FIS launched an armed attack
on the Algerian state, adopting the classic tactics of insurgents everywhere.
Insurgents do not have the resources available to regular armies, and so do
not fight like regular armies. If they tried to fight like regular armies, they
would be quickly defeated. Instead, insurgents hide among the local popu-

lation, launch an attack where it is least expected, and then vanish again. The state they are attacking has to be careful in its response. While pursuing the insurgents, it is easy to alienate the local population and increase support for the insurgents, which is exactly what the insurgents want.

The attacks launched by insurgents are invariably described by the state they are attacking as "terrorism," even when the targets of the attacks are military or governmental. Often, however, insurgents chose other, less well defended targets. These "soft" targets are often civilian, and civilian casualties result. This is what happened with the insurgent groups derived from the FIS, who came to be widely regarded as terrorists, or even as bandits.

Not all Islamist groups which can see no prospect of gaining power through elections resort to insurgency or terrorism, though some do. The Sharia has little to say about such tactics. There is no developed doctrine of justified rebellion, so Islamists instead fall back on the rules of Jihad, which (unsurprisingly) permit the killing of the enemy. Quite who counts as an enemy is not much investigated, because when the doctrine of Jihad was being formulated, the answer to that question seemed obvious. The killing of women and children is forbidden, but only if they are non-combatants, and so insurgents sometimes construct explanations of why the women and children they kill are not actually non-combatants. In the end, the tactics of Islamist insurgents differ little from the tactics of any other type of insurgent (for example, nationalist or Communist), and really have little to do with Islam. The tactics of Islamist political parties also differ little from those used by other political parties in similar circumstances. What is "Islamic" is the inspiration for the utopias such parties seek to construct.

Support for Islamism

As the reader will have gathered, I am not myself at all enthusiastic about Islamism. Neither are some former Islamists, including a man we will call C. W., an Iranian who took an active and leading part in the Islamic revolution in Iran, and who today regrets that the ideals of the revolution have vanished and that the whole idea—once, for C. W., a beautiful and urgent idea—has been hijacked by people who simply want to hang on to power, and who have reduced Islam to police campaigns against alcohol consumption and the harassment of women wearing the wrong sort of head covering. In C. W.'s view, not only was the Iranian regime at the start of the twenty-first century corrupt and in need of replacement, and not only was Islamism a bankrupt ideology, but Islam itself needed to change if it was to survive.

Millions of Muslims across the world, however, are still enthusiastic about Islamism, and we now need to consider why this is the case. One answer is that most of those millions are not sufficiently attentive to the history of the modern world, are not familiar with the disappointing realities of Islamic states such as the Sudan, and fail to understand that Islamism is in essence just another modern political movement, similar to Communism or Fascism. Like most scholars, I draw a careful distinction between Islamism and Islam, between the political movement and the religion. Islamists, however, do not draw this distinction. For them, Islamism is Islam, and Islam is Islamism. This is an error which, ironically, many Western observers also make. For Islamists, it is a very useful error. If I can convince you that my political movement is endorsed by God, that it is your pious duty to support me, and that to oppose me is actually sinful, it is going to be a lot easier to recruit you. It is difficult to make a case to uneducated country folk using unfamiliar concepts like social justice and economic rationality, but if political objectives can somehow be reexpressed in familiar terms—which really means in religious terms—they will sound much more convincing. Islamist leaders are invariably modern Muslims, often quite influenced by Wahhabism, but they can sometimes succeed in winning the support of traditional Muslims in this way.

Another important reason why Islamism attracts many millions is that there seems to be no real alternative. Most Westerners are on the whole content with the political systems in which they live, even if they would prefer some details to be different. On the other hand, almost no Muslims in the Muslim world are content with the political systems in which they live. Most Muslims suffer from poverty, unemployment, and corruption (government and private) of a sort that few Westerners can even imagine. Turkey, Malaysia, and to some extent Indonesia are exceptions,[1] but

---

[1] The final outcome in Iraq remains unknown at the time of writing, but I am not optimistic. I hope that I will be proved wrong.

elsewhere the main objective of the regimes that rule the Muslim world is to stay in power, which they do by a mixture of force and bribery, and by doing their best to ensure that any group which might be a threat is either controlled by them or disbanded. The courts are made into departments of the government, journalists who become too critical of the regime are jailed, and opposition political parties are either banned or reduced to insignificance. It goes further than that, though. Even small local charities are subject to intrusive state control, with the security services vetting candidates for their boards and government ministries monitoring their activities.

State intervention in economic life is ubiquitous. Major industries are often state owned, and used more for patronage than production. They provide jobs of sorts for those the regime favors, and produce low quality goods at a loss. Private business, where it exists, needs ridiculous quantities of official permits for the simplest activities. This not only makes business less efficient, but ensures that businesses can only survive by maintaining good relations with the regime. This means political loyalty on the one hand, and cash and favors to officials on the other.

Islam is not responsible for this sorry state of affairs, or at least is not responsible in any obvious fashion. Equally dreadful or even worse regimes are found in non-Muslim countries in certain parts of the world. There is nothing in Islam that condones fraud, bribery, or theft. Some observers argue that Islam encourages submission to state authority and acceptance of suffering, but others disagree.

Understandably, most Muslims want a new political system to live in. They want governments that are not arbitrary and corrupt, and businesses that provide jobs and are not corrupt. They also want public services that work. The Islamists are the only opposition group with enough strength and conviction to survive state repression, so they are the focus of many Muslims' hopes. Although Islamism has failed to deliver much in the countries where it has actually been implemented, since few Muslims in other countries realize this, the Islamists still have the benefit of the doubt. In many Muslim countries, the best voluntary organizations (subsidized clinics and the like) are run by Islamists, or by modern Muslims sympathetic to Islamism.

University students everywhere tend more toward radical alternatives than their parents' generations. At one point, Western university students demonstrated against war and injustice, and sometimes joined socialist or Communist parties. So did university students in the Muslim world. A radical Western university student today is unlikely to join the Communist party, and can chose from a range of radical alternatives, from feminism to animal liberation. A radical university student in the Muslim world has only one place to go: the Islamists.

Many urban Muslims, then, are either Islamists or regard Islamism with varying degrees of approval. Some of them support the use of violence to achieve political objectives, and some of them reject it. These are personal positions that are hard to predict, and depend on local circumstances. Few Turks will support an Islamist insurgency, since a Turk can simply go to vote for an Islamist party in fair and free elections. In countries where elections are neither free nor fair, there is little point in voting for anyone, and insurgents are more likely to be supported. Once insurgents go too far and are seen as terrorists, they generally lose popular support.

Many Muslims, however, have no sympathy for Islamism. Some traditional Muslims have been recruited by Islamist organizations, but most of them see Islam as having little or nothing to do with politics. Some of the best educated Muslims see Islamism much as I do. Even those Muslims who see Islamism as a disastrous wrong turn in their countries' histories, however, may still hesitate to condemn it, especially in the face of a non-Muslim who confuses Islamism and Islam. Rather than seem to endorse a criticism of Islam, many Muslims will offer a limited defense of Islamism, or of aspects of Islamism.

Alternatives to Islamism

There are some alternatives to despotism in the Muslim world other than radical political Islam. Turkey demonstrates one alternative, and Malaysia demonstrates another. Neither are model democracies, but both are societies that function reasonably well and provide their citizens with reasonable standards of living. It may be significant that many Turks have their eyes focused on the example of nearby Europe, while many Malaysians have their eyes focused on the example of nearby Singapore. The future direction of Iran will also be fascinating to watch. Most Iranians want some other political system in place, and there are many ideas of how different systems might work. At the time of writing, however, there seems to be no plausible alternative to the current regime. That regime is generally disliked, but it still has some supporters, and is probably not disliked enough for it to be overthrown spontaneously. Still, the system seems bound to change.

Prospects for change in other directions in the Arab world are, at present, poor. It is difficult to imagine any Arab regime giving up power voluntarily, and the examples of Iraq and Algeria are not encouraging. Both the destruction of the regime of Saddam Hussein and the attempts at democratization of the Algerian regime led to violence, and little improvement is yet visible.

No significant groups within any Arab country are pressing for Western-style democracy, though there are intriguing signs that the leadership of some formerly radical Islamist groups may be prepared to accept some sort of political pluralism and move closer to the moderate Turkish model, given the chance. At the time of writing, opinion among observers is divided, and it is hard to make any prediction. One problem is that although individual Muslims everywhere are aware of the benefits of democracy—especially those who have received better educations and have traveled or lived in the West—they make up only a small percentage of the total. Few Arabs have the experience to really understand how a democratic system works. Their own regimes often present themselves as democratic, and "elections" are held frequently—during which the ruling party almost invariably receives at least 95 percent of the vote. Nobody, as a result, is very interested in elections. The Egyptian parliamentary election of 2005 was a notable exception to this rule—for the first time since 1952, an opposition party won enough seats to constitute a significant bloc in the parliament. It will be most interesting to see how this trend develops. But in general attention focuses more on who is in power and how they exercise that power than on the mechanisms for a party getting into power—or on what political scientists recognize as much more important, the mechanisms for peacefully removing from power a government that has lost popular support.

Even in the absence of democracy, it seems obvious to most thoughtful Western observers that immediate improvements in the Arab world would result from functioning independent legal systems, a responsible free press, and economic growth. Well educated Muslims who know the West often recognize this. It is not obvious, however, how such improvements can be achieved in the absence of some form of democracy, and few observers are enthusiastic about the period of Islamist rule that would probably result from truly free elections in most Arab countries. There is probably little that the outside world can do about this situation.

One ray of hope exists: the spread of satellite television has removed the most important of the mass media from state control, and may in the end produce a responsible free press.

Summary

Although the Sharia was once the main law in Muslim states, it is relevant today only in Saudi Arabia, Iran, and a few minor states. There are many Islamists, however, who would like to make the Sharia the law of the state in another way—as an ideology more than as a political system. These Islamists are supported by many Muslims mostly because they are the only real alternative to systems that are seen as having failed, and because they can express their arguments in terms that are familiar to unsophisticated audiences that are used to thinking in religious terms and have little understanding of political theory.

Islamist leaders are modern Muslims, often influenced by Wahhabism, though some of their followers may be traditional Muslims. But even though Islamism came out of modern Islam, not all modern Muslims are also Islamists.

In the few functioning democracies in the Muslim world, Islamists follow the democratic path to power. Where no such route exists, they often resort to the classic tactics of insurgents, including terrorism. As innocent casualties of the terrorism grow, the Islamists generally lose popular support—but embattled regimes may lose even more support if they mishandle the insurgency.

Some observers suggest that the form of Islamism discussed in this chapter is in its last days. Islamism has failed, it is argued. In most cases

Islamists have failed to take power, and when they have taken power, they have been unable to deliver their promised utopias. Recognizing this, a new generation of Islamists is bound to turn in new directions. The direction taken by Turkish Islamists may indicate the future: democratic politics where Islam is a source of moral direction. Time will tell, but I myself suspect that Turkey is as much a special case as Iran, though for different reasons.

12

The Clash of Civilizations
Islam and the West

Since 2001, or perhaps since the collapse of the Soviet Union, the idea of a major "clash of civilizations" between Islam and the West has been gaining adherents in both the Muslim world and the West. This is in itself almost enough to produce a clash, but there are other reasons behind the conflict. Some are religious, and some are not.

Certainly, the Muslim world and the West have never been on very good terms. They have fought many wars since the first clash between an Arab Muslim army and a Byzantine Christian army in the year 634 A.D. (which the Arab Muslims won). But that does not mean that a clash between the Muslim world and the West today is inevitable.

The relationship between the two civilizations has inspired many books, so I will restrict myself here to offering some alternative perspectives. I will start with cultural conflict, since cultural conflict between the Muslim world and the West certainly exists. For many observers, this is the fundamental explanation of the clash between the Muslims and the West: Muslims reject Western values, and so are determined to destroy them. Westerners also reject many Muslim values, of course, but are not determined to destroy the Muslim world, because Westerners are tolerant, and will work for peaceful change. Muslims, in contrast, are intolerant and violent.

This argument seems convincing, but is not borne out by the facts. Certainly, disagreement over values produces conflict, and—as we have seen in earlier chapters—tolerance and non-violence are more accepted in the West than in the Muslim world. This book sees Islam as one of three main monotheistic religions, and I have repeatedly pointed out how much of the religious worldview of Muslims is the same as that of religious Westerners. The three monotheistic religions, however, see their positions somewhat differently: each one sees itself not just as one of three main monotheistic religions, but as the only proper monotheistic religion. This is as true of Islam as it is of orthodox Judaism and most varieties of Christianity. But this on its own does not mean that Muslims are any more determined to destroy Christianity than Christians are determined to destroy Islam.

Islam and Non-Muslims

Within the family of monotheistic religions, each religion has an explanation of the religion or religions that came before it. Judaism has little to say about either Christianity or Islam, but Christianity gives Judaism an honored place. The most important Jewish scriptures are incorporated word for word into the Bible, though the interpretation of them sometimes differs. The Jewish prophets are honored by Christians, and the law they brought is not ignored, but rather seen as having been superseded. From a Christian point of view, the law of Moses was right for a time that has now passed.

Similarly, Islam gives both Judaism and Christianity an honored place. Jews and Christians are "peoples of the book," following a book or scripture given to them by God. Although neither the Jewish not the Christian scriptures are incorporated into the Koran word for word, many of the stories and themes found in them are also found in the Koran. Adam, Noah and the flood, Joseph's dreams, Moses and Pharaoh, Jesus and the Jews—all are found in the Koran, though the details and interpretation sometimes differ.

The Jewish prophets and Jesus are honored by Islam, but—and here is an important difference—the law they brought is seen somewhat differently. For Christians, the Jews follow a law that was once right, but has been superseded. For Muslims, the law that Jews and Christians now follow was not that which was originally revealed to them, and has been distorted. Earlier Jews and Christians both departed from the revelation they had been given, and changed the record of that revelation. Jesus, most importantly, never actually claimed to be divine; it was an error of his later followers to see him as divine, and to start to worship him as if he were God. Islam, then, gives Judaism and Christianity honored positions, but rather less honored positions than Christianity gives Judaism. For Christians, the problem with the Jews is that they failed to acknowledge Jesus; for Muslims, the problem with the Christians is not only that they failed to acknowledge Muhammad, but that their Christianity is not even "real" Christianity in the first place. As a result, most Muslims hold that Christians and Jews have no hope of going to heaven, though many of the Iranian Ulema hold otherwise. Christians and Jews are, however, closer to the truth than followers of other paths such as Hindus. Hindus are polytheists, worshipers of idols, and utterly lost.

This is the perspective of the religion of Islam, a perspective which almost all Muslims would acknowledge in theory. In practice, however, individual Muslims' attitudes to other religions generally depend on their personal experiences and understandings of that other religion—as is probably true of non-Muslims' attitudes.

Many Muslim countries have significant non-Muslim religious minorities, which sometimes fit uneasily into the wider community. By contemporary Western standards, Islam is an intolerant religion when it comes to such minorities. The Sharia does not recognize non-Muslims as the equals of Muslims, prohibits Muslim women from marrying non-Muslims, and punishes conversion from Islam to other religions.

Religious tolerance is now acknowledged as a virtue by nearly all Westerners, and no Western legal systems have laws of any importance that distinguish between people on the basis of religion. This was not always the case, however. In comparison to medieval Christianity, Islam appears as a remarkably tolerant religion. In the medieval period, Christian states worked hard to ensure orthodoxy, and tolerance was seen as dangerous laxity. Beliefs that differed from the accepted orthodoxy were a danger to those who held them, to the souls of those who might be infected by them, and to the established order. Steps should be taken—and were taken—to root out heresy. There was no tolerance of unorthodox Christian beliefs, and no tolerance of non-Christian beliefs either. When medieval Christian rulers conquered lands from Muslim rulers, sooner or later non-Christians (Muslims and Jews) were given the choice of converting or leaving. Most left.

Medieval Islam never valued tolerance as such, but was in practice generally less concerned with ensuring orthodoxy. There are no cases of mass expulsions of non-Muslims by medieval Muslim rulers. On the contrary, Jews forced out of Europe often took refuge in lands under Muslim rule.

There was never any idea that Muslims and non-Muslims were or should be equal, however. Christians and Jews lived somewhat apart from other groups, to a large extent managing their own affairs. Sometimes Muslim rulers were pragmatic, making use of skilled men whatever their religion. Sometimes other rulers were more principled (in their own eyes), refusing to employ non-Muslims in important official positions, and on occasion introducing regulations to make clear the second-class status of non-Muslims—for example, forbidding them to carry swords, ride horses, or wear the same clothes as Muslims did. Such persecutions were usually minor and short-lived, though non-Muslims who found themselves engaged in litigation with Muslims were always at a disadvantage. In the end, though, it was much better to be a non-Muslim under medieval Muslim rulers than a non-Christian under medieval Christian rulers. Plenty of Christian and Jewish communities survived in the Arab world, sufficiently integrated to use the majority language (Arabic) in their writings, and to be culturally similar to the Muslim majority. No Muslim communities survived in the Christian world, and the Jews survived only with great difficulty, and not in all parts of Europe. Medieval Jewish culture in Europe had little to do with Christian culture, and European Jews rarely used the majority languages in their writing.

That was the medieval system. Today the positions have been reversed, and it is better to be a non-Christian in the West (since the end of Nazism, at least) than a non-Muslim in the Muslim world. This is not because the Muslim treatment of religious minorities has become worse, but because the Christian (now, Western) treatment of religious minorities has improved beyond all recognition.

Just as Western states no longer have laws of any real importance that distinguish between people on the basis of their religion, few Muslim states have such laws, except for family law (marriage, divorce, inheritance, etc.)—Saudi Arabia, as usual, being an exception. Certainly, Egyptian law prohibits a non-Muslim from becoming president, but then British law also prohibits a Catholic from becoming monarch (though not prime minister). Of course, the Egyptian president has more real power than the British monarch, but neither law effects many people directly. Most Muslim states maintain in public that all their citizens are equal, whatever their religion.

But few individual Muslims really agree. The Sharia's conception of non-Muslims as outside the community somehow persists.

In practice, the other religions that Muslims today encounter are Judaism, Christianity, Hinduism, and Buddhism. Hinduism is an issue only for Muslims in India, and Buddhism is primarily an issue for Muslims in countries such as Thailand.

Many Muslim countries have Christian minorities, and Muslim attitudes toward Christians are thus shaped by personal experience (and, in the case of Western Christians, by politics). In Egypt, for example, about 10 percent of the population is Christian—and relations between Muslim and Christian have less to do with the Sharia than with the dynamics of relations between majority and minority, which are difficult everywhere. To Egyptian Muslims, Christians are different, and somewhat untrustworthy. They are always complaining about discrimination, but how often can you find a Muslim working in an important position in a Christian-owned company? To Egyptian Christians, Muslims are an obscurely threatening majority that excludes them from national life and fails to respect or value their different heritage. Despite this, Muslims meet Christians at school and at work, have friendly relations with each other, and may sometimes even become friends. There are definite limits to their relationship, however. If in his or her right mind, no Muslim parent of a pretty nineteen-year-old daughter is going to invite a Christian friend with a twenty-year-old son to dinner. And sometimes, especially in villages, there are outbreaks of intercommunal violence.

Muslims and Israel

Judaism is quite a different sort of issue. Few Muslims outside Palestine have much contact with Judaism, especially since the mass emigration of Arab Jews to Israel in the 1940s and 1950s. Of all the Muslim countries in the world, only Turkey and Morocco have any significant Jewish community today, and so only Turks and Moroccans have any real chance of personal contact with Jews. Muslim attitudes toward Jews are generally a function of one of the world's most intractable conflicts, that between the

Arabs and Israel. Originally, this conflict was not primarily religious, but over recent decades it has become increasingly religious.

In 1850, neither Jews nor Arabs had any particular sense of nationhood. Jews saw themselves as a religious minority, and often as loyal citizens of their adoptive countries (some adoptive countries, notably Russia, gave them no chance to be or feel like loyal citizens). The Arabs living in Palestine saw themselves as Muslims or Christians (as the case might be), and as inhabitants of particular towns, or as subjects of the Ottoman empire. They were aware of themselves as Arabic-speaking locals rather than Turkish-speaking Ottoman administrators and soldiers, but this had little significance.

At the very end of the nineteenth century, a project emerged among European Jews for the establishment of a Jewish state, so that the Jews could be a regular people like any other. This project was known as Zionism, and at first attracted little support. Many religious Jews, in fact, strongly objected to it: for them, to be Jewish was a matter of religion, not nationality, and the last thing they should aspire to was to be a people like any other (they were, after all, God's chosen people). Such Jews also objected strongly to the choice of location for the proposed Jewish state: the Holy Land. For them, the Jews should return to the Holy Land only when the Messiah appeared.

Support for Zionism grew, however, and the Zionist movement attracted the support of the British government. In 1917, the British cabinet expressed itself in favor of the establishment of a "national home for the Jewish people" in Palestine so long as "nothing shall be done which may prejudice the civil and religious rights of existing non-Jewish communities." This proviso proved, in practice, impossible. The earliest Zionists had assumed, rather optimistically, that the existing inhabitants of Palestine would either welcome the advantages that Zionist-sponsored economic development would bring, or else would leave the small part of the Ottoman empire they inhabited for other Arab-speaking areas of the Ottoman empire. They were mistaken. After the First World War, Britain administered Palestine under the authority of the League of Nations, and Palestine became a state in its own right (though never an independent state). Its inhabitants thus discovered that they were Palestinians, different from French-administered Lebanese and Syrians, just as the first waves of Zionist settlement began.

Between the two world wars, the British struggled to keep an increasingly difficult situation in Palestine under control, as clashes between the established Arab inhabitants and the newly arrived Zionist immigrants escalated, often violently. These clashes were produced by the oldest cause of human conflict: competition for land. The clashes were between two very different communities that had no understanding of each other, could not speak each other's languages, and regarded each other with increasing hostility. Religion was part of the identity of the two communities, but not the most important part. Sometimes the conflict was expressed in religious terms, but religion was not itself the cause of the conflict. Christian Arabs in Palestine were no more enthusiastic about the Zionist immigration than were Muslim Arabs.

Both Arabs and Zionists also regarded the British with hostility. In 1939, the British finally concluded that the plan of 1917 was unworkable—that there was no way that a Jewish state could be established in Palestine with any form of Arab consent. The Second World War then ended British power, and Palestine became one of many formerly British territories to be vacated as quickly as possible. The UN voted for partition, but the Palestinian Arab leadership rejected this. As soon as Britain withdrew from Palestine, the Zionists declared the establishment of the State of Israel, and various Arab armies attacked in defense of their Palestinian brother-Arabs—and lost. Israeli forces were better prepared, better led, and fighting on their own ground. During the conflict, most Palestinian Arabs had fled, under circumstances that remain controversial,[1] leaving Israel with an unproblematic Jewish majority. At this stage, there were still no significant religious elements to the conflict. Most of the original inhabitants of Palestine had left, just as the earlier Zionists had hoped, though under somewhat different circumstances.

In 1967, however, a second war broke out, during which the well trained and excellently led Israeli army performed superbly and the Arab

---

[1] Some argue that they left voluntarily, while others argue that they were deliberately expelled. Circumstances differed from place to place, and the evidence is sometimes unclear, but there were probably both voluntary departures (normal life can hardly be continued in the middle of a war zone) and deliberate expulsions.

armies performed lamentably. The Egyptian air force, for example, was completely unprepared, and was wiped out before it could even take off. From this point, the conflict began to acquire religious significance on both sides. For many Israelis, their victories against all odds were a miracle—a divine gift that gave them almost all the territories of ancient Israel. For many Arabs, their ignominious defeat by a much smaller enemy was divine vengeance—a result and a sign of the deficiencies in their societies and political systems. In Israel, where politics had formerly been dominated by non-observant Jews of Western origin, the rise of other political forces began—of Jews of Arab origin, and of the religious parties that are so important in Israeli politics today. In the Arab world, where politics had formerly been dominated by often non-observant Muslims of military origin, the rise of Islamism began.

The increasingly religious understanding of the conflict by Palestinian Arabs has been very visible in the rise of Hamas, an Islamist group, at the expense of the Palestine Liberation Organization (PLO), a secular nationalist group. Hamas promises both resistance to Israel and an Islamic state, and so is in tune with the times. The PLO is out of tune with the times—and has also lost support because of the various concessions it has made over the years to Israel and the West, concessions which most Palestinians see as having brought them nothing of much use in return.

Whatever views Palestinians might have of Jews in theory, in practice their attitude toward Jews is now determined overwhelmingly by politics and by their own encounters with Israelis. The only sort of Israeli most Palestinians ever encounter is wearing an army uniform, and the encounters are usually not happy ones. A minority of Palestinians are Israeli citizens, and have most (though not quite all) of the rights their Jewish compatriots have. These Israeli Palestinians have some opportunity to reach an informed and nuanced judgment of the Jews they meet at work and sometimes elsewhere. Most Palestinians, however, encounter Israeli Jews only when they are being given orders by them, or perhaps when they are being shot at by them (or are shooting at them). This experience is central to Palestinian views of Israelis, and so of Jews, and so of Judaism.

The wider Muslim attitude toward Judaism today is also conditioned by these events. Arabs identify with Palestinians rather than Israelis, just as most Westerners identify with Israelis rather than Palestinians. When a

Palestinian bombs a bus full of Israelis and the Israeli army demolishes the bomber's family's house, Westerner and Israeli television viewers see people who look and dress like they do suffering from the bombing; the demolition is an incidental detail, and a just reaction to an unjust act. Arabs see people who look and dress like they do suffering from the demolition; the bombing, in comparison, becomes almost an incidental detail. Arabs, then, have come to see Israelis as their enemies, and only rarely make any distinction between Israelis and Jews. American support for Israel has thus been a major cause of Arab hostility to America.

Most Arab Muslims today see the Arab-Israeli conflict in at least partly religious terms. They are convinced that the Jews have always been the enemies of Islam since the days of Yathrib, ignoring the centuries of more or less peaceful coexistence in between. There is no comprehension of the fact that Zionism was initially a secular nationalist movement. For the original Zionists, conflict with Arabs was an unfortunate side effect of the main project of a Jewish state. For today's Arab Muslims, the Jewish state appears to be a side effect of a main project of attacking Muslims.

Non-Arab Muslims do not necessarily view the conflict in quite these terms. Neither Turks nor Indonesians—for example—have any particular reason to identify with Palestinians, who neither look nor dress like they do. As a result, they are less prone to see Jews as their enemies. Many Turks and some Indonesians, however, do sympathize with the Palestinians as fellow Muslims.

The Muslim World and the West

Geography is an alternative way to look at the long and troubled relationship between the Muslim world and the West. Until very recently, civilizations divided by distance could develop without friction. The Chinese could never come into conflict with the pre-Colombian American civilizations, and Japan's great war with America was in the age of the aircraft carrier. The Muslim world and Christian Europe, in contrast, are close neighbors, and have been struggling for control of the Mediterranean Sea for over a thousand years. At the time of the Prophet Muhammad's birth, the Mediterranean was a Christian lake, controlled by the successors of the Roman empire.

The early Arab conquests divided it into a Muslim southern shore and a Christian northern shore, much as it is divided today. In the meantime, the Mediterranean might have become entirely Christian again if the Crusaders had been more successful, or entirely Muslim again if the sailors of the Ottoman empire had been as good as Ottoman soldiers were. The whole Mediterranean did once again come briefly under almost total Christian (or at least European) control between 1918 and 1948: during those thirty years, Turkey was the only Mediterranean state not to be either part of Europe or under European military occupation. That Arabs and Turks, Byzantines and Europeans, have been quarreling neighbors in this way for so many centuries is only possible because of geographical proximity.

The Mediterranean is not the only aspect of geography that has brought the Arabs and the West into contact, and into conflict. More recently, the presence of the world's most important oil supplies under the sands of previously unimportant parts of the Muslim world has kept the two regions engaged with each other—the West has been the major consumer of oil, and the Arab Gulf states have been the key producers. Israel is another geographical issue. The earliest Zionists seriously considered establishing the Jewish state of which they dreamed in Argentina. If this had happened, relations between the West and the Arab world would have been much easier.

Power politics also plays a role. The twentieth century saw three great conflicts. During the First World War, the Muslim world's most powerful state—the Ottoman empire—fought on the side of Germany, partly because this gave them a powerful ally against the Russian empire, an old enemy, and partly in the hope of German reward. As a result of what turned out to be a bad choice on the Ottoman part, most of the Arab countries that had been part of the defeated Ottoman empire were occupied by Britain or France during or after that war. During the Second World War, only one Muslim country actually fought on the German side (Iraq, for a brief thirty days), but sympathies were often with the enemy of the Muslim world's colonial occupiers, Britain and France. The advance of Hitler's Afrika Korps on Cairo was watched with delight by many Egyptians, who knew little or nothing of Hitler's racial theories (which were not in fact at all flattering about Arabs). Later, during the Cold War, many Arab states were more closely aligned with Moscow than with Washington. This was partly because they did not want to be on the same side as their recent European occupiers, Britain and France. It was also partly because Moscow offered support against Israel, and partly because Moscow was more enthusiastic about supporting grandiose state-sponsored industrialization projects. In all three major global conflicts of the twentieth century, then, most Muslim states were in one way or another on the opposite side to the West—not because of religion, but because of the logic of power politics.

Not all Muslim countries sided with the Soviet Union during the Cold War, however. Both Turkey and Iran had frontiers with the Soviet Union, and had been in conflict with Russia during the previous century. When they came under Soviet pressure at the very beginning of the Cold War, it was the West that saved them—not the former imperialists in Europe, but America. Both Turkey and Iran then established close military relations with America. One of these relationships survived, and the other did not. Turkey remains a member of NATO, and its government is generally on excellent terms with the U.S. Iran presents an interesting contrast. Although the Shah's regime remained on excellent terms with the U.S., it ended up on the worst possible terms with its own people. When the Iranian people turned on the Shah during the revolution of 1979, they turned on the U.S. as well.

This is one important way in which anti-American feeling grew up in the Muslim world—because the U.S. was friends with the wrong people. American support for the Shah of Iran made good sense in the context of the Cold War, but made America almost as hated in Iran as the Shah was. An American alliance with Western Europe was essential during the Cold War, but again aligned America with countries that were, from a Muslim point of view, the bad guys—the former colonial occupiers. After the Cold War, American support for unpopular authoritarian regimes has had much the same impact in the Arab world that support for the Shah did in Iran. Many of these regimes are adept at "using" America, demanding American support as the price for mildly friendly relations with Israel or even for the suppression of internal Islamist oppositions that are hostile to America. Many ordinary Muslims, however, see things the other way around: to them, America seems to be using the regimes. The regimes' many sins thus become the fault of America.

Americans were not responsible for the Crusades or for the European imperialism of the late nineteenth and early twentieth centuries, and so tend to ignore it, if they know anything about it. Arabs, however, are more aware of this history, and are inclined to see America as the successor of the European imperialists and even of the Crusaders. The Crusades in reality had very little to do with later European imperialism, being a conflict that took place in a confused period of Muslim history in an area where a dozen rulers were competing for land and power—Arabs and Turks and Kurds, Sunni and Shi'i Muslims, and even an unusual sect of the minority Ismaili denomination known to their enemies as the Assassins. The Crusaders did not at first stand out as particularly different from the other participants, except perhaps as being unusually primitive in cultural terms. Neither religion nor ethnicity were at first much of an issue. This changed when Saladin and others definitively established the control of Sunni Islam over the area, but the change was very much to the disadvantage of the Crusaders, who were ejected from the area without great difficulty. The Crusades were not, then, of much real significance in the history of the Muslims (unlike the later Mongols). When Muslims encountered European imperialism in the nineteenth century, however, the Crusades were remembered, and portrayed in a very different light by nationalist Arab historians.

American behavior has been on the whole very different from British or French behavior, or that of the Crusaders. Until 2003, America had never actually invaded and occupied a Muslim state, although there had been a few punitive raids and although American support for Israel during the 1967 and 1973 wars was seen by many Arabs as aggression by proxy. From an Arab perspective, however, American intervention still looks very similar to earlier European intervention. What matters is not how justified this comparison is, but whether or not people make it.

The conflict between the Muslim world and the West has so far been explained with little reference to religion. Religion, however, clearly matters. Firstly, it is a source of identity: the only reason that the struggle for control of the Mediterranean was a struggle between civilizations rather than between countries is that the Arabs and Turks involved saw themselves as Muslims above and beyond their own political divisions, just as the Europeans involved saw themselves as Christians, at least until the nineteenth century. In the nineteenth century, many Europeans began to define themselves as "civilized" rather than as Christian, but "civilized" still defined a distinct civilization just as "Christian" once had, and defined it by contrast with Islam. Even in the nineteenth century, Arabs often saw the Europeans primarily as Christians, as they often do to this day. This identity is not necessarily fixed, however. Turks today generally see themselves as civilized, or at least as relatively developed and sophisticated, rather than as Muslims, and this makes their alignment with the West much easier—as does the fact that no one in Istanbul has seriously considered conquering Vienna for some centuries now, and that no Western army has ever successfully invaded Turkey.

Religion also exacerbates the conflict by providing a distorting glass through which to see the other side, and by prescribing certain responses on the Muslim side. Muslims are very inclined to interpret international affairs in religious terms. Israel is seen as "the Jews," and Western states as "the Christians," and Israeli and Western policies and actions are then often perceived in terms of Jewish and Christian hostility toward Islam. Westerners, in turn, sometimes perceive Arab policies and actions in terms of Muslim hostility toward non-Muslims. As always, the perception is what matters, not the truth—and as often, there is some truth in the perception. If the Israelis were Muslims, conflict between them and Palestinians would appear an internal conflict, not an attack by outsiders (and there would be less conflict anyhow, as the two groups would tend to merge into one). If the Iranians were Christians, it would have been more difficult for them to see the Shah's modernization policies as an attack on their religion, and modern America would look less alien than it does. Christian Iranians would also be easier for Westerners to understand, and Iranian hostility toward the former supporters of the Shah would have no element of conflict of civilizations. It would look more like Chilean hostility toward the former supporters of General Pinochet.

What is more important, however, is the responses that Islam prescribes for Muslims in the conflict between the Muslim world and the West. Two related aspects of Islam are especially important. One is the doctrine of Jihad, and the other is the conception of the martyr.

The Sharia makes fighting for the faith a religious duty, and envisages a more or less continuous state of war between Muslims and non-Muslim peoples. At the level of government, the Sharia doctrine of Jihad has been almost totally ignored since the sixteenth century. Relations between Muslim and non-Muslim states have been conducted on the standard basis of treaties and alliances, and Muslim states have generally gone to war under the same circumstances that Western ones have (when they judge it necessary or useful). With occasional minor exceptions, governments have referred to the doctrine of Jihad only as part of wartime propaganda.

What is more important is that, as we saw in chapter 1, the history of early Islam (known to all Muslims) is full of stories of battles and heroic deaths. The message is not that might is right, but that right should be supported by might, and that bravery is a religious virtue.

The brave heroes who fall for the faith are martyrs—a rather different type of martyr from those familiar to Christians. The earlier Christian martyrs generally died for truth, choosing awful deaths rather than deny their faith (although some medieval martyrs also died in battle, for example during the Crusades). Very few Muslim martyrs died rather than deny their faith, for the simple reason that the Sharia allows Muslims to deny their faith to save their lives. Nearly all Sunni martyrs died in battle, while many Shi'i martyrs died deaths more similar to Christian martyrs, generally murdered for the truth they stood for, and often because they chose not to deny their faith.

The Islamic concept of Jihad and of martyrdom is rarely challenged. Some recent Muslim writers have tried to reinterpret the terms, stressing that Jihad means struggle, and that one can have a Jihad for development. Although the Islamic Republic of Iran at one point merged its ministry of agriculture with its ministry of Jihad, since the ministry of Jihad was primarily concerned with rural development, nearly all Muslims continue to understand Jihad primarily in a military sense. Some liberal Muslims have tried to reinterpret martyrdom as a form of "bearing witness," or as the opposite of keeping silent in the face of injustice—but rather more Muslim commentators have reinforced the primarily military meaning of the term. This is understandable when it comes to states: it is an effective way of motivating soldiers.

The result of this is that most Muslims, whether traditional or modern, devout or not, tend to see an armed response as an appropriate response to any sort of attack. This is in many ways anachronistic: what is needed against laser-guided bombs is not individual bravery but technological, financial, and industrial capacity. These capacities are beyond the reach of nearly all Muslim states today, however, and so the individual response is emphasized instead. And the most effective individual response seems to be the terrorist, and especially the "suicide bomber."

Terrorism and suicide bombing are not in themselves Islamic. The first modern terrorists were European and American anarchists at the end of the nineteenth century, and it was from Europe that Muslims learned the techniques of terrorism. Some of the earliest Arab terrorists—the Palestinian airplane hijackers of the 1970s—were not in any way devout Muslims; in fact, most were Marxist atheists, sometimes of Christian origin. The group with the largest tally of suicide bombing techniques at the time of writing is the Tamil Tigers, a Hindu separatist group in Sri Lanka, and the world's most famous suicide bombers were probably the Japanese kamikaze pilots.

A number of Muslims, however, have been especially enthusiastic terrorists and suicide bombers. Most Muslims' views on these terrorists depend not on religion but on politics. The same is true of most of us (though we may not realize it). When Islamists were blowing up Soviet soldiers and civilian "advisors" in Afghanistan during the 1980s, they were heroes not just for Muslims, but also for most Americans (though not, obviously, for many Russians). In 1985, one Islamist leader, Gulbuddin Hekmatyar, was even invited to the White House to meet President Reagan (he declined). When Islamists started blowing up American soldiers and civilians in Afghanistan and Iraq at the start of the twenty-first century, no American saw them as heroes. In 2003, American forces tried (without success) to kill Gulbuddin Hekmatyar, 18 years after he had declined his invitation to the White House. For those Muslims who saw little difference between Soviet actions in Afghanistan and American actions there and in Iraq (of whom there were many), nothing much had changed, however. Those who the West sees as terrorists are often seen by Muslims as freedom fighters, and Muslim suicide bombers are often seen as martyrs. This has nothing much to do with religion, and everything to do with politics. Islam condemns suicide just as any other monotheistic religion does, but praises the self-sacrifice of the martyr.

The conflict between the Muslim world and the West, then, is in some senses a religious conflict. It is also a political conflict brought about by geography and history. While religious differences in general exacerbate conflicts that exist for other reasons, religious differences on their own do not produce conflicts between Muslims and the West.

Just as religion on its own does not produce conflict, religion on its own does not resolve conflict—though many religious people try. At the highest level, the answer to the question of how to turn conflict into peace is a purely political question, and lies beyond the scope of this book. At a lower level, the questions of the most useful approaches to insurgency and terrorism (which are not the same thing) are military or security questions—also subjects for another book entirely.

Muslims in the West

Paradoxically, just as a small number of Muslims have been enthusiastic terrorists in the conflict between the Muslim world and the West, a larger number of Muslims have been enthusiastic immigrants into the West. Well-educated Muslims have generally chosen America and Canada, where they see the greatest opportunities. Less educated Muslims are to be found principally in the richer countries of Europe, which are generally easier for them to enter than America or Canada are. This has created a form of reverse colonialism, whereby people from countries such as Algeria that were once colonized by France now establish colonies in France, and people from Britain's former Indian empire establish colonies in Britain.

Islam in the West has already been referred to many times in this book. What I am concerned with here is the political implications of Muslim minorities in the West. These are more problematic in Europe than in America. America is used to receiving immigrants, while European countries are not. American Muslims are on the whole well educated and fit in reasonably well, while European Muslims are often poor and alienated. And alienation gives rise to hostility. Of course, there are alienated and hostile Muslims in America, and successful and integrated Muslims in Europe, but these exceptions to the general rule have little political significance.

Because most American Muslims are relatively well integrated, they do not form a significant distinct group within American society. As a result, they have little impact on the political system. They may, of course, lobby for their interests, but these interests do not generally make much difference to other groups. America is full of groups lobbying for their interests, after all. Alienated Muslims in America also have little impact on politics, because there are so few of them. Some of these alienated individuals may be of concern to the security services, of course, but that is another question.

The situation in Europe is different. In many European cities there are areas inhabited by large numbers of young unemployed Muslims who are dangerously alienated from the societies and systems of the countries they inhabit. Many are also alienated from the cultures of their countries of origin, or more frequently from the cultures of the countries of origin of their parents or even grandparents. Many such Muslims are Muslims only in the sense that they are not Christian, and fall into depressingly familiar patterns of behavior that are unequivocally condemned by the Sharia and by Muslim societies—drug use and crime. Some studies suggest that the French prison population is now predominantly Muslim. Public housing projects on the edge of some French cities are the European equivalents of America's worst inner cities—and they are inhabited almost exclusively by Muslims. There are similar areas in other countries, especially Britain and Germany. Race riots break out from time to time, sometimes lasting for days.

This situation is of great concern to European policy makers, politicians, and publics. It is primarily a social problem, and is generally seen as such, though in recent years it has fueled the growth of right-wing political parties that horrify many Europeans, reminding them of the racist fascism of the 1930s. There are, however, religious aspects to the problem. Even if most of these unemployed and alienated Muslims are not particularly religious, Islam clearly plays a role in reinforcing their separate identity, and is a bar to the most effective form of integration—intermarriage. More worryingly for many policymakers, some individuals escape from drugs and crime through the rediscovery of Islam. This would normally be a cause for rejoicing rather than alarm, but the Islam that is rediscovered is likely to be modern or Wahhabi, and probably politically radical. Traditional Islam is to be found in the West among first-generation immigrants, but rarely survives into the second generation. There are Muslim community leaders and organizations in Europe that are in no sense politically radical, and work to make the practice of Islam as easy as the practice of other minority religions such as Judaism. Such leaders and organizations, however, are of little interest to the alienated. The risk of the political-religious radicalization of substantial sections of their population thus keeps many Europeans awake at night. It has not happened yet, but it might happen one day.

The Sharia is of little help in determining how Muslims should relate to Western states and societies. It concerns itself at length with how non-Muslims should be treated in the Muslim world, both as a group and as individuals, but has little to say about how Muslims should live in the non-Muslim world. To the extent that this question was addressed at all in previous centuries, the most frequent view was that Muslims should not live in non-Muslim countries in the first place, though it was permitted to visit them for trade or similar purposes. This made sense in earlier centuries, when Christian conquerors of previously Muslim areas such as Spain usually ended up giving Muslims the choice of conversion to Christianity, emigration, or death. It makes little sense today.

Various approaches to the problem exist. At one extreme are integrationists who argue that Muslims in the West are subject to the local laws and customs just like anyone else, but should do what they can to make adjustments for the sake of their religion. They should persuade schools to provide areas for Muslims to pray in and offer alternatives to pork in the cafeteria. They can go to bars with their colleagues, but should drink soft drinks if they do. At the other extreme are separatists, radicals who argue that Muslims are subject to no law but the Sharia, and should actively work to make the Sharia the law of the land in which they live. This position is theoretically defensible in terms of the Sharia, but is recognized by most Muslims as being ridiculous. Clearly, the only way that the Sharia could become the law of America is if the majority of the American people converted to Islam, or if America were conquered and occupied by a Muslim state, neither of which seem at present even remotely possible. Equally, people who ignore the laws of the country they are living in will inevitably have a hard time. Positions between these two extremes are more frequent. Such intermediate positions accept that Muslims must follow local laws, but hesitate over questions such as whether Muslims should volunteer to serve in the armies of non-Muslim countries.

Whatever the position Muslim communities in the West take, they are unlikely to have any significant impact on political or social structures, if only because they are minorities. Minorities can only shape events if they are dominant minorities, as the French were once dominant in Algeria or the British in India. Otherwise, minorities are more likely to be shaped or excluded by a majority. Even if Muslims in the West who maintain that they are not subject to national law are a minority within a minority, they risk bringing down the wrath of the majority on their fellow Muslims, and in the end it is Muslims who will suffer, not the West.

Summary

Cultural conflict between the Muslim world and the West exists, but is not on its own enough to explain the "clash of civilizations." Attention has to be paid to geography and history and politics as well.

When it comes to non-Muslims, Islam is an intolerant religion by contemporary Western standards, though tolerant by medieval standards. The Sharia regards non-Muslims as outside the community, and at an individual level, most Muslims today retain this approach. Individual relations between Muslims and non-Muslims can, however, be good, and the laws of most Muslim states other than Saudi Arabia distinguish between persons on the basis of religion only in matters of family law.

The longest-running conflict between Muslims and non-Muslims is the Arab-Israeli conflict. At the start, this was a conflict between two different groups over land; it then became a nationalist conflict; by now it has also become in many ways a religious conflict. Although the religious element exacerbates the conflict and makes it harder to solve, the conflict determines the religious element more than religion guides the conflict. Palestinians, for example, usually understand Judaism primarily in terms of their experiences of the Israeli army. Other Arabs' understandings are similar. Non-Arab Muslims feel less involved, and are more likely to take detached views.

For geographical reasons, there has also been competition between the Muslim (Arab and then Ottoman) world and Europe. Religion defines the two blocs, but proximity was more important than religion in producing competition. This competition seemed finally to have been won by Europe at the end of the First World War, when all important Arab states had come under British or French control, as well as many Muslim states in other parts of the world. This is one reason why alignment of Arab and Muslim states during the Second World War and the Cold War was often on the opposite side to their former masters.

America got involved in this after the Second World War partly because of the priorities of the Cold War, partly because of the need to protect oil supplies, and partly in support of Israel. Many Arabs and some other Muslims came to see America as the successor of Britain and France, a view that was cemented in 2003 when America for the first time invaded and occupied an Arab state.

Islam plays a part in actual conflict between Muslims and the West, with the concepts of Jihad and of martyrdom encouraging Muslims to think in terms of armed responses, including terrorism. Armed responses, however, are not exclusive to Islam, and politics and history are in the end probably more important.

Some Muslims in the West, especially in Europe, are alienated from a system they do not fit in to, and the more radical among them argue for solutions which, if implemented, would severely undermine the states and societies they live in. Such radicals, however, stand no realistic chance at all of putting their solutions into practice, and so even radical and alienated Muslims in the West pose no significant threat on a group level. They might, however, pose an indirect threat to other Muslims, since they risk bringing down the wrath of the majority on all concerned.

Conclusion

Islam is one of the major world religions, and is the non-Western religion of which Westerners are most aware, largely as the result of conflict. It was once the religion of a sophisticated and powerful world empire, but is today the religion of some of the least dynamic parts of the world, often found in countries that have deliberately avoided integration into an increasingly globalized world. Islam often seems to Westerners to be very different, and not very appealing.

Islam, however, has much in common with Judaism and Christianity. Like the other monotheistic religions, it is based on a God-given sacred text (the Koran) and on the teachings of its founder (the Prophet Muhammad, whose life and words are recorded in the *hadith*). In practice, though, what Muslims follow is not so much Islam as the Sharia, the result of interpretations of the Koran and *hadith* over the centuries. The Sharia is no longer the national law in most Muslim countries, but it is still the standard to which Muslims refer in their daily lives. Much of this book has discussed the Sharia and its application in everyday life.

The Sharia was originally constructed by the Ulema, scholars who are not priests, as they have no sacramental functions and are not primarily responsible for encouraging good and religious behavior. This responsibility lies with all members of the local Muslim community, which in the Muslim world is based around villages and urban neighborhoods, and in the West is based around the mosque or Islamic Center. This community role of the mosque is giving Imams a new importance in the West, but in the Muslim world the Ulema are now much less important than they once were, and no longer attract the finest talent available. Muslim intellectuals trained in modern sciences are increasingly taking their place.

There are several different versions of the Sharia, producing several different denominations of Islam. Most important is the Sunni Islam of the majority, and the Shi'i Islam found in Iran, Iraq, Lebanon, Pakistan, and the West. Then there are also smaller denominations like the Ismailis.

Some argue that Wahhabism is a new denomination; it is certainly a different version of Sunni Islam from that practiced by traditional Muslims.

The difference between Sunni and Shi'i Islam is important, but in many ways is less important than the difference between traditional and modern Islam, a difference produced over the last 150 years by an invisible reaction to the coming of modernity, in a process similar to the European Reformation. When it comes to everyday life, the most important difference of all is the one between devout and less devout Muslims. Devout modern Muslims (whether Sunni, Shi'i or Wahhabi) are generally called "fundamentalists," but it is not their attitude to fundamentals that makes them different. It is based on their attitude to the more spiritual aspects of traditional Islam, which they reject, and to the relatively strict application of Islam to social and political questions, on which they often insist. Not all devout modern Muslims are terrorists or even politically active, but all Muslim terrorists are modern (or Wahhabi) Muslims. Their motivation is ultimately political more than religious.

The aspects of Islam that most worry Westerners concern the treatment of followers of other religions, violence, and relations between the sexes. The Sharia regards non-Muslims as essentially different from Muslims, and as outside the community. There is no widespread movement advocating non-violence, and few Muslims see any objection in principle to corporal punishment, whether of criminals, children, or disobedient wives. Islam's view of women as inferior to men and in need of male guidance and protection has few echoes in the modern West, and the segregation of men and women to avoid circumstances where sexual desire might be unduly and illegitimately aroused is also alien to Western practice.

The differences in practice, however, are not as great as the differences in theory. Individual relations between Muslims and non-Muslims can be good, the legal systems of most Muslim countries are based around laws very similar to those in force in the West, and individual Muslims generally object to the excessive use of violence. Although women are often at a disadvantage to men both legally and culturally, individual women and individual families still arrange their lives in ways that they find entirely satisfactory. Some Muslim feminists are calling for women to receive the rights they are given by Islam, and may make more progress in the future.

A more important difference between the Muslim world and the West at present is over politics. Islamists are important in the politics of the Muslim world, and aim to establish states where the Sharia and Islam operate as an all-embracing ideology. They are supported by many Muslims, mostly because they seem the only real alternative to discredited and unpopular systems. When no democratic path to power exists, Islamists may resort to revolutionary and insurgent tactics, including terrorism. Generally, as the innocent casualties of terrorism grow, the Islamists then lose support.

Although the conflict between Islamists and non-Islamist regimes is a conflict within the Muslim world, sometimes it spills out into other areas, getting entwined with new forms of the long-established conflict between the Muslim world and the West. This conflict is partly cultural, but also results from geography, history, and politics. The Muslim world and Europe are close neighbors, and have been in conflict in one way or another for over a thousand years. During the Second World War and the Cold War, many Arab and Muslim states took the opposite side to that of their former colonial masters—which also meant, against America. American-Muslim relations are also complicated by the long-running Arab-Israeli conflict, which was once a nationalist conflict, but is now in many ways also a religious conflict.

As a result of these conflicts, many Westerners, especially in Europe, are worried about the long-term presence of Muslims in Western societies. Alienated radical Islamists in the West clearly pose an immediate security threat, but it is hard to imagine any circumstances in which Muslim immigrants could fundamentally change the West. It is more likely that the West will change the immigrants, either by integrating them into the mainstream as non-observant or partly-observant Muslims, or even by encouraging the development of a new, postmodern Islam. Views of sacred texts as containing primarily symbolic truth, and of the tenets of religion as historical developments, are widespread in the West. Such views are increasingly available to Muslim intellectuals in contact with the West, as well. The forces that in the nineteenth century produced Reform Judaism may, in the end, do something similar to Islam.

While writing this book, I was sitting one day with two Americans. One, Danny, was talking of converting to Islam in order to marry Rana, his Palestinian girlfriend. Rana was not particularly devout, but her parents were, and Danny had accepted that for their sake, he had to become Muslim before he and Rana could marry. The other American, Abdulla, had converted to Islam—for spiritual rather than marital reasons—some years before. Danny went through the obvious issues with Abdullah, and Abdullah gave a number of reassuring responses, similar to some of the views represented in this book. Danny still looked unconvinced. "Yes," he said, "but . . . can' t you tell me something *good* about Islam?"

Abdullah thought for a while. "In the end," he said, "the best thing about Islam is that it gives you access to God. Perhaps other religions do too, but Islam does it better than any other I know. That's the point of all these rules—if you follow them, you can go places you couldn't otherwise go. Access to God is something that's hard for many people to understand. Perhaps you've felt something like it sometimes, perhaps while contemplating nature. It's a feeling that Freud called "the oceanic," though he understood it rather differently. Before I became Muslim, I once felt it sitting by the edge of a lake during a beautiful sunset. Anyhow, that's the point about Islam: instead of happening by chance once or twice in a lifetime, that can happen all the time."

One can see something of this access to God—or to the oceanic—in the faces of many Muslims in the Muslim world—in what the British poet Kathleen Raine called "faces of radiant beauty and the joy of life." In cities like Cairo, despite the poverty and the disorder, it is sometimes possible to glimpse something magically beautiful. The tawdry and ugly and commonplace is transformed into the special, the glowing. That, in the end, may be the real point about Islam.

Glossary

Note: The alternative spellings (given in brackets) follow the transliteration system used by most scholars. These are the spellings that will generally be used in dictionaries, encyclopedias, and more or less scholarly works.

baraka: divine grace, much as understood by Catholics. An imaterial force for good, emanating from God. Contrast *hasad*.

bida (bid'a): innovation, the opposite of *sunna*.

Caliph: originally, a Sunni successor of the Prophet. Also a title of later Ottoman rulers.

corrupt: see *fasih*.

discouraged: see *makruh*.

dua (du'a): prayer in the normal Western sense of an internal appeal to God. Contrast *sala* and *zikr*.

ego: see *nafs*.

fasih: corrupt, a non-observant Muslim. Contrast *salih*.

Fatwa: the non-binding "opinion" of a Mufti on the proper interpretation and application of the Sharia.

fiqh: the codified law of the Sharia, including civil and criminal law.

Fundamentalist: popular term for a devout modern (or perhaps Wahhabi) Muslim.

hadith: the record of what the Prophet did and said, collected in books quite separate from the Koran, and of entirely human composition.

Hajj: annual pilgrimage performed in Mecca. Contrast *umra*.

halal: an act that is allowed; the opposite of *haram*.

haram: an act that is forbidden in Islam.

hasad: envy, the "evil eye," an immaterial force for evil. Contrast *baraka*.

Imam: a Muslim who leads others in prayer. Sometimes also the person in charge of a mosque. In Shi'i Islam, one of the divinely protected successors of the Prophet, starting with Ali.

Islam: the religion of the Muslims.

Islamist: a person subscribing to a political ideology derived from Islam.

Jihad: struggle, either "just war" against the enemies of the Muslims (the "lesser" Jihad), or the struggle against the ego (the "greater" Jihad).

jinn: created beings that—like angels—are in another dimension, and that—like humans—have the power to chose between good and evil.

Kaba (ka'ba): the small and very ancient building in Mecca that Muslims believe was established by the prophet Abraham for the worship of the one God, toward which all Muslims turn to perform the *sala*.

Koran (Qur'an): the sacred text of the Muslims, containing the revelations transmitted by God to the Prophet Muhammad through an angel.

makruh: discouraged. An act which is not forbidden, but which it is better not to do.

marj'a taqlid. Model for emulation. An outstanding member of the Ulema selected by Shi'i Muslims as their ultimate authority in religious matters.

mawlid: anniversary celebration for a dead saint. See also *ziyara*.

mazhab (madhhab): accumulated body of opinions of the Ulema, akin to the accumulated case law of a particular U.S. state, including methodological decisions.

model for emulation: see *marja taqlid*.

monotheism: a religion such as Islam, Christianity, or Judaism that recognizes one God, maker of heaven and earth.

mubah: a religiously neutral act, like talking on the telephone.

Muhammad: the prophet of Islam, who Muslims believe to be the last prophet sent by God. Also spelled "Mohamed."

Mufti: senior member of the Ulema who delivers non-binding "opinions" on the proper interpretation and application of the Sharia.

Muslim: a person who follows the religion of Islam to any extent, or an inhabitant of a Muslim country who does not follow another religion. Sometimes restricted by more devout Muslims to the more devout.

nafs, ego, the lower or animal self. Contrasted with the mind, the heart, and the soul.

order, Sufi. See *tariqa*.

Ottoman: the ruling family of the great empire established by Turks in the years after 1300, which collapsed at the end of the First World War. Also used to describe the culture and systems of that empire.

pilgrimage: see Hajj, *ziyara* and *umra*.

polytheism: a religion such as that of the Greeks or the Indians which is not monotheistic and recognizes various gods.

prayer: see *dua*, *sala*, and *zikr*.

prophet: in Islamic usage, a human being appointed by God to spread a religion. The first prophet was Adam; the last was Muhammad, referred to as "*the* Prophet." Other prophets include Moses and Jesus.

righteous: see *salih*.

ritual prayer: see *sala*.

sabr: virtuous endurance of misfortune.

sadaqa: alms, given voluntarily and according to inclination. Contrast *zakat*.

sala: prayer in the ritual sense, as discussed in chapter 6. The *sala* should be performed five times a day in a specific fashion. Contrast *dua* and *zikr*.

salih: righteous. An observant Muslim. Contrast *fasih*.

Sharia: the totality of the rules that tell a Muslim how to live properly, including ethical rules and the *fiqh*. Often (wrongly) understood in the West to refer only to the penalties of the criminal law of the *fiqh*.

Shaykh: a senior and respected figure of any sort, but especially used to describe the leader of a Sufi order.

Shi'i: a Muslim who accepts the authority in religious matters of the Imam Ali and of the Imams who followed him; not a Sunni or member of any smaller sect.

sidq: the virtue of straightforwardness.

Sufi: a Sunni or Shi'i Muslim, usually traditional, who observes certain extra spiritual practices and follows a Shaykh or spiritual master.

sunna: exemplary tradition. Either the practice of the Prophet (and so by implication the *hadith* that record this) or something that it is not essential to do, but that it is a good idea to do.

Sunni: a Muslim who is not Shi'i, and rejects the authority of the Shi'i Imams.

taqwa: respect for God bolstered by fear of God, and resulting in piety.

tariqa: A group of Sufis following a Shaykh or spiritual master.

tawba: repentance, especially practical repentance, with an aspect of turning to God.

Testimony of faith: "There is no god other than God, and Muhammad is the Prophet of God." The two beliefs that are the beginning of Islam, and which in their implications make up a lot of Islam.

Ulema (*'ulama*): scholars specializing in Islam who, until recently, collectively exercised authority in religious matters, and in other areas of life as well.

umma: worldwide Muslim community.

umra: lesser, voluntary pilgrimage performed in Mecca. Contrast Hajj.

Wahhabi: follower of the teachings of Ibn Abd al-Wahhab, discussed in chapter 4.

zakat: alms, an obligatory act of worship, calculated according to specific formulas. Contrast *sadaqa*.

Zionist: a person supporting the project of the establishment of a Jewish state. Now used by some Arabs as a pejorative alternative to "Israeli."

zikr (*dhikr*): repetitive prayers of remembrance, the speciality of the Sufis. Contrast *sala* and *dua*.

ziyara: pilgrimage performed by a Shi'i Muslim at the tomb of an infallible Imam, or by a Sunni Sufi at the tomb of a saint.

Muslim Populations by Region

A: Indian Subcontinent

Indic countries with Muslim populations over 1 million:

Country	Muslims (m)	Notes
Pakistan	143 (97%)	Includes 30 m Shi'a
India	124 (12%)	
Bangladesh	119 (88%)	
Afghanistan	28 (99%)	Includes 5 m Shi'a
Nepal	1 (4%)	

Percentages in brackets are Muslims as a percentage of total population.

Indic countries with Muslim populations of less than 1 million:

Bhutan (negligible).

B: Middle East & North Africa

Middle East & North African countries with Muslim populations over 1 million:

Country	Muslims (m)	Notes
Egypt	69 (94%)	Also a very small number of Shi'a
Turkey	67 (99%)	Including about 8 m Alevis
Iran	66 (98%)	Mostly Shi'a. Includes about 6 m Sunnis
Algeria	32 (99%)	
Morocco	31 (99%)	
Saudi Arabia	24 (99%)	Including about 2 m Shi'a
Iraq	24 (98%)	Mostly Shi'a. Includes about 8 m Sunnis
Syria	15 (90%)	Including about 3 m Alawi and Druze
Yemen	19 (95%)	Including about 5 m Zaidis
Tunisia	10 (98%)	
Libya	5 (97%)	
Jordan	5 (92%)	

Country	Muslims (m)	Notes
Oman	3 (95%)	Mostly Ibadi. Includes ½ m Sunnis
Lebanon	3 (70%)	Mostly Shi'a. Includes ¾ m Sunnis and some Druze
United Arab Emirates	2 (96%)	Includes about ½ m Shi'a
Kuwait	2 (84%)	Mostly Shi'a. Includes ½ m Sunnis
West Bank	2 (75%)	
Gaza Strip	1 (99%)	
Israel	1 (15%)	Includes some Druze
Bahrain	1 (100%)	Mostly Shi'a. Includes ¼ m Sunnis

Middle East & North African countries with Muslim populations of less than 1 million:

Qatar (750,000) and Western Sahara (270,000).

Middle East & North African countries without significant Muslim populations:

Malta (Malta is Catholic and a member of the European Union, but Maltese is actually an Arabic dialect).

C: Africa

African countries with Muslim populations over 1 million:

Country	Muslims (m)
Nigeria	65 (50%)
Ethiopia	31 (48%)
Sudan	26 (70%)
Tanzania	12 (35%)
Mali	10 (90%)
Senegal	10 (94%)
Niger	9 (80%)
Somalia	8 (100%)
Guinea	8 (85%)
Burkina Faso	6 (50%)
Côte d'Ivoire	6 (38%)
Congo, Democratic Rep	6 (10%)

Country	Muslims (m)
Chad	5 (51%)
Uganda	4 (16%)
Ghana	4 (20%)
Sierra Leone	3 (60%)
Kenya	3 (10%)
Mozambique	3 (17%)
Cameroon	3 (20%)
Mauritania	3 (100%)
Zambia	3 (25%)
Eritrea	2 (50%)
Malawi	2 (12%)
Benin	1 (20%)
Gambia, The	1 (90%)
Madagascar	1 (7%)
Togo	1 (20%)

African countries with Muslim populations of less than 1 million:

Liberia, Comoros, South Africa, Burundi, Guinea-Bissau, Central African Republic, Rwanda, Djibouti, Maldives, Mayotte, Congo, Rep of, Zimbabwe, and Swaziland.

African countries without significant Muslim populations:

Angola, Botswana, Equatorial Guinea, Gabon, Lesotho, Namibia, and Reunion.

D: Southeast Asia

Southeast Asian countries with Muslim populations over 1 million:

Country	Muslims (m)
Indonesia	204 (88%)
Malaysia	14 (60%)
Burma	6 (14%)
Philippines	4 (5%)
Thailand	3 (5%)
Sri Lanka	1 (7%)

Southeast Asian countries with Muslim populations of less than 1 million:

Cambodia (700,000), Singapore (700,000), Australia (300,000), Brunei (200,000), Vietnam (100,000)

Southeast Asian countries without significant Muslim populations:

East Timor, Laos, New Zealand, and Papua New Guinea.

E: Central Asia

Central Asian countries with Muslim populations over 1 million:

Country	Muslims (m)	Notes
Uzbekistan	23 (88%)	
Kazakhstan	8 (47%)	
Azerbaijan	7 (93%)	70% of Azerbaijani Muslims are Shi'i
Tajikistan	6 (90%)	
Turkmenistan	4 (89%)	
Kyrgyzstan	4 (75%)	

Central Asian countries with Muslim populations of less than 1 million:

Georgia (about 500,000), and Armenia (small).

Central Asian countries without significant Muslim populations:

None.

F: Europe

European countries with Muslim populations over 1 million:

Country	Muslims (m)	Notes
Russia	20 (14%)	Long-established: Tartars and inhabitants of the Caucasus and Volgar regions.
France	5 (7.5%)	Immigrants, mostly North African
Germany	3 (3.7%)	Immigrants, mostly Turks
Albania	3 (70%)	Long-established
Serbia & Montenegro	2 (19%)	Long-established
Bosnia & Herzegovina	2 (40%)	Long-established

Country	Muslims (m)	Notes
United Kingdom	2 (2.7%)	Immigrants, mostly from Indian subcontinent
Italy	1 (1.8%)	Immigrants
Netherlands	1 (5.5%)	Immigrants
Bulgaria	1 (12%)	Long-established

European countries with Muslim populations of less than 1 million:

About 900,000: Netherlands, Bulgaria; Spain (about 700,000); Macedonia (about 600,000); Belgium (about 400,000); about 300,000: Austria, Switzerland, Sweden; Romania (about 200,000); about 100,000: Croatia, Cyprus, Denmark, Greece, and Norway.

European countries without significant Muslim populations:

Andorra, Belarus, Czech Republic, Estonia, Faroe Islands, Finland, Gibraltar, Greenland, Guernsey, Hungary, Iceland, Ireland, Latvia, Liechtenstein, Lithuania, Luxembourg, Moldova, Poland, Portugal, Slovakia, Slovenia, and Ukraine.

Note on Sources

In many cases, figures are approximate. Most Western countries publish reliable statistics for population, but not all publish statistics for religious denominations. Some other countries' statistics are far less reliable. Figures for religion are often politically sensitive and disputed. In some cases, such as that of the Democratic Republic of the Congo, all figures are no more than intelligent guesses.

Population figures are for mid 2002, and are taken from the U.S. Census Bureau (International Programs Center, International Data Base, released March 2004).

Religious denominations are taken initially from the CIA's *World Factbook*, refined as necessary from the "Religious Demography" sections of the State Department's *Religious Freedom Report* for 2004, and from other sources.

Suggested Further Reading

Chapter 1: What is Islam?

For the similarities between Islam and other monotheistic religions, and between the monotheistic religions and other religions, two widely appreciated books are Huston Smith, *The World's Religions* (Harper, 1991) and Karen Armstrong's *A History of God* (Ballantine, 1994). The early history of Islam is dealt with in almost any book on Arab history. Ira M. Lapidus's *A History of Islamic Societies* (Cambridge University Press, 2002) is an excellent treatment of an enormous subject, starting with the origins of Islam and ending at the present day; at over 1,000 pages, it is more of a reference work than beach reading. An even more extensive treatment is Marshall Hodgson's magisterial *The Venture of Islam* (three volumes, University of Chicago Press, 1975).

The Koran itself is difficult for non-Muslim readers to make much sense of without the relevant background. Many translations exist: among the best are that of Arthur J. Arberry (which attempts to retain some of the poetry of the original) and that of Mohammed Marmaduke Pickthall, which is sometimes more precise. Kerry Brown and Martin Palmer's *The Essential Teachings of Islam: Daily Readings from the Sacred Texts* (Century Hutchinson, 1989) is much more accessible, with extracts from the Koran and *hadith* arranged by subject. Shi'i perspectives are reflected in the fine new translation of Ali Quli Qara'i, which can be difficult to obtain, but may be ordered online from www.qurannewtranslation.com.

For the life of the Prophet, an excellent work (written from a Muslim perspective) is Martin Lings's *Muhammad* (Inner Traditions, 1987).

Chapter 2: The Construction of Islam

Almost any standard history of Islam covers this material. Little has been written specifically on the decline of the Ulema, but surrounding circumstances are dealt with in all modern histories. For the Arab world, see William Cleveland, *A History of the Modern Middle East* (Westview, 1999).

For the Ottomans, Bernard Lewis's *The Emergence of Modern Turkey* (Oxford University Press, 1991) is a classic.

Chapter 3: Types of Muslim

Albert Hourani's *Arabic Thought in the Liberal Age* (Cambridge University Press, new edition, 1983) is the classic account of the Muslim encounter with modern Europe and of its consequences. Despite its age, this beautifully written book is still well worth reading. Little has yet appeared on the Islamic Reformation as such. See Michaelle Browers and Charles Kurzman, *An Islamic Reformation?* (Rowman and Littlefield, 2004).

There are no good books on Muslim religiosity. Some idea of the varieties of religiosity may however be gained through fiction. Tayyib Saleh's *Season of Migration to the North* (Heinemann, 1970) gives an interesting view of the place of religion in the encounter of old and new, and Alaa al-Aswany's *The Yacoubian Building* (AUC Press, 2005) gives a beautiful, if rather scandalous, picture of less devout varieties of Muslim in contemporary Egypt. Salman Rushdie's *Satanic Verses* (Picador, 2000) is not a book that I would recommend taking into a Muslim country or showing to most Muslims, but it is the fascinating product of a sensitive non-observant Muslim's struggle with faith and culture.

Chapter 4: The Muslim Worldview

The Islamic worldview is rarely written about as such, but may be found in any number of introductions to Islam written by Muslims. For Sufis, saints, and miracles, see Mark Sedgwick, *Sufism: The Essentials* (AUC Press, 2001). See also Carl Ernst, *The Shambhala Guide to Sufism* (Shambhala, 1997) and—for a long and detailed treatment—Anne-Marie Schimmel, *Mystical Dimensions of Islam* (UNC Press, 1971). See also Rumi's poems, available in many different editions.

Chapter 5: Worship

The "five pillars" are covered in most introductions to Islam. For *sala*, see Mamdouh N. Mohamed, *The Islamic Prayer from A to Z* (2003). For a deeper view, see Abu Hamid al-Ghazali, *Mysteries of Worship in Islam* (out of print, but perhaps available in a library). For the pilgrimage, see F. E. Peters, *The Hajj* (Princeton University Press, 1995).

Chapter 6: The Family

Most books on the Muslim family are either indictments by Western-style feminists or somewhat dry books by anthropologists, tending to concentrate on the practices of traditional, rural societies. One exception is Carolyn Fluehr-Lobban's *Islamic Society in Practice* (University Press of Florida, 1994), which has two chapters on rural families in Sudan and Egypt, written very much in the spirit of this book. See also Abu Hamid al-Ghazali, *The Proper Conduct of Marriage in Islam* (Al-Baz, 1998).

The classic indictments are those of Nawal al-Saadawi, who has a wide following in the West but almost none in the Muslim world. See, for example, *The Hidden Face of Eve* (Zed Books, 1980). Another classic indictment, Betty Mahmoudi's *Not Without my Daughter* (St Martin's, 1991), is not really recommended, as its portrayal of Islam owes more to its author's personal sufferings than to anything else.

For Islamic feminism, see Asma Barlas' *Believing Women in Islam* (University of Texas Press, 2002) or Fatima Mernissi, *The Veil and the Male Elite* (Perseus Books, 1992). For something more radically liberal, see the article by Sa'diyya Shaikh in Omid Safi's *Progressive Muslims* (Oneworld, 2003).

Chapter 7: Daily Life

The rules of the Sharia are covered in dozens of books aimed at educating young Muslims. For the arts, my own two favorite coffee table books are Martin Frishman and Hasan-Uddin Khan, *The Mosque* (Thames & Hudson, 1994) and Dominique Clevenot, *Splendors of Islam* (Vendome, 2000).

Chapter 8: Community Life

For *mazhabs* and Muftis, see almost any standard work. For a scholarly examination of virtue promotion, see Michael Cook, *Forbidding Wrong in Islam* (Cambridge University Press, 2003). I know of no good books on race, crime, punishment, or violence—though there are many bad books on Islam and violence.

Chapter 9: Ethics

See almost any of the works of Abu Hamid al-Ghazali, and T. J. Winter, *Al-Ghazali on Disciplining the Soul and Breaking the Two Desires* (Islamic Texts Society, 1997). For a sophisticated discussion by a leading Iranian

Ayatollah, see Murtada Mutahhari, *Understanding Islamic Sciences: Philosophy, Theology, Mysticism, Morality, Jurisprudence* (Palgrave Macmillan, 2002). Those with access to a suitable library might want to look at either of two scholarly works, Majid Fakhry's *Ethical Theories in Islam* (Brill, 1997) or Baber Johansen's *Contingency in a Sacred Law: Legal and Ethical Norms in the Muslim Fiqh* (Brill, 1998).

Chapter 10: Other Denominations
For almost everything to do with Shi'ism or Iran, one of the best and most readable books is Roy Mottahedeh, *The Mantle of the Prophet* (Oneworld, 2000). A visit to www.al-islam.org may also be interesting. There are surprisingly few books on Wahhabism, given its importance. See Hamid Algar, *Wahhabism* (Islamic Publications International, 2002). The Baha'is are well covered in Juan Cole, *Modernity and the Millennium* (Columbia University Press, 1998). For Traditionalism, see Mark Sedgwick, *Against the Modern World* (Oxford University Press, 2004).

Chapter 11: Islam and Politics
The medieval Islamic state is covered in many books such as that by Lapidus, recommended for chapter 1 (above). An excellent book for modern politics is L. Carl Brown's *Religion and State: The Muslim Approach to Politics* (Columbia University Press, 2001). For more detail on political Islam in one important country, see Gilles Kepel's well-written and sometimes entertaining *Muslim Extremism in Egypt* (University of California Press, 2003). Kepel's other works are also worth reading.

Chapter 12: Islam and the West
The classic book on the "clash of civilizations" is Samuel P. Huntington, *The Clash of Civilizations* (Simon & Schuster, 1998). This book is extremely influential, but regarded by many scholars as being both fundamentally wrong and also dangerously close to self-fulfilling prophecy. For those who want to understand the relationship between Islam and the West in the context of recent history, an account such as that by William Cleveland, recommended above for chapter 2, will be useful. For alternative views of Israeli history, see Benny Morris, *Righteous Victims* (Vintage, 2001).

Index